Meet John Doe

Meet John Doe

Frank Capra, director

Charles Wolfe, editor

Rutgers University Press

New Brunswick and London

Meet John Doe is volume 13 in Rutgers Films in Print

Copyright © 1989 by Rutgers, The State University

Manufactured in the United States of America

Library of Congress Cataloging-in-Publication Data

Meet John Doe : Frank Capra, director / Charles Wolfe, editor.
    p. cm.—(Rutgers films in print)
    Filmography: p.
    Bibliography: p.
    ISBN 0-8135-1386-3
    ISBN 0-8135-1387-1 (pbk.)
    1. Meet John Doe. I. Wolfe, Charles, 1949–   . II. Series.
PN1997.M4273M44 1989
791.43'72—dc19   88-23502
                                CIP

British Cataloging-in-Publication information available

Illustrations on pages 23 and 24 reproduced courtesy of Warner Brothers Archive, USC Cinema-Television Library.
Editorial entitled "An Inspiring Experiment," *Film Bulletin* (6 April 1940). Lewis Jacobs, "Film Directors at Work: Frank Capra," *Theatre Arts* 25, no. 1 (January 1941):43–48. Theodore Strauss, "Mr. Riskin Hits the Road," *The New York Times* (26 January 1941), used by permission of The New York Times Company, copyright © 1941. *Meet John Doe* correspondence files, Frank Capra Collection, Wesleyan University Cinema Archives. Frank Capra, *The Name Above the Title* (New York: Macmillan, 1971), used by permission of the William Morris Agency, Inc., on behalf of the author; copyright © 1971 by Frank Capra.
Bosley Crowther, *The New York Times* (31 March 1941), used by permission of The New York Times Company, copyright © 1941. Edwin Schallert, "Meet John Doe Hailed as Capra Victory," *Los Angeles Times* (31 March 1941), reprinted by permission of Los Angeles Times, copyright © 1941. James Shelley Hamilton, *New Movies: The National Board of Review Magazine* (April 1941). Jay Leyda, "Courage in Films," *Direction* 4, no. 4 (April-May 1941), used by permission of Kraus Reprint. Herbert Biberman, "Frank Capra's Characters," *New Masses* (8 July 1941). Otis Ferguson, "Democracy at the Box Office," *The New Republic* 1373 (24 March 1941).
Richard Glatzer, "*Meet John Doe:* An End to Social Mythmaking," in *Frank Capra: The Man and His Films,* ed. Richard Glatzer and John Raeburn (Ann Arbor: University of Michigan Press, 1975):139–148. Dudley Andrew, "Productive Discord in the System: Hollywood *Meets John Doe,*" in *Film in the Aura of Art* (Princeton: Princeton University Press, 1984); reprinted from *Enclitic,* nos. 10 and 11 (Fall 1981 and Spring 1982). Nick Browne, "System of Production/System of Representation: Industry Context and Ideological Form in Capra's Meet John Doe," originally published as "Sistem di produzione/sistema di representazione: *Meet John Doe,*" in *Hollywood in Progress,* ed. Vito Zagarrio (Venice: Marsilio Editori, 1984).

Acknowledgments

Many individuals assisted me on this project. I am especially indebted to Jeanine Basinger, curator of the Frank Capra Collection at Wesleyan University's Cinema Archive, whose wise and generous advice made this a better book. During my visits to Wesleyan, I also was aided in my research by Candace Bothwell and Alicia Springer. At Princeton University, Mary Ann Jensen, curator of the William Seymour Theater Collection, guided me to the Warner Brothers New York legal files; her assistant, Andy Thomson, guided me through them. Leith Adams, curator of the Warner Brothers Archive at the University of Southern California, enabled me to examine the studio's production files for *Meet John Doe,* and Ned Comstock of the Archive of the Performing Arts at USC led me to other collections of great value. Anthony Slide of the Margaret Herrick Library, Academy of Motion Picture Arts and Sciences, gave me access to the Production Code Administration file for *Meet John Doe.* Eleanore Tannen kindly arranged for the screening of a 35mm print of *Meet John Doe* at the University of California, Los Angeles, Film Archive. Roger Kelly carefully checked the continuity script prepared for this book against the UCLA print. Like the students we share at the University of California, Santa Barbara, I benefited from the powers of recollection of Paul N. Lazarus, who as a vice-president at Warner Brothers in 1941 oversaw the advertising campaign for *Meet John Doe.* For a close reading of the introductory essay, and valuable suggestions concerning it, I am in the debt of Edward Branigan. At different stages of the project, support of various kinds was provided by Al LaValley, Naomi Greene, Kathyrn Carnahan, and Ronald Magliozzi. Deborah Scott Wolfe helped from beginning to end; this is her book too. Finally, I am deeply grateful to Frank Capra, who backed the idea for a book on *Meet John Doe* when I first proposed it several years ago, and to Leslie Mitchner of Rutgers University Press who kept the idea alive.

Contents

Filmography and Bibliography

Introduction

Meet John Doe:
Authors, Audiences,
and Endings
Charles Wolfe

oday, the reputation of *Meet John Doe* is that of an ambitious but troubled work, the film in which director Frank Capra's fabled optimism failed him as an adequate guide to topical, political fiction-making. The perceived deficiency of the ending has been singled out for special attention in this regard. Capra himself has spoken candidly and written at some length on the difficulties he and screenwriter Robert Riskin experienced in resolving the plot lines that converge on a City Hall roof on Christmas Eve at the close of the fiction.[1] In the wake of revisions by Capra after the film was first released in March 1941, the question of an appropriate ending was a matter of lively debate among reviewers, and scores of viewers took the liberty to write to Capra offering alternative suggestions of their own. For critical commentators, the ending has been less a problem to be solved than a symptom of underlying issues. It has

1. See "Five Endings in Search of an Audience," the excerpt from his autobiography that is reprinted in this volume. Capra also speaks about these difficulties in the following interviews: Arthur Bressan and Michael Moran, "Mr. Capra Goes to College," *Inter/View,* 22 (1 June 1972), pp. 25–30; James R. Silke and Bruce Henstell, eds., *Frank Capra: One Man—One Film,* Discussion No. 3 (Washington D.C.: American Film Institute, 1972); Donald W. MacCaffrey, "Frank Capra: The Ideal and the Real," in Donald E. Staples, ed., *The American Cinema* (Washington, D.C.: Voice of America, 1973), pp. 127–143; Richard Glatzer, "A Conversation with Frank Capra," in Glatzer and John Raeburn, eds., *Frank Capra: The Man and His Films* (Ann Arbor: University of Michigan Press, 1975), pp. 24–39; Richard Schickel, "Frank Capra," in his *The Men Who Made the Movies* (New York: Atheneum, 1975), pp. 57–92; and John F. Mariani, "Frank Capra," *Focus on Film,* no. 27 (1977), pp. 41–47.

served biographically as a sign of Capra's artistic ambitions or limitations, institutionally as a sign of contradictions within a system of studio film production, and historically as a "sign of the times," marking a transitional moment when anxieties generated by the Great Depression had been complicated and modified by America's drift toward engagement in international conflict, with no ending to that story in sight.

The weight placed on the ending over and above other aspects of *Meet John Doe* as a fictional text can in part be attributed to certain assumptions concerning the function of closure in conventional narrative form. The end ties up the main plot lines with sufficient clarity and credibility, allowing the viewer comfortably to take leave of the fiction. Making sense, retrospectively, of preceding events, it is a point beyond which no crucial questions need to be answered or addressed. From this perspective, the problem of *Meet John Doe*'s ending might seem technical, a function of certain lapses in the architectonics of the work that could be exposed by retracing the plot lines in full knowledge of its problematic destination. But many Hollywood fictions seem flawed in this regard; indeed, the undermotivated "happy ending" constitutes something of a Hollywood convention in and of itself.[2] Thus, for Parker Tyler, writing in 1944, the "false ending" of *Meet John Doe* is indicative of a moral and aesthetic laxity in Hollywood films in general, of a greater concern for action than logical closure, of setting things in motion rather than tying things up.[3] The special emphasis placed on the ending to *Meet John Doe* over the years suggests, however, that the stakes riding on this particular ending have been perceived as unusually high. If so, what raises them? Why has it mattered so much that something at the end of *Meet John Doe* appears to go wrong? The remarks that follow take the ending of *Meet John Doe* as a focal point in considering various sources and contexts that may help to clarify the "troubles" of the text.

The suicide plot in *Meet John Doe* can be traced to "A Reputation," a work of short fiction by Richard Connell, first published in *Century Magazine* in August 1922.[4] At the outset of the story, an inconspicuous New Yorker, Saunders Rook,

2. See David Bordwell, "Happily Ever After, Part Two," *The Velvet Light Trap*, No. 19 (1982), pp. 2–7.

3. See Parker Tyler, *The Hollywood Hallucination* (New York: Creative Age Press, 1944), pp. 176–177.

4. "A Reputation" is reprinted in Connell's anthology of short stories, *Apes and Angels* (New York: Minton, Blach & Co., 1924), pp. 35–62.

wins the attention of the members of the Heterogeneous Club by announcing his decision to commit suicide on the Fourth of July to protest the state of civilization in America. His life is transformed: he is courted by high society, consulted by literati and politicians, and revered around the world. Savoring every moment of his fame, Rook awakens on Independence Day to realize that in order to save his reputation he must take his life. He walks to the Central Park reservoir, climbs above it, and contemplates his dilemma. "Still, after all, a reputation is a reputation," Rook reminds himself, then jumps in. Written in a tone of cool detachment, the story sketches a character without passion, except a desire to be known, in an urban milieu with no fixed values. All that hangs in the balance in his final gesture is "a reputation," the pursuit of which is figured as a self-annihilating act.

Fifteen years later, Connell's story served as the premise for a play by Jo Swerling, a Hollywood screenwriter who had collaborated with Capra on a series of romantic comedies and melodramas at Columbia Pictures in the early 1930s. Swerling never completed the play, and there are no surviving archival copies, but records suggest that Swerling's version, titled *The World Is an Eightball*, used the premise of the short story in large measure to satirize contemporary social events. In a twist suggestive of work in the 1940s by director-writer Preston Sturges, Swerling recast the protagonist as "Ferdinand Katzmellenbogen," a shy photographer whose inhibitions drop with a single drink and who has no memory of his eccentric behavior when sober. Tongue loosened at a high-toned party, Ferdinand denounces Germany and Italy in front of countesses from these countries, then announces his decision to commit suicide to protest the world's state. Hailed as a new messiah by a Hindu mystic, he is rechristened "John Doe" and a publicity campaign is launched by a newspaperwoman (Jane) and radio columnist (Tristram Erskine) with whom he resides. Jane writes and John delivers a radio address that spawns the formation of John Doe clubs throughout the country. Plans for mass suicides are drawn up. Paramount Pictures buys the movie rights to John's life story and arranges to stage his suicide at the theater where the film will premiere on the Fourth of July. At the close of Swerling's second act, an FBI agent, sent by the government to prevent the suicide, arrests the leaders of the movement for fraudulent fundraising. Here Swerling's plot appears to have run aground; no third act was written.[5]

---

5. This synopsis is drawn from documents in the Warner Brothers (New York) Legal Department Files, Box 12689, held at Princeton University.

In the spring of 1939, Connell returned to the material, collaborating on a treatment with Robert Presnell. Titled *The Life and Death of John Doe,* the treatment picks up the topical allusions of Swerling's play, but shies away from the satire. The protagonist now is simply John Doe, an anonymous information clerk at Grand Central Station who secretly craves the limelight. By chance, he has the opportunity to rescue his favorite movie star from a mob of fans at the station. When he discovers that she has left her purse behind, he is emboldened to crash a party she is hosting to return it. There, in a desperate attempt to attract the attention of her socially prominent guests, he announces his intention to take his own life in order to protest the state of the modern world. Thanks to an ambitious reporter (Nan), his remarks make the morning paper and create a stir. To exploit the incident further, Nan collaborates with John on a daily column for the paper, and ghostwrites a radio speech in which he summons ordinary people to join in common cause against war, poverty, and injustice. In response, a John Doe movement, based on principles of Christian brotherhood, springs up and spreads around the world. Wall Street panics, foreign dictators fume, and a co-alition of corporate capitalists and political leaders conspire to suppress the movement. John rejects their bribes, but, with the suicide date approaching, considers escaping west with Nan, with whom he has fallen in love. The sincerity of the club members, however, turn John and Nan into true believers. The con-spirators kidnap John and hide him in a jail on the top floor of City Hall. Nan rouses the people to action, then accepts John's decision to leap from the building on the Fourth of July, a martyr to peace, as his followers sing "The Battle Hymn of the Republic" on the street below. No Hindu mystics, no mass suicides, no staged death scene; Connell and Presnell play the motif of religious and political martyrdom straight.[6]

The differences between "A Reputation" and *The Life and Death of John Doe* seem, in part, a function of the contrasting formal demands of a short story and screen treatment, with the latter work opening up a character sketch to a broader range of social actors and groups placed in dramatic conflict. But the differences surely are also historical, a measure of a changing perspective on "the state of civilization" between 1922 and 1938. The Great Depression, congressional in-vestigations into war profiteering, and the rise of international fascism are ex-plicit reference points for a social concern that was left wholly undefined in "A

---

6. Copies of the treatment are held in the script collection of the UCLA Theater Arts Library, and in the Warners Legal Files (Box 12689), Princeton.

Reputation." More particularly, the idea of a national John Doe Club seems drawn from a cluster of popular movements in the mid-to-late thirties that promised economic and social salvation: the Townsend Plan for a national pension, Huey Long's Share Our Wealth clubs, and radio priest Father Coughlin's National Union for Social Justice.[7] Connell's original suicide plot is thus transformed into a social allegory, in the first instance satiric, in the second, religious.

In November 1939, Capra and Riskin purchased the rights to both "A Reputation" and *The Life and Death of John Doe,* and announced that the material would form the basis for the first project of their new, independent film company, Frank Capra Productions.[8] The attractions of the treatment were probably several. A plot in which an ordinary "John Doe" was catapulted to the center of a social crisis of which he had been previously unaware, only to emerge as maligned but genuine martyr and hero, retraced the narrative trajectories of two of Capra's most celebrated works of the 1930s: *Mr. Deeds Goes to Town* (scripted by Riskin for Capra in 1936) and *Mr. Smith Goes to Washington* (in release at the time of the purchase of *The Life and Death of John Doe*). Integrating conventions of romantic comedy and social melodrama, the films absorbed topical social problems—in *Mr. Deeds,* the plight of dispossessed farmers; in *Mr. Smith,* political corruption extending from state government to the nation's capital—and configured these problems to enable the triumph of the hero and to create a sense of social recovery. Moreover, the idea of a John Doe movement, founded on a Christian precept of neighborly love, bore a resemblance to the Shangri-La of James Hilton's *Lost Horizon,* which Capra and Riskin brought to the screen in 1937. In a comic but no less fanciful vein, an extended family with similar values had combated the encroachment of a munitions manufacturer in *You Can't Take It with You* (1938), which Capra and Riskin adapted from the play by George S. Kaufman and Moss Hart. The fact that *The Life and Death of John Doe* located this utopian impulse in a nonsectarian Christian movement would have seemed especially timely in 1939, when media attention had turned to the Oxford Group,

---

7. See Alan Brinkley, *Voices of Protest: Huey Long, Father Coughlin, and the Great Depression* (New York: Alfred A. Knopf, 1982).

8. Although *The World Is an Eightball* was not announced to be part of this agreement, a subsequent copyright infringement suit against Frank Capra Productions and Warner Brothers by Robert Shurr and Pat A. Leonard, authors of an unproduced play, *The Stuffed Shirt,* was dismissed by the federal courts in part because material in question was traceable to Swerling's play (*Box Office,* 27 May 1943).

a movement for Moral Re-armament that had held a major rally, with live radio coverage, at the Hollywood Bowl in June.[9]

The Life and Death of John Doe, however, posed problems that Capra and Riskin had not heretofore faced in their topical fictions. First of all, the story derived much of its narrative impact from the execution of the suicide threat.[10] As its title suggested, the treatment called for the hero's actual death as the necessary price for social renewal in contemporary America, a darker variant of a martyrdom motif than, say, the incarceration of Longfellow Deeds in a psychiatric hospital or the humiliation of Jefferson Smith on the floor of the United States Senate. Secondly, by suggesting that the suicide threat of John Doe was an eccentric, attention-seeking act, it complicated the motives of the hero in ways Capra's earlier films had not. Yet these difficulties also appear to have been part of the appeal of the material; Capra claims in his autobiography, for example, that working with a protagonist of uncertain motives was a challenge he welcomed in the hope of demonstrating to critics that he could handle "hard-nosed brutality." Staking a claim for creative independence within the Hollywood studio system, Capra and Riskin sought to test their capacity to tackle more difficult material without losing touch with the audience for whom Capra claimed great affinity. Competing pressures thus influenced the project from its very inception.

Production of a screen version of *The Life and Death of John Doe* became possible with the signing of a set of interlocking agreements among Frank Capra

9. Capra drew an analogy between the John Doe movement and the Oxford Group in an interview with Victor Saint-Clair: "Un quart d'heure avec Frank Capra," *Cinémonde* (Paris), 24 April 1940. From this perspective, the "source" material for *Meet John Doe* does not appear wholly defined by the literary properties Capra and Riskin purchased. It is interesting to note, for example, that when copyright infringements suits were filed against Warners by Shurr and Leonard (see note 8) and by Henry W. Clune (author of the 1940 novel, *Monkey on a Stick*) a defense considered by a Warners consultant was that stories of media-based, third-party movements were so pervasive that they were not protectable under copyright. Another defense under study was that the similarities between *Meet John Doe* and Capra's previous films clearly marked the new work as authored by him. In the Clune case, however, Warners ended up settling the case out of court for $2,500 (Warners Legal Files, Box 12689, Princeton).

10. Suicide was by no means alien to Capra's work. *The Bitter Tea of General Yen* (1933) ends with the title character, a Chinese warlord, taking his life in an almost luxurious fashion, but the implications of the event are more personal and philosophical than social or political. Suicide is also attempted by the heroine in *Ladies of Leisure* (1932) and contemplated by the hero in *American Madness* (1932). And a Christmas Eve impulse to jump to one's death would later resurface as the narrative premise of Capra's *It's a Wonderful Life* (1946).

Productions, Warner Brothers, Vitagraph (Warner's distribution company), and the Bank of America on 21 February 1940. The original contracts were highly favorable to Capra and Riskin, securing funding, studio facilities and personnel, and access to a prime distribution circuit, while at the same time guaranteeing the director and screenwriter complete control over the writing, shooting, and editing of the film.[11] Work on the screenplay, however, was not as swift as the collaborators had hoped. Begun in December 1939, an unfinished draft was prepared as early as 26 January, but a complete script was not ready until four months later, on 22 April. Capra was dissatisfied with it and invited Myles Connolly, a friend and frequent script consultant, to join him and Riskin in the High Sierras to work on revisions. They returned three weeks later with a second version, dated 13 May, then worked on the script for another full month before a copy was ready for submission to the Production Code Administration, the industry's self-regulating censorship agency. Dated 13 June, the script was sent to the PCA on 24 June and came back two days later with only minor suggestions for revision, focusing on the use of slang terms. Meanwhile, Capra and Riskin had continued to rework the script. On 27 June a new version titled *Meet John Doe* was printed up, from which the production budget and shooting schedule were prepared.[12]

Filming began 8 July, but Capra and Riskin continued to tinker with the script while it was being shot. Principal photography was completed on 18 September, and Capra had a rough cut ready by early November, but the release schedule for

11. A complete set of contracts are located in the Warners Legal Files, Box 12723, Princeton. Photocopies of the key contracts can also be found in the production files for *Meet John Doe* which are held at the Warner Brothers Archives, University of Southern California. It is clear from correspondence in the legal files that some officials at Warners thought the deal was overly favorable to Capra and Riskin. The contracts were amended by letter agreement on 31 March 1941 so as to guarantee Warner Brothers 25 percent of the net revenue above a $2 million dollar gross. The agreement also indicated that both parties considered additional production at Warners "problematic." Although Capra went on to produce and direct *Arsenic and Old Lace* at Warners in the fall of 1941, the film was designed to be shot quickly and cheaply, and Capra retained no rights to it. A subsequent proposal for independent production by Warners promised Capra the freedom to select his own script, with the proviso that it not be "of a political or controversial nature." By this time World War II had intervened, and Capra went to work as a filmmaker for the United States Army instead. For an analysis of the original contracts, see Nick Browne's article in this volume.

12. Letter, R. J. Obringer to Morris Ebenstein, 21 July 1941, Warners legal files, Box 12689, Princeton; Production Code Administration files, Margaret Herrick Library, Academy of Motion Picture Arts and Sciences, Beverly Hills; *Meet John Doe* "estimating" script, Frank Capra Collection, Wesleyan University Cinema Archive; *Hollywood Reporter,* 1 May 1940 and 31 May 1940.

the film was repeatedly pushed back. On 3 January 1941, Capra reassembled key members of the cast to film additional material for the closing scene on the City Hall roof, and three weeks later reshot footage for the first scene between Ann Mitchell and her mother.[13] Robert Riskin journeyed to New York to begin negotiating a distribution package, but admitted to the press that final plans would await further test screenings of the film; audience response would dictate whether a prestigious road-show release would be undertaken. Deciding against it, Capra and Riskin finally opened *Meet John Doe* at seven theaters in four cities on 12 March, an unusual distribution strategy at that time.[14]

At first, Capra attempted to turn these delays to his advantage by suggesting to the trade press that he had decided, as an independent producer, to make films in an entirely new way, taking his time with postproduction decisions, shooting additional material when necessary, and fine-tuning the final version before releasing it. But by early 1941, it had become well known in the industry that Capra was having difficulty with the ending, and was previewing and reshooting. When Capra ordered the ending to all prints altered on 14 March, two days after the release, the difficulty became obvious to reviewers and audiences as well. Then, in an exceptional move given standard studio procedure, Capra reassembled key cast members again on 23 March and shot additional footage for the closing scene. Intercut with existing material, this new ending was tested in Los Angeles, then went into national distribution in April.[15]

It is impossible to reconstruct the full range of endings Capra and Riskin contemplated during the course of these revisions, but existing documents point to several major alterations. The 27 June shooting script ended with D. B. Norton and his cohorts confronting John on the City Hall roof, and Ann arriving on the scene and persuading John not to jump. An epilogue was appended to this in which Ann and John announce the formation of a John Doe Club in a neighborhood store, where the Colonel is also present. When a poster for this club is

13. "Estimating" script, Capra Collection, Wesleyan; Daily Production and Progress Report for *Meet John Doe*, Warners Archives, USC.

14. Theodore Strauss, "Mr. Riskin Hits the Road," *The New York Times*, 26 January 1941, sec. 10, p. 5; *Variety*, 29 January 1941, p. 4.

15. *Hollywood Reporter*, 19 September 1940; 18 October 1940; 11 November 1940; 25 November 1940; 20 December 1940; 27 December 1940; 10 January 1941; 15 January 1941; 14 March 1941; 24 April 1941; 10 April 1941; *Daily Variety*, 7 November 1940; New York *Herald-Tribune*, 8 October 1940; 10 January 1941; *Box Office*, 5 April 1941; *Film Daily*, 13 February 1941; *Showman's Trade Review*, 4 January 1941; unidentified clips, *Meet John Doe* scrapbook, Capra Collection, Wesleyan; Daily Production and Progress Report for *Meet John Doe*, Warners Archive, USC.

mocked by passersby, the Colonel turns to the camera and delivers the final lines of the film: "Listen, you Heelots. I'm giving you just one more chance." Production was suspended in September without the epilogue being shot; thus, any previews that took place in late 1940 most likely ended with the original City Hall scene. The revised ending shot on 3 January was also set on the City Hall roof, but added several new elements, including an extended argument by Ann, an order by D.B. to Connell to publish John's letter on the front page of *The Bulletin,* and, amid a celebratory atmosphere, a revised, transplanted parting line by the Colonel: "Well, I guess I'll have to give the Heelots one more chance." By the time of the 12 March release, the last line had been cut, to be replaced simply by the Colonel's exclamation, "Long John!" and some choral singing. Two days later, D.B.'s statement of conversion was excised from all prints in circulation. Then on 23 March, Capra filmed the Millville club members driving to City Hall and apologizing to John, and added a new tag line, delivered by Connell: "There you are, Norton! The people! Try and lick that!" This new material was deftly interwoven with existing footage of Barbara Stanwyck and Edward Arnold, neither of whom was present for the retakes.[16]

Notably absent from any of these variations is an ending in which John leaps to his death. In the aftermath of the postrelease revision, it was widely reported that such an ending had been shot and previewed, but the production records offer no evidence for this.[17] Capra has given a variety of reasons for his rejection of such an ending; most revolve around his belief that a suicide, however logical, powerful, or couched in imagery of Christian redemption, would have signaled defeat to the audience. Here Capra speaks as a filmmaker whose desire to inspire an audience is clearly paramount, and who questions how a suicide could be set forth as a model resolution, especially at a time when the political problem posed

16. On 23 March Capra also filmed Bert Hansen and Sourpuss Smithers driving home from the John Doe convention, a scene that helps to set up the revised ending. Prior to his distribution of a new version in April, Capra also cut three brief passages from the original release: 1) an assertion by John during his confrontation with Norton at the dinner party that he now understood why people took up arms to protect themselves from "vultures" like the men present, 2) several vicious catcalls aimed at John by disillusioned followers at the John Doe convention, 3) a second Christmas carol sung outside Norton's house on New Year's Eve. See notes 28, 30, and 35 to the continuity script.

17. John's suicide could have been improvised on the set during the day in which the script was shot. It is even conceivable, although highly improbable, that Capra shot footage for which no records were kept. But why then would the other revisions be so well documented? It is interesting to note, moreover, that as early as February 1940, two months before a complete script had been written, Capra retitled the project *The Life of John Doe,* dropping the key words that would have obligated him to conclude the film with John's death.

in the fiction was applicable to the contemporary social scene. This presumed social need, moreover, was most likely reinforced by a generic precedent (with social roots of a less topical kind): Capra's own reliance on the conventions of romantic comedy to resolve the social melodramas his previous films had plotted.[18]

Given the narrative dynamics of the story leading up to the closing scene, the lack of a suicide was likely to be to some extent disappointing. Capra and Riskin's interest in staging a scene of John's defeat and humiliation at the convention had only intensified the pressure for this ending; suicide was now an act that could authenticate John's identity among those who had abandoned him. Narrative construction had been perversely logical on this score: events at the close would make a sensational scenario planted at the outset seem a matter of psychological necessity, motivated by a crisis of identity and given special force in the montage sequence that precedes the final scene. Moreover, the irony implicit in Connell's original story—that to save his reputation, Saunders Rook must take his life—had been translated into a martyr's triumph, in which an individual life assumes its greatest social power upon its termination. And the presence of Norton and his cabal on the City Hall roof at the close only heightened the sense that John's leap from the parapet was a victory of a kind; silenced at the convention, John's final confrontation with D.B. allows him briefly to recover his voice, and even to appear to outsmart his otherwise all-powerful antagonist.

From this perspective, the problem of the ending may seem a byproduct of a conflict between an intrinsic demand for the hero's death and extrinsic demands (based on perceived social need and generic precedent) for the character to live, an impasse forged at the moment of closure. Yet it is important to keep in mind that Capra and Riskin, in shaping the original treatment into a screenplay, altered the premises of the story in ways that generated contradictory pressures from within the narrative itself. Central here are the implications of their decision to convert the capitalists, who in the treatment are bent on suppressing the John Doe movement, into fifth columnists capable of exploiting such a movement for its own fascistic ends. In Capra and Riskin's version, the movement is never placed in unambiguous opposition to the corporate conspirators. In lieu of clearly defined, antagonistic forces engaged in political combat, the script to *Meet John Doe* cultivates tensions within a movement that now consists of three tiers, with

18. Although the problem of defining this film in terms of conventional genre fiction is suggested by the label assigned to *Meet John Doe* by the Production Code Administration: "melodrama-comedy (newspaper story) with social implications" (PCA File for *Meet John Doe*, Herrick Library).

the John Does on the bottom, at the mercy of an unseen cabal on top, and a media apparatus in between. D.B. acquires political capital by underwriting the development of a national network of members. Conflicting values and desires propel the movement forward as a social and political force.

Moreover, the John Doe club members are in and of themselves a volatile force. As good-hearted neighbors, they play a pivotal role in shaping John's acceptance of the role of leader, but their unruly abandonment of the movement at the convention plays no less a role in motivating John's journey to the City Hall roof at the close. However resonant John's metaphor of "family" may be to describe their potential relation to one another, they ultimately seem an unstable confederation seeking some broader social connection than an individual or marital life provides. The fact that the revival of the movement appears to require John's death in the end only reinforces the notion that its members are dependent on charismatic leaders and sensational acts to sustain their belief. In contrast to *The Life and Death of John Doe,* Capra and Riskin emphasize that if John should jump, the club members, far more than corporate conspirators, would bear the brunt of the blame. The role John internalizes thus taps a dark side of the Christian mythos: beyond fellowship and altruism looms a scenario of persecution, martyrdom, and guilt.

Guilt for John's final predicament in *Meet John Doe* also falls heavily on the character of the Ann, whose role in the film is considerably expanded and altered. The protagonists of "A Reputation" and *The Life and Death of John Doe* write their own death scripts: their early pronouncements generate the plot lines that eventually conclude with their suicides, an event that in some sense seems self-willed. From the very first drafts of the film script, however, Ann authors a fictional suicide threat in response to her firing at the *Bulletin;* John is then cast for the part, and gradually takes on the character as his own. Thus, whatever sense of autonomy may accrue around John's journey to the parapet at the close of *Meet John Doe,* it is a journey scripted for him by Ann.

In Capra and Riskin's revision of the treatment, moreover, Ann is a medium for the visions of her late father, preserved in the diary to which her mother gives Ann access. From this follow some of the more intriguing complications of character in the fiction. "Behind" John's voice is not simply the prose of a female ghostwriter, but the spectral voice of her father, whose absent image she projects (at the suggestion of her mother) upon the figure of John. Through the motif of the absent father, *Meet John Doe* weaves together two disconnected strands of the Connell-Presnell treatment: the romance plot between speechwriter and performer, and their invocation of a political and spiritual past to be reclaimed.[19] The voiced text of the father serves to bridge the past and present, the ideal and the mundane. Ann inhabits two spheres: an all-male society (the high-powered world of media and politics defined by Norton and his cabal, and Ted Sheldon and his troopers, a world in which she thrives) and the familial world of her mother and sisters, in whom are reposited a utopian morality. John, in turn, moves back and forth between two male societies: Norton's world of media and politics, and a world of adolescent male bonding and play. This second society is spoken for by the Colonel, but is also attractive to lower echelon figures of the first world such as Beany and Angelface, for whom a mimed ballgame is pleasurable diversion. If Ann, as emblem of sexual difference, lures John to occupy the world of media and political power, it is also at the service of her other role as conduit of familial values.

The effect of this on Ann's role in the fiction is twofold. It places her at the center of the narrative for the first third of the film, in a position of narrative agency but split by an internalized narrative conflict. Her ambitions, as defined at the outset, are ambiguous. How are we to understand the letter she fabricates? Does it give imaginative expression to the injustice experienced by the departing employees, thereby rechanneling personal anger into a fictional statement with broad social resonance? Or is it simply a clever and exploitive exercise that she concocts out of the events of her own predicament into a sensational fiction, the journalistic "fireworks" Connell has prescribed? Does her imaginative writing bear the seed of an authentic morality tale, or is her performance simply the point, demonstrating talents that might be parlayed into a career? Ann's fiction seems something of both, and as the film progresses this ambivalence underpins a conflict between Ann as ambitious survivor and Ann as keeper of her father's flame. In pursuit of power by way of an ethos of service and altruism, positioned between the audience and employer for whom she writes, Ann embodies the central contradictions of the John Doe movement itself.

At the same time, Ann's role is progressively diminished by the system of social relations mapped out by the fiction; as father's daughter, she is eventually dislodged from a place of power as narrative interest shifts to the character and identity of the male hero. The allusions to founding fathers and the legacy of Christ that she scripts are taken up by John and become his own; her projection of

---

19. The motif of the absent father, as Raymond Carney has astutely observed, is central to much of Capra's fiction. See Carney's *American Vision: The Films of Frank Capra* (Cambridge: Cambridge University Press, 1986), pp. 40–45.

a role of paternal authority upon him returns in the form of his dream of her wedding, where he imagines himself alternately as father of the bride and justice of the peace. A direct male lineage for the transmission of familial values is established, moreover, in the scene in which an inebriated Connell reveals his paternal side, invoking the memories of Washington, Jefferson, and Lincoln ("lighthouses in a foggy world"), before moving in seemingly desultory fashion toward his indictment of Norton by recalling the death of his own father, witnessed by the son on the battlefields of the First World War. Desultory, but with unerring dramatic logic, a few moments later, disabused of his faith in Norton's good intentions, John will confront Norton directly (speaking extemporaneously while Ann, now voiceless, watches), and will await a second confrontation with Norton in a public arena by standing at the convention podium, stunned, mouthing "land where my fathers died" as the audience sings a national hymn.

This dense cluster of motifs—interwoven so as to make the movement toward romantic and social integration, and spiritual and national renewal, appear all of a piece—paradoxically function so as to make resolution problematic. For how can the roles of Ann's double script—John as romantic partner, John as social martyr—be aligned? The demand for the consummation of the suicide plot entails the abstraction of John's social function so as to make a martyr's "future" more desirable than the domestic happiness signalled by the conventional gesture of a "romantic clinch." The romance is so freighted by a social problematic that romance alone cannot function as a narrative resolution; yet, without shoring up the romantic plot line at the close, the social model constructed on a metaphor of a national family collapses.

As if in recognition of the price of social inscription of this kind, Capra and Riskin introduce a figure who, like the absent father, does not appear in any previous version. As Dudley Andrew notes in an essay included in this volume, the Colonel argues from a position outside the system of values that otherwise propels the narrative. Indeed, one might say that it is his special function to articulate the degree to which the oppositions that structure a conventional social melodrama—ambition versus self-sacrifice, acquisition versus charity, cynicism versus innocence, exploited versus exploiter—are all part of a system of relations, each term dependent on the other, which constitutes a social trap. The Colonel refuses to distinguish between the schemes of Norton and the dreams of the people, between Ann as hustler and Ann as visionary. His counterproposition is an escape from romance, an escape from neighborhoods, and an escape from the binding force of the media.

As filmed by Capra, the scenes in which the trajectories of these characters and groups intersect are articulated visually so as to emphasize the tensions within this social configuration. Most telling here is Capra's orchestration of reaction shots so as to highlight the competing pull on John at moments when questions of social integration are foregrounded in the plot. There are multiple points of entry into major scenes, most notably John's first radio address, his meeting with the Millville club, and the convention. Capra plays the facial reactions of Ann, Connell, the Colonel, D.B., and the John Does off one another contrapuntally, with John the pivotal figure, and the object of the glances of others whether speaking or listening. The Colonel, meanwhile, stands or sits to the side, looking askance, undercutting the exploitable sentiment of the moment. He signals an escape route out of the social logic of these events, a logic into which all other figures, unwittingly or not, are locked. John's entrapment at the Millville City Hall is the apex of this pattern; with the Colonel's departure, John becomes available for packaging on a media tour, represented by means of a dizzying montage passage, where his body (not simply his photograph or his voice) is transported and circulated.

Having inscribed John within this system, Capra moreover effects a crucial reversal of the plot lines and stylistic patterning of *Mr. Deeds* and *Mr. Smith*. In the earlier films, scenes of isolation and estrangement precede the hero's revival as a persuasive performer in a climactic public spectacle. Emerging from incarceration and protracted silence, Deeds finally speaks at a public hearing, winning legal confirmation of his sanity and the right to redistribute his windfall fortune to impoverished farmers. Contemplating his betrayal in the shadows of the Lincoln Memorial, Smith is prompted by the heroine to return to the Senate floor to stage a filibuster, and finally exact a public confession of corruption from his betrayer. A sense of persecution in both instances gives way to an act of self-defense and social heroism. The parallel scene in *Meet John Doe* is the convention, but instead of winning over his audience, John loses them; instead of public celebration, there is hostility and violence. Reversing the pattern of the earlier films, John now slips into melancholic despondency. Where the earlier films build to a whirlwind climax, the convention passage, set off by John's blow to Ted Sheldon, and visually choreographed and sonically orchestrated for maximum dramatic impact, resolves nothing. The third of Slavko Vorkapich's three montage passages for the film turns subjective. Headlines are grotesquely distorted and past scenes are recycled as memories and supplanted by hallucinations of mockery.

The pace of events is then eerily suspended; the plot seems to hesitate. Cacophony and vocal mockery give way to the singing of "Silent Night"; rain-slick city streets now are covered with snow, occasioning a shift to what Dudley Andrew labels the "hieratic" register of the final scene. Having inherited the public spectacle on the City Hall rooftop from the original treatment, Capra takes great pains to re-imagine the scene in a setting at once open and secluded, on the eve of a holiday both secular and religious (in contrast to the singularly political connotations of the Fourth of July).[20] Public space, first represented at the convention as a hellhole of accusation, betrayal, and violence, is now a public building with an aerial view of the city skyline. William Cameron Menzies's elaborate set, with its monumental columns, might double for that of a cathedral, with churchbells ringing in the distance.

Given this setting and atmosphere, who was to appear in this scene? And to what effect? The process of revision highlights two issues: one concerning the resolution of the central narrative question—will John jump?—and the other concerning the implications of the epilogue or tag line. From the time of the original shooting script, the central argument against jumping had been given by Ann. Rebuffed by John, apprehended by Norton's troopers, detained at the police station, and then cloistered at home, Ann had been immobilized as the power struggle within the John Doe movement unfolded. The climb to the City Hall roof, against the counsel of mother and doctor, thus represents Ann's return to narrative power at the moment when an alternative ending to the fiction she had first crafted must be proposed. She arrives at City Hall, however, not as brash storyteller, but as pleading penitent, afflicted with unexplained fevers. What perhaps arrests attention in this passage is less the logic of her appeal than the sheer force of her performance, which turns John away from the railing.

Yet if the power Ann musters at the close is largely indebted to melodramatic expression, we might also pay attention to what the character is given to say. In the original shooting script, Ann's appeal has four parts: a confession of love, an assertion that she and John can rebuild the movement together, an observation that the presence of Norton's group on the roof is a sign of the lingering vitality of the movement, and a final plea that a movement worth dying for is worth living for (or else she will die too). Her first two points might suffice for conventional, romantic closure, but these may seem of slight consequence in light of the ques-

20. In the 13 June script the date in Ann's letter is originally Labor Day, but as if to shift the nature of the crisis from unemployment to a spiritual malaise, Ann changes the date to Christmas Eve.

tions concerning John's public identity and the fate of all John Does that the fiction has raised. Ann's interpretation of Norton's appearance on the roof, however, opens up another line of argument: that the movement can be remobilized without the consummation of the suicide act. In the 27 June script, it is this observation that ostensibly wins John over. Moreover, its appeal is buttressed in the script by descriptive commentary suggesting that D.B.'s world view has been altered by what he has witnessed, a transformation of the villain for which the only preparation is his ambiguous response to the Christmas carolers a short while before.

The suggestion that Christmas Eve might occasion a conversion experience was seized on by Capra and Riskin in the script composed 2 January and shot the next day, perhaps not coincidentally at the close of what for the director and writer was also a holiday season. In it, Ann, at wit's end, asks for divine help and is promptly inspired by a Christian trope: the death of Christ stands in for John's martyrdom. Her conflicting projection of John as both social martyr and lover is resolved, in effect, by insisting that John need not reenact a death scene; the image of John as Christ-like and, reciprocally, Christ as the "first John Doe" suffices. The terms of this metaphorical move dissolves the very need for temporal endings: whatever the historical contingencies, Ann claims, Christ will "go on keeping it alive forever and always!" No longer the secular weaver of plots, Ann emerges as hermeneutic interpreter, finding in inscrutable faces, in the sound of ringing bells, signs of the presence of another Father, absent but eternal, a source of immanent meaning. As scripted, the tone of the scene was immediately to shift; transformed by a "warm Christmas spirit" (the powers of which were first noted in the radio speech), John wishes Norton, "Merry Christmas"; D.B. orders the publication of John's letter and exchanges Christmas greetings with an elated Connell, and the once recalcitrant Colonel now "gaily" delivers his tag line. In effect, a beatific spell was to be cast over the scene by the invocation of a metaphor. But could a conversion of this kind take the place of a causally motivated resolution, one grounded in the traits of the characters as they had been developed to this point? In the weeks to follow, Capra and Riskin obviously had doubts. Whether responding to the reactions of preview audiences, or to their own sense of the inadequacy of the new material, they trimmed much of it back. Two days after the premiere, they cut Norton's closing conversion, surrendering any hope that he could be brought into the fold. By this point Capra had essentially settled for a stalemate at the finish.

Revisions to the epilogue and tag line are no less illuminating. Serving a conventional function, Capra and Riskin's original epilogue had pointed toward future events and had drawn a lesson from past ones. But it was also marked by a striking ambivalence. A storefront John Doe Club, John and Ann's excitement about a neighborhood meeting, and the apparent domestication of the Colonel all suggest a new application of the John Doe principle on a smaller scale. Yet the club announcement they post is mocked, and the final declaration of the Colonel is discordant and threatening. Moreover, the target of the Colonel's parting challenge—"Listen, you Heelots. I'm giving you one more chance"—is no longer simply the disillusioned townspeople, but the audience for the film, presumably Heelots all. The Colonel's access to that audience, concomitantly, suggests a narrational power unavailable to any other character, a capacity to speak across the boundaries of a fictional, diegetic space and time and comment on the audience's relation to what they have witnessed. Coming in the wake of the spectator's reprieve from the darker implications of the plot, as part of a "happy ending" in which the Colonel himself has been inscribed, his remark has particular resonance. A film that opens with an invitation to "meet John Doe" closes with a warning from its most intransigent character: we have "one more chance." If we fail this test, will the next John Doe jump? Guilt for the fate of John, and the John Doe movement, is redirected toward the audience.

In the January revision, however, the epilogue has been jettisoned and the Colonel's closing remark tacked onto a scene in which the Christmas spirit has prevailed. Moreover, a minor change in wording and a fundamental shift in address transforms an aggressive assertion into playful self-rebuke—"Well, looks like I gotta give the Heelots one more chance"—contained within the realm of the diegesis and the private ruminations of a character. The Colonel has learned a lesson; the Heelots may not be such a bad lot after all. By the time of the premiere, moreover, the Colonel's role has been further reduced to a simple expression of relief ("Long John!") after his friend decides not to jump. And the idea of an epilogue or tag line has been wholly replaced by the voices of a nondiegetic chorus, filling a void with a compensatory song about faith and brotherhood as Ann and John depart to an unknown fate.

The 23 March material, however, lays the groundwork for a different epilogue, entirely contained within the closing scene. The arrival of the Millville club members on the roof does not appear to motivate, as Capra, among others, has often suggested, John's decision not to jump. Their reactions are foregrounded as Ann's argument takes its metaphorical turn, but they themselves do not speak, indeed do not appear even recognized by John, until he has lifted Ann up in his arms. Their confession, pleas, and offer of assistance, however, provide the ground for the possibility of a new social order extending precariously beyond the embrace of Ann and John. In lieu of the Colonel, who is relegated to the background, Connell now steps forward to formulate precisely the social conflict that the fiction has never dramatized: "There you are, Norton. The people! Try and lick that." By April 1941, the John Does have been recast as "the people," and a source of power; aggression, in turn, is belatedly redirected toward Norton.

1ST MAN (*off*): Paging John Doe! . . . Paging John Doe!
CHAUFFEUR: Who is John Doe?
1ST WOMAN: Who is John Doe?
2ND MAN: Who is John Doe?
—transcript of promotional trailer for *Meet John Doe* [21]

"He's the man the ads are written for. He's the fellow everybody sells things to. He's the Joe Doakes, the world's greatest stooge and the world's greatest strength."
—John's radio address in *Meet John Doe*

Announced in bold letters over the entranceway to the Rivoli Theatre in New York for the opening run of *Meet John Doe* in March 1941 was not only the title of the film but the names of producer-director Frank Capra and the film's principal stars, Gary Cooper and Barbara Stanwyck. On opposite ends of the entrance display were two sets of oversized photographic cut-outs, each pairing the stars. On the left, Cooper's hand was lifted as if in a wave; on the right, it reached forward as if to shake the hand of another. Scripted over both pairs of figures was the film's invitational title: "Meet John Doe Now!" [22]

Arranged for the eye of the passing pedestrian or motorist, this sidewalk display was very much in keeping with the broader promotional campaign for the film. Coordinated across various outlets for advertising—marquees, trailers, and the media channels of newspaper, magazines, and radio—was the reminder that Capra was as much an attraction in *Meet John Doe* as were the two stars, that (as one ad phrased it) his was the "one magic name" behind a host of Academy Award–winning films. Moreover, Capra was now introducing a new character,

21. Trailer transcript, *Meet John Doe* file, Warners Archives, USC.
22. A photograph of the front of the Rivoli Theatre during the opening run of the film was published in Warners' Publicity Campaign Book for *Meet John Doe* (Advertising and Publicity File, Warners Archives, USC). The specific ads I discuss here are also from this book.

not simply a new film. "In a little New England town," the copy to one ad in the Warners campaign book read, "Capra's all-seeing camera-eye found 'Mr. Deeds.' Further West, it discovered 'Mr. Smith.' Now the eyes of Capra rove the country to seek out 'Mr. Doe.'" "To all Friends of Mr. Deeds . . . Meet John Doe," read the headline to another. At the Rivoli Theatre, this rhetorical device was translated into a sidewalk gimmick. John Doe was poised to greet the patron; although the figure was cardboard, his handshake inanimate, on the moviehouse screen John Doe came to "life." [23]

But who *was* "John Doe"? Absent from the promotional material was any concrete notion of character, setting, subject matter, or narrative premise. No mention was made of Long John Willoughby, or of the role of politics, religion, or the media in the fiction. Beyond a suggestion of conventional romance, there was no indication of genre or plot, or of the nature of Stanwyck's role in support of the main figure. [24] Attention was instead directed outside the fiction to two entities: Gary Cooper as star, and the audience who might come to see him. As with all star-centered fictions, a certain ambiguity between star and role was exploited: meet Gary Cooper (a celebrated actor) *as* John Doe (a construct of this particular fiction). But the ambiguity was complicated in this instance by the wedding of the image of the star to a name that connoted the very opposite of stardom: the anonymous American citizen. Consider, for example, two more ads. In one, a full-figure sketch of Cooper is matched by a silhouetted outline, which in turn is "fleshed in" with line drawings of hundreds of tiny figures.

23. It is difficult to calculate the exact scope or impact of a publicity campaign of this kind, or to gauge the degree to which it responded to popular thought about Capra's films or shaped the debate about them. It is likely, moreover, that some of the ads designed for the campaign were used infrequently, if at all, by exhibitors around the country. But the campaign book constitutes a kind of "first reading" of the film by the publicity department at Warners, which sought to find the proper "fit" for the film in economic and cultural sectors.

24. Doe gained a certain status by virtue of his association with Longfellow Deeds and Jefferson Smith, but lacked their regional definition. Where did he come from? "He's 3,000 miles wide and 1,000 miles tall," one ad asserted, superimposing a sketch of Cooper over a map of America. Character in this instance was simply conflated with country, his dimensions graphable only in terms of its outermost boundaries. Paul N. Lazarus, who was vice-president in charge of advertising at Warners in 1941, and who designed the *Meet John Doe* campaign, recalls that Robert Riskin lobbied to have more details concerning the story included in the ads, but that Lazarus himself was convinced that focusing on Capra, Cooper, and Stanwyck was the best way to market a potentially downbeat film. Those ads that depicted the John Does as a collective body seeking a hero, Lazarus speculates, were likely a concession to Riskin (Interview with author, Santa Barbara, California, 19 January 1988).

Posted over Cooper and his silhouette is the slogan: "One Man in a Million! . . . A Million Men in One!" In the other, Cooper bends over to greet a field of similarly drawn miniatures, beneath the headline: "John Doe . . . Meet America!" (Fig. 1). If the first encouraged a certain play between the extraordinary and the ordinary, the larger and the smaller than life, the second suggested that the larger-than-life figure was positioned to meet the multitudes he represented on the screen: Americans met themselves in the figure of Gary Cooper/John Doe.

As advertisements for motion picture patronage, these verbal and graphic texts made it clear that a theater was the appropriate location for such a transaction. America was an *audience,* and the only hand an audience could give to a celluloid John Doe was one of applause. Overseeing this transaction was Capra. At the top of the ad in which Capra's search across the breadth of America for a new character was described, there was a sketch of the director, script in hand, sitting behind a disproportionately large camera lens, from which flowed a stream of tiny figures (Fig. 2). The image suggested with striking economy that Capra's camera-eye allowed for the eventual projection of not simply a hero, but of the anonymous crowd out of which such a figure emerged, and the audience for whom such a figure was cinematographically displayed. To enter the front door of a movie theater and meet John Doe was perhaps to discover yourself, or your neighbor, or yourself as part of the national neighborhood that Capra's "camera eye" envisioned.

Throughout this promotional material, the referent for "John Doe" was mobile and shifting. As a social fiction, the term gave a name to the idea of an ordinary American, an individuated (male) subject within an otherwise undifferentiated citizenry. In the case of these ads, the very instability of the notion of a specific, embodied John Doe allowed for the transfer of the term among a variety of figures—as visible as a star, as anonymous as a spectator—within a national community defined by the motion picture industry. In this fashion, the cultural notion of "John Doe" was translated into the language of commercial movie-making and movie-going.[25]

The willingness of viewers to identify with the John Doe label is evident in the

25. The rhetoric of promotion and publicity also appears to have provided a convenient framework for reviewers. Consider, for example, Bosley Crowther's initial response, reprinted in this volume, in which "John Doe" is used interchangeably to identify the average American citizen, the character in the fiction, and the audience—"you and countless other John Does" whom Crowther instructs to see the film. Crowther's follow-up review in *The New York Times*, 16 March 1941, sec. 10, p. 5, was titled "How to Be a Good American."

Figure 1

Figure 2

mail Capra received in the weeks following the release of the film. Numerous people noted that they had been inspired to form John Doe clubs. Others vigorously—and in a few cases vehemently—opposed the depiction of the John Doe club members as a mob, considering it a betrayal by Capra of the John Does in the audience. Alternative endings were suggested: Norton's servants could inform other John Does of the confrontation they had witnessed at the mansion; Ann could deliver her confession over a loudspeaker set up for caroling on the streets outside City Hall, and her amplified voice could be picked up by a radio network; John could return to Millville and organize a new club with Sourpuss Smithers. Their comments, in turn, prompted Capra's decision to return to a sound stage on 23 March and shoot new footage that cast the Millville John Doe Club in a more favorable light.[26] The decision was remarkable. *Meet John Doe* was already a substantial critical and moderate commercial success, and "word-of-mouth" on the film had already been set; by rereleasing the film with a different ending, Capra opened himself up to mild ridicule in the press.[27] Capra's bid for "independence" from a conventional system of studio production now extended to protocols of distribution and exhibition; indeed, the boundary line between production and exhibition had become somewhat blurred. Dialogue of a kind opened up between the director and this self-selecting group of correspondents. In the figure of Capra, viewers and reviewers located someone of singular

26. *Meet John Doe* Correspondence Files, Capra Collection, Wesleyan. Capra replied fairly promptly to the first round of letters he received, but delayed answering those with suggestions for alternative endings until 8 April, when his revised version was in distribution. In the excerpt from his autobiography reprinted in this volume, Capra quotes from a single letter, signed "John Doe," which he claims sparked his decision to shoot a "fifth" ending with the John Doe Club on the roof. The correspondence files at the Wesleyan do not contain this letter, although several letters express related sentiments, and a couple are signed "John Doe." It is possible that Capra synthesized various responses in a composite letter, ostensibly authored by single individual. If so, Capra employs a storytelling license not unrelated to the one assumed by Ann in the film.

27. Capra, moreover, claims to have disliked reshooting scenes after filming had been completed: "I'd gotten out of that shell. I'd gotten out of that cocoon. It was difficult for me and for the actors too." Transcript of interview conducted at the Academy of Motion Picture Arts and Sciences, 2 November 1968; reprinted in Jeanine Basinger, *The It's a Wonderful Life Book* (New York: Alfred A. Knopf, 1986). The problems and possibilities of ending (and continuing) the plot to *Meet John Doe* may have continued to fascinate him, however. On 7 May 1941, Douglas W. Churchill reported in *The New York Times* that Capra and Riskin were preparing a scenario for a sequel, titled *The Further Adventures of John Doe*. In June, it was also reported that stage actress Maude Adams was negotiating with Capra to star in *Meet Jane Doe, Mother of John Doe*.

responsibility, an author they could hold accountable for the fiction, and to whom they could propose endings of their own design.

Yet the very terms of this relationship were contingent upon a media apparatus that accommodated such an exchange. It was, after all, the publicity machinery of Hollywood, and related organs of the press and radio, that made it possible for viewers to identify Capra as an author in the first place. As eye behind the camera, master of the machinery, and magic name behind the screen, Capra himself was promoted and packaged by the system from which he would claim "independence." Furthermore, as Nick Browne suggests in an essay in this volume, the national audience to whom Capra might address his claim of directorial autonomy was a function of a exhibition circuit that was a central component of the Hollywood studio system during these years. As a product circulating within this system, *Meet John Doe* was enmeshed in a nexus of promotional activities and media tie-ins. Warners radio affiliate KWFB in Los Angeles billed themselves as "Mr. John Doe's station" for the two weeks prior to the opening, and actor James Gleason plugged the film over the air. An opening night tribute to Capra was devised for the radio, featuring the "transcribed voices" of Gary Cooper, Walter Brennan, and other stars, and the premiere was broadcast live from the lobby of Warner's Hollywood theater by Knox Manning, an announcer who appears at the John Doe convention in the film. The motorcycle corps of actor Victor McLaglen, used as D. B. Norton's paramilitary troopers in *Meet John Doe*, supplemented Warner's "police staff" at the opening. The head of Warner's Pacific Coast theaters launched a special tie-in campaign with the *Los Angeles News;* their ad featured a photograph of Cooper and his signed endorsement of the daily paper, under the headline, "Meet John Doe and his newspaper." John Doe contests were sponsored by other papers in Los Angeles and New York.[28] *Life* magazine published a photo-essay on Dorothy Andree, cast in the film in the fleeting, satirized role of "Miss Average Girl," and speculated that by uttering four words in a Frank Capra movie she might be on a path to stardom.[29] And *Time* magazine,

---

28. *Motion Picture Herald,* 29 March 1941, p. 6; 12 April 1941, p. 59; *Los Angeles Times,* 13 March 1941, p. 16. In 1942, a condensed radio adaptation of *Meet John Doe* was broadcast on the Philip Morris Program. Moreover, the sale of broadcast rights to television was to help bolster profits from the film. By 1949, when *Meet John Doe* premiered on KTLA in Los Angeles on Christmas Day, Capra and Riskin were reported to have earned over $1 million from television, reissue, and 16mm sales (Warners Legal Files, Box 12723, Princeton; *Variety,* 20 December 1949).

29. "Dorothy Andree Gets Her Big Chance: Four Words in a Frank Capra Picture," *Life,* 17 March 1941, p. 59.

whose front cover had been appropriated by Capra and Riskin in *Meet John Doe* to mark the national celebrity of their protagonist, reappropriated the device for their own report on the film and its newsworthy star. The photograph of John used in the film was recaptioned, "Gary Cooper—John Doe/He made the cover," and the article inside recounted how an ordinary man from Montana "went to Hollywood and became the most popular man in America," elevated to a position of national prominence because he had never lost touch with an "indestructible naturalness." Cooper's biography was thus retraced over the celebrity saga of the fictional folk hero he portrayed.[30]

As a work of social reform fiction, *Meet John Doe* reconfigured media relations of this kind so as to render them both dramatic and problematic. The label "John Doe" is dispersed in the film over a body politic of ambiguous character (the world's greatest stooges as well as the world's greatest strength) and is attached to a media hero whose fraudulent character must be exposed. The very premise of the film calls into question the possibility of an authentic relationship between the "hero" and the "people" by transposing the former into a performer and the latter into an audience. Moreover, to the extent that a commercial media binds—by way of the modern technology of printing, photography, and vocal transmission—a national (and international) audience, the notion of a "good neighbor" has been crucially redefined. Even as the ending to *Meet John Doe* courts the possibility of transparent or transcendent relations, the force of the media stubbornly holds sway. John's anonymous burial in potter's field, Norton notes, would nullify his bid to revive the John Doe movement. At risk is his public image, not his soul, as John acknowledges in leaving behind a letter for the *Bulletin* that ensures that his fictive self will endure.

In contrast to Jo Swerling's incomplete play, *The World Is an Eightball*, in which John's death scene at a Paramount theater is linked to the gala premiere of his filmed biography, the role of Hollywood in this social problematic is never addressed. Cinema remains exempt from the explicit media critique *Meet John Doe* otherwise advances. Yet by foregrounding the work of an author, actor, producer, and audience in the construction and promotion of a hero, and elevating the question of the authorship and authenticity of media fictions to the status of a narrative problem, *Meet John Doe* invites critical appraisal of the media context that secured its own ground as a commercial object in 1941. To see this has perhaps required time, and a vantage point on the relationship of cinema to

30. "Coop," *Time*, 3 March 1941, cover and pp. 78–82.

various strands of technological, social, and political history in the twentieth century. It has also required that critics approach films (including those from Hollywood) with an eye for signs of self-consciousness, a dimension highly prized in commentaries on works of "high art" in the modern age. Indeed, if there has been a central dynamic to criticism of *Meet John Doe* in recent years, it has been the pursuit of this dimension, and an attempt to ground the film's heightened self-consciousness in the details of Capra's biography, the relation of Capra as director to his collaborators in Hollywood, or the institutional relation of the studio system to other media.[31]

In "John Doe; or, the False Ending," Parker Tyler argues that the journey of John away from the parapet is indicative of Hollywood's debasement of forms of classical drama in pursuit of the "pseudo-divine." Death is symbolic, not terminal: the demand for a happy ending results in the death of a certain conception of the heroic, with John Doe at the close transformed into Gary Cooper, an impersonator of the classical hero from Hollywood.[32] To insist on John's suicide as a clarifying act, however, is to cling to the notion that his audience requires, for its moral instruction or aesthetic satisfaction, the recycling of a myth in a mass medium. "Fictions can degenerate into myths when they are not consciously held to be fictive," writes Frank Kermode in *A Sense of an Ending*, proposing that whereas assent to a myth is absolute, assent to a fiction is conditional.[33] In the revised ending to *Meet John Doe,* the club members from Millville seem to be groping toward a distinction of this kind ("anyway, what he stood for wasn't a fake," Mrs. Hansen asserts), as the film itself seems to grope toward the salvaging of a fiction out of a mythic martyrdom that cannot be countenanced. Alternately hailed by the Colonel and Mrs. Hansen as "Long John" and "Mr. Doe," John does not appear headed toward a world in which his identity has been any more sharply defined, yet the movement away from the parapet is in the direction of something more tempered than the wild flights of imagination and shifts in mood that have dominated the film to this moment. Only conditional assent to the

---

31. See the essays by Richard Glatzer, Dudley Andrew, and Nick Browne included in this volume for examples of each of these approaches. A detailed discussion of the self-reflexive dimension of *Meet John Doe,* within the context of Capra's career as a filmmaker, also appears in Raymond Carney's *American Vision: The Films of Frank Capra,* pp. 347–376.

32. Tyler, *The Hollywood Hallucination,* pp. 182–187.

33. Frank Kermode, *The Sense of an Ending: Studies in the Theory of Fiction* (New York: Oxford University Press, 1967), p. 39.

idea of Long John's worthiness seems required of the John Does in the fiction; audiences for the fiction need not give more. From this perspective, the blemishes of reworking this ending (many times over) may signal a salutary, if inadvertent, skepticism about social messiahs in an era when the idea of absolute authority and "final solutions" carried with it an especially pernicious political charge.

Frank Capra
A Biographical Sketch

Born to Sicilian peasants in 1897, Frank Capra immigrated with his family to the United States when he was six, and grew up in an Italian neighborhood in Los Angeles. A bright student, he was the first member of his family to complete high school and received a scholarship to attend the California Institute of Technology, from which he earned a bachelor's degree in chemical engineering in 1918. During the waning months of World War I, he served in the Coast Artillery in San Francisco, but then found himself unemployed amid the postwar recession. He spent much of the next three years traveling the western states, peddling self-improvement books, photographs, and blue-sky mining stocks, and playing poker and performing on the guitar in various cities and small towns.

In December 1921, Capra was hired by an aspiring film producer in San Francisco to direct a twelve-minute adaptation of a poem by Rudyard Kipling. No more experienced in motion pictures than his employer, Capra nevertheless directed the film with sufficient skill that it was sold to a distributor, Pathé, for a substantial profit. The success prompted Capra to pursue a film apprenticeship in earnest, first as an assistant in a photo lab, then as a properties manager, editor, and writer for Bob Eddy, a Hollywood producer filming comedy shorts in San Francisco. In 1924 he returned to Los Angeles to work as a gag writer for Hal Roach and Mack Sennett. When comic star Harry Langdon left Sennett to produce his own films in 1926, he took Capra with him. Capra directed two of Langdon's features (*The Strong Man* [1926], *Long Pants* [1927]), and in 1928 was hired as a contract director at Columbia Pictures.

Over the next few years, Capra honed his craft on a series of quickly produced, low-budget features at Columbia, directed economically yet with felicitous "touches" that soon caught the eye of critics. He also emerged as a key figure in the plan of studio chief Harry Cohn to elevate the financial and social status of the "poverty row" studio, and established close working relationships with some of the most promising talent Columbia had under contract, including cinematographer Joseph Walker, screenwriters Jo Swerling and Robert Riskin, actors Ralph Graves and Jack Holt, and actress Barbara Stanwyck. In 1933, Capra's opulently designed melodrama with Stanwyck and Nils Asther, *The Bitter Tea of General Yen,* was selected to inaugurate a new all-movie policy at the year-old Radio City Music Hall in New York, and his adaptation of a Damon Runyon urban comedy, *Lady for a Day,* released at the Music Hall nine months later, went on to garner Academy Award nominations in four of the top five categories. Capra's next film, *It Happened One Night,* paired Clark Gable and Claudette Colbert in an unassuming romantic "road" comedy that was the box-office surprise of 1934; the following spring it swept the top five Academy Awards, including Best Director.

By the time of the award, Capra had established a critical reputation as a comic stylist with a sure sense of pace and a facility for eliciting offbeat, charming performances. Capra claims, however, that this period was a time of stock-taking (and of an undiagnosed physical ailment), after which the social relevance of his work became a more pressing concern. As early as *The Miracle Woman* (1931) and *American Madness* (1932), he had evidenced a willingness to tackle topical issues on the screen (the career of radio evangelist Aimee Semple MacPherson in the first film, a depression-era bank run in the second), but it was not until *Mr. Deeds Goes to Town* in 1936 that Capra, with his by then favorite screenwriter Robert Riskin, hit upon a formula for combining comedy and social melodrama in a story with broad popular appeal. His next three films—*Lost Horizon* (1937), *You Can't Take It with You* (1938), and *Mr. Smith Goes to Washington* (1939)—were all celebrated works, and *Mr. Smith,* in particular, generated critical debate about the possibility of a Hollywood filmmaker giving serious treatment to topical political material and at the same time retaining a hold on the box-office.

During the 1930s, Capra also carved out a unique position for himself within the Hollywood studio system. At Columbia, he exercised primary control over the writing, casting, and editing of his films, consolidated a loyal crew, and commanded increasingly larger budgets and longer production schedules. He also assumed a prominent role in the industry at large, serving as president of the Academy of Motion Picture Arts and Science from 1935 to 1939, and as head of the Directors Guild from 1938 to 1940, during which time the organization won hard-fought recognition from the studio heads. He emerged as an outspoken

critic of standard studio production practices and defender of the creative autonomy of the director. The subject of both a cover story in *Time* and a photo-spread
in *Life* in 1938, Capra was extensively interviewed and profiled in the press,
enjoying a popular reputation as a "star" director.

On the eve of the release of *Mr. Smith* in October 1939, Capra put his faith in
directorial autonomy to the test when he and Riskin formed Frank Capra Productions, the company that was to produce *Meet John Doe* at Warner Brothers in
1940–1941. But Capra's problems with resolving the plot to *Meet John Doe*
shook his confidence, and, although the film was profitable, the tax structure
under which the production company operated was financially debilitating. Parting ways with Riskin, Capra pursued a variety of offers for independent deals at
other studios, and, perhaps in search of other options, also offered his services to
the Army in July of 1941. A few months later, he directed *Arsenic and Old Lace*
at Warners to make some quick cash, and was inducted into the Army on the set
the day after Pearl Harbor. Assigned to the Morale Branch of the Signal Corps,
Capra by June 1942 had set up a film unit in Los Angeles, where he supervised
the production of the Army orientation series, *Why We Fight,* as well as several
related indoctrination projects. In September 1943, he was appointed head of a
special unit to improve photographic coverage of battlefronts, and remained on
special assignment for the duration of the war.

Back in Hollywood in 1945, Capra ventured into independent production for a
second time, forming Liberty Films with Samuel Briskin (a former Columbia
producer who had worked as a production manager in Capra's film unit during
the war) and two prominent directors back from the battlefront, William Wyler
and George Stevens. For the next year-and-a-half, Capra devoted his energies to
making *It's a Wonderful Life.* Today, the film is perhaps Capra's most widely
known work, but its reception in December 1946 fell far short of Capra's expectations. By the spring of 1947, with the first films of Wyler and Stevens not yet
completed, the company was in financial trouble. Capra and Briskin convinced
their colleagues to accept an offer from Paramount to buy Liberty, including the
services of its founders. Following the release of *The State of the Union* (1948),
his second and last film for Liberty, Capra was again under contract to a Hollywood studio. The arrangement was not a happy one; finding most of the projects
he proposed vetoed by Paramount executives, Capra completed two modest
comedies with Bing Crosby, then terminated his contract with the studio.

Frustrated by the experience, Capra reluctantly withdrew from the industry,
selling off story ideas and retreating with his family to their avocado ranch south

of Los Angeles. He kept his hand in filmmaking during the mid-fifties, however, by producing, writing, and directing four science documentaries for Bell Telephone, all of which were broadcast on network television and later distributed to schools. Then in 1957, in an effort to return to directing features, Capra set up an independent, co-production deal with Frank Sinatra for the making of *A Hole in the Head.* He also resumed an active role in industry politics, serving a second term as president of the Directors Guild and overseeing the merger of the screen branch with that of radio and television in 1959. As a director, however, he found "independent" production in the new Hollywood to be contingent on the schedules and whims of "bankable" stars, and a co-production with Glenn Ford to remake *Lady for a Day* as *Pocketful of Miracles* in 1961 was fraught with conflict. After struggling to get various feature films off the ground over the next few years, a demoralized Capra decided to retire for good in 1967.

The writing and publication of Capra's autobiography, *The Name Above the Title,* however, paved the way for a new career. Part comedy, part melodrama, and part moral fable, the book traced the ups and downs of his career in a fashion not dissimilar to the roller coaster plot of some of his films, and was a popular success. Embarking on a tour of colleges and universities, Capra also discovered a new audience for his films and took up the cause of film education in academia. Retrospectives of his films were mounted (including screenings of his previously neglected early films), and a new body of critical writing emerged that assured a place for that work in histories of film and American popular culture. Honored at a variety of festivals and tributes, Capra maintained a busy schedule until the mid-1980s, when failing health finally slowed him down. Now in his nineties, he resides in the desert community of La Quinta, California.

Meet John Doe

Meet John Doe

The composition of this continuity script is based on a close examination of various 16mm prints and videotapes of *Meet John Doe,* and the script has been checked against a 35mm print held by the UCLA Film Archive. Although versions with variant endings were in circulation in March and April of 1941, and truncated prints have been reissued and broadcast on television over the years, I have taken the "definitive" version of *Meet John Doe* to be the last one worked on by Capra and Riskin. Encompassing new material shot by Capra on 23 March, eleven days after the film had officially opened, it was distributed to theaters in early April and was the version used for the film's general release on 4 May. After that time, Capra made no further changes.

In July 1941, Frank Capra Productions prepared a "final script" for the film, designed to bring the shooting script into conformity with the version in general release. It is a curious, hybrid work, combining dialogue from the film, prose passages and shot sequences culled from various shooting scripts, and descriptions of actions and significant gestures that are not mentioned in the script but appear in the film. (The last are often misdescribed.) Copies of this script are held by various archives, and it has recently been reprinted (with minor changes in format) in an anthology edited by Sam Thomas, *Best American Screenplays* (New York: Crown, 1986). Students and scholars should keep in mind that it is neither an accurate shooting script *nor* an accurate continuity script.

Although I have occasionally drawn on information supplied in the shooting script (such as names of unidentified characters or settings), in general I have restricted myself to the images and sounds of the film as these bear on the unfolding of the plot. This involves considerable selection and compression, but I think a reader familiar with *Meet John Doe* should be able to reconstruct a fuller sense of the film from the material presented here.

The scale of individual shots are indicated by the following abbreviations:

CU   close-up
MCU   medium close-up
MS   medium shot
MLS   medium long shot
LS   long shot
ELS   extreme long shot

As is conventional practice, these descriptions are cued to the relation of camera distance to the central object of interest in the shot (usually a human subject), but particular shots may have multiple and shifting centers of interest, and markings of this kind are always approximate. Unless otherwise noted, transitions between shots should be assumed to be straight cuts. Transitions involving a spatial and temporal shift in the action are signaled by double spacing. The only exceptions to this general rule are the three montage sequences, which I have bracketed as autonomous segments. It is also important to note that the use of rapid dissolves and multiple images within these passages make the delineation of individual shots difficult. My general procedure in such cases has been to treat any image that lingers, while other images emerge and fade, as the base image for a single "shot."

Credits and Cast

Credits

Production Company:
Frank Capra Productions

Producers:
Frank Capra and Robert Riskin

Director:
Frank Capra

Screenplay:
Robert Riskin [and, uncredited, Myles Connolly], from a treatment, "The Life and Death of John Doe," by Richard Connell and Robert Presnell, based on Connell's short story, "A Reputation"

Photography:
George Barnes

Editor:
Daniel Mandell

Montage Effects:
Slavko Vorkapich

Special Effects:
Jack Cosgrove

Art Director:
Stephen Goosson

Production Design:
William Cameron Menzies

Gowns:
Natalie Visart

Musical Score:
Dimitri Tiomkin

Musical Director:
Leo F. Forbstein

Choral Arrangements:
Hall Johnson

Sound:
C. A. Riggs

Assistant Director:
Arthur S. Black

Locations:
Warner Brothers Studio, Burbank, Ca.; Wrigley Field, Los Angeles (the convention); Griffith Park, Los Angeles (scenes by the bridge); Pasadena, Ca. (Norton's estate); ice house, 525 Clayton Street, Los Angeles (City Hall roof)

Distributor:
Warner Brothers, through Vitagraph, Inc.

Released:
March 12, 1941 (Rivoli and Hollywood theatres, New York City; Warners-Hollywood and Warners-

Downtown theatres, Los Angeles;
Paramount and Beach theatres,
Miami; Criterion Theatre, Oklahoma
City)

Running time:
Running times ranging from 123 to
129 minutes were reported in
newspapers and the trade press at the
time of the film's initial release. The
variations perhaps reflect the fact that
Capra was still tinkering with the
film. Although the April release
introduced new material, the overall
length of the film was reportedly
reduced. 16mm prints currently run
approximately 121 minutes.

Cast

**Long John Willoughby/
"John Doe"**
Gary Cooper

Ann Mitchell
Barbara Stanwyck

D. B. Norton
Edward Arnold

Colonel
Walter Brennan

Henry Connell
James Gleason

Mrs. Mitchell
Spring Byington

Ted Sheldon
Rod La Rocque

Office boy
Bennie Bartlett

Sign painter
Garry Owen

Newspaper secretary
Bess Flowers

Pop Dwyer
Aldrich Bowker

Joe
Edward MacWade

Governor
Vaughan Glaser

Jim, Governor's associate
John Hamilton

Governor's associate
William Forrest

Spencer
Andrew Tombes

Mayor Lovett
Gene Lockhart

Mayor's secretary
Edward Hearn

Mrs. Brewster
Mrs. Gardner Crane

Beany
Irving Bacon

Angelface
Warren Hymer

Eddie, a photographer
Hank Mann

Ann's sisters
Carlotta Jelm, Tina Thayer

Mike
Pat Flaherty

Miss Average Girl
Dorothy Andree

Male midget
Billy Curtis

Female midget
Johnny Fern

Radio station director
Edward Earle

Radio station announcer
Mike Frankovich

Dan
Sterling Holloway

Mayor Hawkins
Harry Holman

Mrs. Hawkins
Sarah Edwards

Bert Hansen
Regis Toomey

Mrs. Hansen
Ann Doran

"Sourpuss" Smithers
J. Farrell MacDonald

Grubbell
Frank Austin

Mrs. Delaney
Emma Tansey

Mr. Delaney
Lafe McKee

Charlie
Charles C. Wilson

Wall Street tycoon
Ed Kane

Relief administrator
Edward Keane

Republican
Paul Everton

Democrat
Ed Stanley

Legislator
Forbes Murray

Convention radio announcers
Selmer Jackson, Knox Manning,
John B. Hughes

Hammett
Pierre Watkin

Weston
Stanley Andrews

Bennett
Mitchell Lewis

Barrington
Walter Soderling

Butler
Cyril Thornton

Sheriff
James McNamara

Doctor
John Ince

Police Commissioner
Richard Kipling

Sergeant
William Gould

Policemen
Earl Bunn, Eddie Cobb, Jack Cheatham

The Continuity Script

Credits are printed over a series of "stock shots" of American life linked by dissolves. The images include: a throng viewed from above, workers punching timecards, farmhands sowing seeds, miners walking through an underground tunnel, women at work in a garment factory, switchboard operators, a crowded urban street, a crowded boardwalk and beachfront, spectators cheering, students passing through a campus archway, civilians led by a uniformed soldier at a campsite, West Point cadets marching smartly in parade formation, and children at play in a schoolyard. The orchestral accompaniment to these images incorporates three American folk tunes: "Roll Out the Barrel," "Take Me Out to the Ballgame," and "Oh Susanna." [1] The sequence ends with Frank Capra's directorial credit over an image of rows of babies in bassinets. As the credit fades out, the camera tracks left and there is a dissolve in closer to a single baby. The music softens to an accordion solo of "Take Me Out to the Ballgame" and the crying of the babies rises up on the soundtrack. Fade out.

1. *Fade in on* MS *of a weathered plaque: "Est. 1862/THE BULLETIN/'A free press means a free people.'" A worker attacks the lettering with a pneumatic chisel.*

2. CU: *the words "free press" are chiseled off.*

3. *Dissolve to* MS *of the plaque with its lettering removed. A new sign with modern lettering is lifted into place: "THE NEW BULLETIN/A streamlined newspaper for a streamlined era." [2]*

4. *Dissolve to* MS *of the frosted glass window of the door to the office of the Managing Editor. The name of "Henry Connell" is being painted. An office boy exits, interrupting the work of the sign painter.*

5. MCU *of office workers in a newsroom, looking up as the door slams.*

6. LS, *panning with the office boy as he comes to the center of the newsroom.*

7. MCU *of the office boy. He checks his clipboard, then points to and whistles at a figure offscreen left.*

8. MCU *of a senior employee by the Sports Art Department door.*

9. MCU *of the office boy, who crosses his throat with his finger and makes a popping sound to signal that the man has been "axed."*

10. MCU *of the fired employee, who salutes ironically.*
11. MCU *of the office boy, who repeats the gesture for another employee.*
12. CU: *another veteran lowers his head despondently.*
13. CU: *yet another employee nods sadly in response to the boy's whistle.*
14. MLS *of the newsroom. The office boy's whistle summons a woman from her seat in the background as her colleagues turn to watch.*
15. MCU *of the office boy; he gives the "ax" sign two more times.*
16. MS *of Connell's door. The painter is again interrupted as a stream of people exit: two older men, an older woman who is weeping, and the young Ann Mitchell, who is solemn. The painter waits for the door to swing shut.*
17. MCU *of Ann, thinking. Suddenly, she spins around and heads back to the door.*
18. MS *of the door as Ann passes through. When it closes, we see that the last letter on Connell's name has smeared, to the considerable chagrin of the painter.*
19. LS, *inside Connell's office, panning with Ann as she crosses to his desk, where he stands with his silent, pipe-smoking assistant, Pop.*[3]
    CONNELL *(on the phone)*: Yeah, D.B. Oh, just cleaning out the deadwood.
20. MS *of the three of them, favoring Ann.*
    CONNELL: Okay.
    Hanging up, Connell takes a sip of milk.
    ANN: Look, Mr. Connell. I just can't afford to be without work right now, not even for a day. I've got a mother and two kid sisters to . . .
    SECRETARY *(handing Connell papers from offscreen)*: More good luck telegrams.
    ANN: Well you know how it is, I, I've just got to keep on working. See?
    CONNELL: Sorry, sister . . .
21. MS *of all three, favoring Connell.*
    CONNELL: . . . I was sent down here to clean house. I told you I can't use your column anymore. *(He flicks on intercom.)* It's lavender . . .
22. MS, *as 20.*
    CONNELL: . . . and old lace.
    SECRETARY *(over intercom)*: Yeah?
    CONNELL: Send in those people.
    SECRETARY *(over intercom)*: Okay.

ANN: I'll tell you what I'll do.

23. MCU *of Ann leaning forward, pleading.*

ANN: I get thirty dollars a week. I'll take twenty-five, twenty if necessary. I'll do anything you say.

CONNELL: It isn't the money. We're after circulation.

24. MS, *as 21.*

CONNELL: What we need is fireworks. People who can hit with a sledge hammer, . . .

25. MCU *of Ann, as 23.*

CONNELL: . . . start arguments.

ANN: Oh, I can do that. I know this town inside out. Oh, give me a chance, please.

CONNELL *(as the newly fired file into the office behind Ann)*: All right, come in, come in, come in! *(To Ann:)* Cashier's got your check. *(She stares for a moment, then turns away.)* Who are these people?

26. LS, *panning with Ann to door.*

CONNELL *(off)*: Gibbs, Frowley, Cunningham, Giles. *(To Ann at door:)* Hey you, sister.

Ann turns.

27. MS *of Connell and Pop.*

CONNELL: Don't forget to get out your last column before you pick up your check.

28. MS *of Ann at door. She exits angrily, ruining the last letter of the sign painter's handiwork. Through the glass he can be seen slashing out Connell's entire name in frustration.*

29. LS, *inside Ann's office as she enters, slams the door, and kicks over a wastepaper basket in frustration. As she paces furiously, Joe, an elderly typesetter, enters.*

JOE: You're a couple sticks shy in your column, Ann.

ANN *(to herself)*: Big, rich slob like D. B. Norton buys a paper and forty heads are chopped off!

JOE: Did you get it, too?

ANN *(to Joe)*: Yeah. You, too?

30. MCU *of Joe nodding.*

ANN *(off)*: Oh, Joe. *(Ann comes over and embraces him.)* Oh, I'm sorry, darling. Why don't we tear the building down?

JOE: Before you do, Ann, perhaps you'd better finish this column.

31. MS *of Ann and Joe.*
    ANN *(picking up her column)*: Yeah. Lavender and old lace! *(As Joe starts to go, Ann's eyes light up.)* Wait, Joe . . .
32. MS *of Joe at the doorway.*
    ANN *(off)*: . . . wait.
33. MS *of Ann as she sits down at her typewriter.*
    ANN: Wants fireworks, huh? Okay! *(She begins to type.)*
34. MS *of Joe at the door, bewildered.*
35. CU *of Ann, her eyes and forehead visible above the typewriter carriage. The scene around her darkens, intensifying the light reflecting in her eyes.*
36. MS *of Joe, panning with him as he walks back to the desk.*
37. *Dissolve to canted* CU *of Ann, as she types with great intensity.*
38. *Dissolve to* MS *of Ann and Joe. Finishing, she whips the paper out of the typewriter.*
    ANN *(handing the paper to Joe)*: Here.
    Ann empties her desk as Joe reads what she has written.

JOE: "Below is a letter which reached my desk this morning. It's a commentary on what we laughingly call the civilized world."

39. MS *of Joe, as he reads.*

JOE: "'Dear Miss Mitchell: Four years ago I was fired out of my job. Since then I haven't been able to get another one.'"

40. MS *of Ann by her desk, panning with her as she moves around the office, collecting her possessions.*

JOE: "'At first I was sore at the state administration because it's on account of the slimy politics here we have all this unemployment. But in looking around, it seems the whole world's going to pot, so in protest I'm going to commit suicide by jumping off the City Hall roof.' Signed, 'a disgusted American citizen, John Doe.' Editor's note: If you ask this column, the wrong people are jumping off the roofs." *(Joe glances up at Ann, who is poised to exit.)* Hey, Ann, this is the old fakeroo, isn't it?

ANN: Never mind that, Joe. Go ahead.

As Ann leaves, Joe chuckles.

41. MLS *of the newsroom, tracking with Ann as she briskly walks through it, acknowledging words of farewell from her colleagues. Suddenly she comes to a halt.*

42. MS *of Connell's office door from Ann's point of view. The sign painter, having finished his handiwork, bends down.*

43. MLS *of Ann as she takes a book from the stack in her arms and hurls it at the door.*

44. MCU *of the other side of the window as the book crashes through. The painter rises; visible through the hole, he screws up his face and counts to himself in exasperation. Offscreen, people in the newsroom laugh.*

45. *Dissolve to* ECU *of the front page of* The New Bulletin.

MAN'S VOICE *(reading the paper)*: ". . . and it's because of the slimy politics that we have all this unemployment here . . ." *(Pull back to reveal two assistants in the office of Governor Jackson, one reading aloud.)* There it is. That's D. B. Norton's opening attack on the Governor.

2ND MAN: Why, Jim, it's just a letter sent into a column.

JIM: No, no. I can smell it. That's Norton!

The Governor enters.

GOVERNOR: Good morning, gentlemen.

MEN: Good morning, Governor.

GOVERNOR *(panning with him as circles around to his desk)*: You're rather early.

All three are framed in a MLS. *Jim hands the Governor the paper.*

JIM: Governor, did you happen to see this in *The New Bulletin?*

GOVERNOR: Um, yes. I had it served with my breakfast this morning.

2ND MAN: Jim thinks it's D. B. Norton at work.

JIM *(as the Governor sits down)*: Of course it is.

GOVERNOR: Oh, come, Jim.

46. MS *of the Governor behind his desk.*

GOVERNOR: *That* little item? D. B. Norton does things in a much bigger way.

47. MLS *of all three.*

JIM: This is his attack on you, Governor. Take my word for it. What did he buy a paper for? What did he engage a high-pressure editor like Connell for? He's in the oil business. I tell you, Governor, he's after your scalp!

48. MS, *as 46.*

GOVERNOR: All right, Jim, all right. Don't burst a blood vessel. I'll attend to it.

He flips on intercom.

VOICE OVER INTERCOM: Yes, sir?

GOVERNOR *(into intercom):* Get me Spencer of *The Daily Chronicle*, please.

49. *Wipe dissolve to* MS *of Spencer at his desk, on the telephone.*

SPENCER: Yes, yes. I saw it, Governor. And if you ask me that's a phony letter. Why, that gag has got whiskers on it. Hum? Okay. I'll get the Mayor and maybe the Chamber of Commerce to go after them. *(He turns to his intercom.)* Get Mayor Lovett on the phone.

50. *Wipe dissolve to* MCU *of the Mayor's secretary.*

SECRETARY *(into phone)*: Sorry, the Mayor's busy on the other phone.

The camera tilts down to the Mayor, seated behind his desk.

MAYOR *(on a second phone)*: Yes, I know, Mrs. Brewster. It's a terrible reflection on our city. I've had a dozen calls already.

SECRETARY *(off)*: Spencer at the *Chronicle*.

MAYOR: Hold it.

SECRETARY *(off)*: Just a minute.

MAYOR: Yes, Mrs. Brewster, I'm listening.

51. *Dissolve to* MS *of Mrs. Brewster, propped in a bed, feeding her Pekinese from a breakfast tray on her lap.*

    MRS. BREWSTER: I insist that this John Doe man be found and given a job at once. Now, if something isn't done about it, I'll call out the whole Auxiliary.

52. MS *of the Mayor listening.*

    MRS. BREWSTER *(heard over the phone)*: Yes, and the Junior Auxiliary, too. We'll hold a meeting and see that . . .

    The Mayor picks up the receiver handed to him by his secretary.

    MAYOR: Yes, Spencer. Who? The Governor?

53. MLS *of the Mayor and his secretary.*

    MAYOR *(excitedly)*: Well, what about me? It's *my* building he's jumping off of! And *I'm* up for reelection too!

    MAYOR'S SECRETARY *(covering the receiver of the phone to Mrs. Brewster)*: Shh!

    MAYOR *(to secretary)*: What are you doing? Get Connell at the *Bulletin*. *(He returns to Spencer.)* Why, why he's liable to go right past my window.

    SECRETARY *(into third phone)*: Get me Connell.

    MAYOR *(glancing toward window)*: What was that?

    SECRETARY: What?

    MAYOR: Out the window! Something just flew by!

    SECRETARY: I didn't see anything.

    MAYOR: Well, don't stand there, you idiot! Go and look!

54. MS *of the Mayor, near hysteria.*

    MAYOR: Open the window! Oh, why did he have to pick on my building?

55. MLS *of the back of the secretary, who opens the window and looks out.*

    MAYOR: Is there a crowd in the street?

    SECRETARY: No, sir.

    MAYOR: Then maybe he's caught on the ledge. Look again.

    SECRETARY *(leaning out further)*: I think it must have been a sea gull.

    MAYOR: A sea gull? What's a sea gull doing around the City Hall? *(The secretary closes the window.)* That's, that's a bad omen, isn't it?

    SECRETARY *(returning to the phones)*: Oh, no sir. The sea gull is a lovely bird.

MAYOR *(to Mrs. Brewster's phone)*: It's all right, Mrs. Brewster. It's just a sea gull.

SECRETARY *(on phone)*: Connell?

MAYOR *(to Mrs. Brewster)*: Nothing's happened yet. No. I'm watching. Don't worry. Ju-just leave it all to me. *(The secretary holds out Connell's line; the Mayor turns to Spencer's.)* Spencer, I'll call you back. *(He takes the phone from the secretary.)* Hello, Connell! This is— *(He turns to the secretary, who is attempting to retrieve the other phone from him.)* What are you doing? *(He returns to Connell.)* This is the Mayor.

56. MS *of Connell standing behind his desk, on the phone.*

CONNELL: Yes, Mayor Lovett. How many times are you gonna call me?

57. MLS *of Pop, beside Connell, comparing newspapers.*

CONNELL: I've got everybody and his brother and sister out looking for him. *(He takes a paper from Pop.)* Did you see the box I'm running? *(He begins to read.)* "Appeal to John Doe. 'Think it over, John. Life can be beautiful,' says Mayor. 'If you need a job, apply to the editor of this paper—,'" and so forth and so forth. Okay, Mayor. I'll let you know as soon as I have something. What? Well, pull down the blinds! *(He hangs up.)*

58. LS *as Beany enters the office, talking a mile-a-minute.*

BEANY *(walking to desk)*: I went up to Miss Mitchell's house, boss. Boy, she's in a bad way.

CONNELL: Where is she?

BEANY: Hey, do you know something? She supports a mother and two kids.

59. MS *of Connell, over Beany's shoulder.*

BEANY: What do you know about that?

CONNELL: Did you find her?

BEANY: No. Her mother's awful worried about her.

60. MS *of Beany, over Connell's shoulder. Not listening, Connell shuffles papers on his desk.*

BEANY: When she left the house, she said she was going on a roaring drunk. Er, the girl, I mean.

CONNELL: Go out and find her!

BEANY: Sure.

61. MS *of Connell, Pop, and Beany, as Beany turns to go. Suddenly, he's reminded of something else.*

BEANY: Hey, but the biggest thing I didn't tell you. Her old man was Doc Mitchell.

CONNELL *(answering the phone, overlapping)*: Hello! . . . Yeah?

BEANY: You know the Doc that saved my mother's life and wouldn't take any money for it? You remember that? *(Connell picks up an object from his desk, as if to throw it.)* Okay, boss, I'll go and look for her.

The camera pans with Beany as he exits. He noisily knocks over an ash-stand.

62. LS, *with Connell on the phone in foreground, as Beany departs.*

CONNELL *(on phone)*: Holy smokes, commissioner. You've had twenty-four hours!

63. MS *of Connell.*

CONNELL *(on phone)*: Okay, Hawkshaw, grab a pencil. Here it is again. About five foot five, brown eyes, light chestnut hair, and as fine a pair of legs as . . .

64. LS *of Ann as she comes through the door. Connell momentarily pauses.*

CONNELL *(slowly)*: . . . ever walked into this office.

The camera pans with Ann as she strides blithely to the desk.

ANN *(with mock innocence)*: Did you want to see me?

CONNELL *(sarcastically)*: No . . .

65. MS *of Connell over Ann's shoulder.*

CONNELL: . . . I've had the whole army and navy searching for you because that's a game we play here every day.

66. LS *of Ann. Enjoying the moment, she plunks herself down in a chair.*

ANN: I remember distinctly being fired.

CONNELL: That's right. But you have a piece of property that still belongs to this newspaper, and I'd like to have it.

ANN: What's that?

CONNELL: The letter.

ANN: What letter?

CONNELL: The letter from John Doe.

67. MS *of Ann from a slightly high angle.*

ANN: Oh.

CONNELL *(off)*: The whole town's in an uproar. We've got to find him. The letter's our only clue.

ANN *(smiling sweetly)*: There *is* no letter.

68. MCU *of Connell behind his desk*

CONNELL: We'll get a handwriting expert to—*(he suddenly realizes what she has said)* What?

69. *High angle* MCU *of Ann.*

ANN: There is no letter.

70. MCU *of Connell, panning as he comes around desk to Ann and ending with a* MLS *of Connell, Pop, and Ann.*

CONNELL: Say that again.

ANN: There is no letter. I made it up.

CONNELL *(echoing her, incredulous)*: You made it up.

ANN: Uh-huh. You said you wanted fireworks.

71. *High angle* MCU *of Ann over Connell's shoulder.*

CONNELL: Don't you know there are nine jobs waiting for this guy?

72. MCU *of Connell from above Ann.*

CONNELL: Twenty-two families want to board him free? Five women want to marry him, and the Mayor's practically ready to adopt him? And you—

73. MLS *of Connell standing over Ann as Beany comes through the door.*

BEANY: I just called the morgue, boss.

74. MCU *of Ann, as 71. She glances at Beany with interest.*

BEANY *(off)*: They say there's a girl there—

CONNELL *(cutting Beany off)*: Shut up!

75. MLS *of Connell, as 73. Noticing Ann, Beany does a doubletake.*

BEANY: Ann!

76. MCU *of Connell, as 72.*

BEANY *(off)*: Say, why didn't you . . .

CONNELL *(cutting him off again)*: Beany!

77. MLS *of Connell, as 73.*

POP *(finally speaking)*: Only one thing to do, Hank. Drop the whole business quickly.

CONNELL: How?

POP *(gently)*: Run a story. Say John Doe was in here . . .

78. MCU *of Ann, listening intently.*

POP *(off)*: . . . and he's sorry he wrote the letter, and . . .

CONNELL *(off)*: That's right.

79. MLS *of Connell returning to his desk as he talks excitedly.*

CONNELL: You got it. Sure. He came in here and I made him change his mind. "*Bulletin* editor . . .

80. *High angle* MCU *of Ann, as 69. She is thinking.*

CONNELL *(off)*: . . . saves John Doe's life." Why, it's perfect. I'll have Ned write it up. *(Ann looks up as Connell speaks into intercom.)* Oh, Ned?

NED'S VOICE: Yeah?

81. MLS *of Connell and Pop at desk.*

CONNELL: I've got a story I want you to . . .

ANN *(racing over to shut off intercom)*: Wait a minute!

82. MS *of Ann and Connell; she leans toward him over the intercom.*

ANN *(very animated)*: Listen, you great big wonderful genius of a newspaperman. You came down here to shoot some life into this dying paper, didn't you? Well, the whole town's curious about John Doe and, boom, just like that you're going to bury him. There's enough circulation in that man to start a shortage in the ink . . .

83. MCU *of Connell from behind Ann.*

ANN: . . . market!

CONNELL: In *what* man?

ANN: John Doe.

CONNELL: What . . .

84. MLS *of Connell and Pop, as 81, with Beany now joining them.*

CONNELL: . . . John Doe?

ANN: Our John Doe! The one I made up! Look, genius, now look. Suppose there *was* a John Doe, and he walked into this office. What would you do? Find him a job and forget the whole business I suppose. Huh! Not me. I'd make a deal with him.

85. MCU *of Connell from behind Ann and Beany.*

CONNELL *(sitting down)*: A deal?

ANN: Sure! When you get hold of a stunt that sells papers you don't drop it like a hot potato.

86. MS *of Beany and Connell with Ann between them.*

ANN: Why, this is good for at least a couple of months. You know what I'd do? Between now and, let's say, Christmas,[4] when he's gonna jump, I'd run a daily yarn, starting with his boyhood, his schooling, his first job. A wide-eyed youngster . . .

87. MCU *of Connell, as 85.*

ANN: . . . facing a chaotic world. The problem of the average man, of all the John Does in the world.

88. MCU *of Ann over Connell's shoulder as her sales pitch builds.*

ANN: Now, then comes the drama. He meets discouragement. He finds the world has feet of clay. His ideals crumble. So what does he do? He decides to commit suicide in protest against the state of civilization. He thinks of the river! But no, no, he has a better idea. The City Hall. Why? Because he wants to attract attention. He wants to get a few things off his chest, and that's the only way he can get himself heard.

CONNELL: So?

ANN: So! So he writes me a letter and I dig him up. He pours out his soul to me. And from now on we quote: "I protest, by John Doe." He protests against all the evils in the world. The greed, . . .

89. ECU *of Beany, dazed, and Pop, sighing wearily, in response to Ann's spiel.*

ANN: . . . the lust, the hate, the fear, all of man's inhumanity to man.

90. MS *of Ann, Connell, and Beany, as 86.*

ANN: Arguments will start. Should he commit suicide or should he not? People will write in pleading with him. But no! *(Ann slaps the desk hard.)* No sir! John Doe will remain adamant! On Christmas Eve, hot or cold, he goes! See?

Finishing, she pauses expectantly.

91. MCU *of Connell, as 85.*

CONNELL: Very pretty. Very pretty, indeed, Miss Mitchell. But would you mind telling me who goes on Christmas Eve?

ANN: John Doe.

CONNELL *(rising, shouting)*: *What* John Doe?

92. MCU *of Ann from behind Connell.*

ANN *(shouting back)*: The one we hire for the job, you lunkhead!

93. MCU *of Connell as he sits back down. He rubs his face.*

CONNELL: Wait a minute. Wait a minute. Let me get this through this lame brain of mine. Are you suggesting that we go out and hire somebody to go out and say he's going to commit suicide on Christmas Eve?

94. MLS *of everyone gathered at Connell's desk.*

CONNELL: Is that it?

ANN *(hand on hip, flippantly)*: Well, you're catching on.

CONNELL: Who, for instance?

ANN: Anybody! Er— *(She turns to the nearest person.)* Beany'll do.

BEANY: Why sure— *(He catches himself.)* Who? Me? Jump off a— Oh, no! Any time but Christmas. I'm superstitious.

He departs hastily. From offscreen is heard the sound of the toppling ash-stand. Connell, Ann, and Pop glance at the scene of the crash, but do not respond.

95. MS *of Connell. He sits back down wearily as Ann watches him intently.*

CONNELL: Miss Mitchell, do me a favor, will you? Go on out and get married, have a lot of babies, and stay out of the newspaper business.

POP *(off)*: Better get that story in, Hank, it's getting late.

ANN *(to Connell)*: You're supposed to be a smart guy! If it was raining hundred dollar bills, you'd be out looking for a dime you lost someplace.

The camera pans with Ann as she passes Pop on the way toward the door, defeated. Entering from the other direction is Ned.

CONNELL *(off)*: Holy smokes! Wasting my time listening to this mad woman.

NED *(off)*: Look, Chief. Look what the *Chronicle* is running on John Doe. *(Ann turns around sharply, in MCU. She brightens at Ned's remark.)* They say it's a fake!

96. MLS *of Connell and Ned. Connell takes the newspaper from him.*

CONNELL *(rising, furious)*: Why, the no-good, the— *(He reads aloud snatches of the article.)* "John Doe story amateur journalism. It's palpably phony."

97. MCU *of Ann listening.*

CONNELL *(off)*: "It's a wonder anyone is taking it seriously." What do you think of those guys!

ANN: That's fine! That's fine! *(The camera tracks with Ann as she rejoins Connell at his desk.)* Now fall right into their laps. Go ahead. Say John Doe walked in and called the whole thing off. *(Now in a MS with Connell, goading him.)* You know what that's going to sound like on top of this.

CONNELL: That's all, Ned.

98. MLS *of Connell and Ned.*

CONNELL: Thank you.

NED: All right.

Ned turns and goes. Pan with Connell as he leaves his desk, agitated.

CONNELL *(combatively)*: "Amateur journalism," huh! Why, the bunch of sophomores! I can teach them more about . . .

99. MCU *of Beany as he flings the door open.*

BEANY: Hey, boss. *(He points behind him.)* Get a load of this.

100. MLS: *Connell looks toward the door.*

CONNELL: What?

BEANY (*off*): Look!

The camera pans with Connell to the doorway. Ann and Pop quickly follow behind. Outside the door is a cluster of down-and-out men.

CONNELL: What do they want?

101. MLS *of the men, very still, staring into the office.*

BEANY (*off*): They all say they wrote the John Doe letter.

The men suddenly come alive, clamoring for attention.

102. MS *of Connell, Ann, and Beany.*

CONNELL (*to Beany*): Oh, they *all* wrote the letter?

Meanwhile, Ann is staring straight ahead, thinking hard.

103. MLS *from above and behind the trio as Ann pushes Beany back out the door.*

ANN (*to Beany*): Tell them all to wait. Look Mr. Connell. (*She shuts the door behind him and pulls Connell a few steps back.*) One of those men is your John Doe. They're desperate and will do anything for a cup of coffee. Pick out one, and you can make the *Chronicle* eat their words.

CONNELL (*her idea registering*): I'm beginning . . .

104. MS *of Connell, panning with him as comes back toward Pop, Ann at his sleeve.*

CONNELL: . . . to like this.

POP (*his brow knit*): If you ask me, Hank, you're playing around with dynamite.

CONNELL: No, no, no, the gal's right. We can't let the *Chronicle* get the laugh on us. We've got to produce a John Doe now.

105. MCU *of Ann beaming beside Connell.*

CONNELL: Amateur journalism, huh! I'll show those guys. (*He turns back toward the door, but is stopped by Ann's knowing look.*)

ANN: Sure, and there's no reason for them to find out the truth, either. Because, naturally, *I* won't say anything.

CONNELL (*eyeing her briefly, then grinning*): Okay, sister. You get your job back.

ANN (*as he again heads toward the door*): Plus the bonus.

CONNELL (*spinning back around*): What bonus?

ANN (*reaching into her purse*): Oh, the bonus of a thousand dollars the *Chronicle* was going to pay me for this little document. (*She hands a paper to Connell.*) You'll find it says, er—"I, Ann Mitchell, hereby certify that the John Doe letter was created by me—"

CONNELL *(testily)*: I can read. I can read.

ANN: Sorry.

She backs away, but looks on smugly as Connell finishes reading.

CONNELL: You think this is worth a thousand dollars to you, do you?

ANN *(in complete control)*: Oh, the *Chronicle* would consider it dirt cheap.

106. MLS *of Ann, Connell, and Pop.*

CONNELL *(to Pop)*: Packs everything, including a gun. *(Pop nods in agreement.)* Okay, sister, you've got yourself a deal. *(Pan with Connell as he leaves them to go to his desk, where he tosses the* Chronicle *aside.)* Now let's take a look at the candidates. The one we pick has got to be the typical average man. *(He takes a swig of milk.)* Typical American[5] that can keep his mouth shut.

POP *(off)*: Show me an American who can keep his mouth shut and I'll eat him.

The camera pans with Connell as he passes Ann and Pop on the way to the door. He flings it open.

CONNELL: Okay, Beany, bring 'em in one at a time.

107. *Connell steps back from the door into a* MS *as Beany ushers the first job-seeker into the office, then closes the door and stands guard outside. The candidate—stout, unkempt, and a bit confused—steps forward, as comic music rises up on the soundtrack.*

108. CU *of Connell; he checks Ann's reaction.*

109. CU *of Ann: she shakes her head "no."*

110. CU *of Connell, who concurs.*

111–113. *Three hoboes, introduced with three successive, soft, rightward wipes. Each figure steps forward into* CU *where their faces are mildly distorted by a wide-angle lens. The three appear progressively strange; the last has a slightly crazed look in his eyes. (Comic music accompanies the sequence.)*

114. CU *of Ann, who has a decidedly negative response to the last candidate.*

115. CU *of Connell, who again concurs.*

116. *Soft rightward wipe as another figure walks through the door: he is Long John Willoughby. Tall and ruggedly handsome, he is also shy and somewhat battered. (As he approaches the foreground, the music shifts to a western folk theme.)*

117. CU *of Ann, who is immediately interested.*

118. CU *of John. Under inspection, he nervously removes his hat.*
119. CU *of Ann. Clearly delighted, she signals her approval to Connell.*
120. CU *of Connell, who nods back to her in agreement.*
121. CU *of Ann. Fascinated by this prospect, she moves closer to him.*
122. MLS *from further back as Ann and Connell approach John; Pop watches at a distance. Circling around John, Ann glances down at his pant leg.*
123. CU *of John's hand, groping to cover a tear in his pants.*
124. MS *of Ann and John as she continues to examine him. She lets Connell know with a glance that she is still satisfied. As she circles back around John, he is reframed in a* MCU *between Ann and Connell.*
     CONNELL: Did you write the letter to Miss Mitchell?
     JOHN: No, I didn't.
     CONNELL: What are you doing here, then?
     JOHN: Well, the paper said there were some jobs around loose. Thought there might be one left over.
     ANN *(eagerly)*: Had any schooling?
     JOHN *(looking at her directly for the first time)*: Yeah, a little.
     ANN: What do you do when you work?

JOHN *(responding slowly)*: I used to pitch.

ANN *(questioning rapidly)*: Baseball?

JOHN: Yeah. Till my wing went bad.

ANN: Where'd you play?

JOHN: Bush leagues, mostly.

125. MLS *of them all, as 122.*

CONNELL: How about family? Got any family?

JOHN *(guardedly)*: No.

CONNELL: Oh, just traveling through, huh?

JOHN: Yeah. Me and a friend of mine. *(He is suddenly animated.)* He's outside.

Ann signals to the others to join her off to the side. The camera pans left with her as the two men follow, ending on a MCU *of Ann from behind Connell and Pop.*

CONNELL *(whispering)*: Looks all right.

ANN *(softly, but excitedly)*: He's perfect! A baseball player!

126. CU *of John, who remains in place but surveys the office.*

ANN *(off)*: What could be more American?

127. CU *of the lunch tray on Connell's desk from John's point of view.*

CONNELL *(off)*: I wish he had a family, though.

POP *(off)*: Be less complicated . . .

128. CU *of John. He stares at the food hungrily.*

POP *(off)*: . . . *without* a family.

ANN *(off)*: That face is wonderful.

129. MCU *of Ann, from behind Connell and Pop.*

ANN: They'll believe *him.* Come on.

The camera pans with them as they return to their original positions around John, in MLS.

CONNELL *(to John)*: What's your name?

JOHN: Willoughby. John Willoughby.[6]

130. MCU *of John between Ann and Connell.*

JOHN: Long John Willoughby, they call me in baseball.

ANN: Er, would you, er, would you like to make some money?

JOHN *(cautiously)*: Yeah. Maybe.

ANN: Would you be willing to say you wrote that letter, and stick by it?

JOHN *(glances at Connell, sizing up the score)*: Oh, I get the idea. Yeah. Maybe.

Ann again signals Connell and Pop to confer with her off to the side.

131. MLS, *as the camera pans left with her, back to their former spot, ending on the same* MCU *of Ann from behind the two newsmen.*

 ANN *(grabbing Connell's lapel in excitement)*: That's our man. He's made to order.

 CONNELL: I don't know. He don't seem like the kind of a guy . . .

132. CU *of John, staring at the tray of food. As Connell speaks, John's body begins to sway.*

 CONNELL *(off)*: . . . that'd fall into line.

 ANN *(off)*: When you're desperate for money, you do a lot of things, Mr. Connell.

133. MCU *of Ann, from behind Connell and Pop.*

 ANN: He's our man, I tell you. *(There is a thud from across the room. They all rush over.)* He's fainted!

134. MLS *of John, trying to pull himself up off the floor with the arm of the chair. The others rush to aid him.*

 ANN *(on the run)*: Get some water, quickly!

 CONNELL: Hurry up, Pop.

 ANN *(with exertion)*: Oh.

 CONNELL *(helping John up)*: Right here. Sit down.

 ANN: Are you all right?

 JOHN *(a bit dazed)*: Yeah, I'm all right.

135. *Dissolve to Ann's office, where John sits in* MS *at her desk, polishing off a large meal. He is fully recovered.*

 ANN (pouring him some tea): How many is that? Six?

 He smiles up at her shyly. She then circles around to the other side of the desk to fill the cup held by an outstretched hand.

136. *Reverse angle* MS *of John's friend, older and shorter in stature, the Colonel,[7] holding out his cup. He nods a silent "thank you" to Ann.*

137. MCU *of John, as he reaches for another hard-boiled egg.*

 ANN: Pretty hungry, weren't you?

138. LS *of Ann's office. Her colleagues peer in through the glass windows in an effort to catch a glimpse of John. She shoos them away.*

 COLONEL *(leaning across the desk, to John)*: All this John Doe business is batty, if you ask me.

 ANN *(her back to them, from the other side of the room)*: Well, nobody asked you.

139. MS *of the Colonel, over John's shoulder.*

COLONEL *(ignoring her)*: Trying to improve the world by jumping off buildings. You couldn't improve the world if the buildings jumped on you.

140. MS *of John, from behind the Colonel.*
     JOHN *(to Ann)*: Don't mind the Colonel. He hates people.

141. MS, *angled behind Ann, as she scoops out some ice cream.*
     ANN: He likes you well enough to stick around.

142. MS *of John, as 140.*
     JOHN: Oh, that's because we both play doo-hickies. *(John pulls out a harmonica from his shirt pocket, as Ann brings them the ice cream.)* I met him in a boxcar a couple of years ago. I was fooling around with my harmonica, and he comes over and joins in. I haven't been able to shake him since.
     John runs the scale on the harmonica.

143. MCU *of the Colonel. His face lighting up in reaction to John's playing, he pulls an ocarina from the inside of his jacket.*

144. MCU *of John, as 140. They begin to play the "William Tell Overture" on their instruments, to Ann's amusement.*

145. *Reverse* MS *of the Colonel, between Ann and John, as the tempo quickens.*

146. MLS *of all, the office door behind them. Connell bursts in, followed by Beany and a cluster of reporters. John and the Colonel stop playing.*
     CONNELL: All right, boys, here he is.
     ANN *(spinning around to confront them)*: No, no, no! You can't take pictures of him like that, eating a sandwich, and with a beard.
     She ushers the reporters back out.
     CONNELL *(as Ann closes the door)*: But he's going to jump off a building!
     ANN: Yes, but not because he's out of a job.

147. *Ann moves forward into a* MCU *with Connell as the reporters hover on the other side of the glass.*
     ANN: That's not news. This man's going to jump as a matter of principle.
     CONNELL: Well, maybe you're right. *(He waves the reporters away.)*
     ANN: We'll clean him up and put him in a hotel room under body-guards. We'll make a mystery out of him. Did you speak to Mr. Norton?
     CONNELL *(he nods yes)*: Thinks it's terrific. Says for us to go to the limit. Wants us to build a bonfire under every big shot in the state.

ANN: Oh, swell! *(She notices something in Connell's hand.)* Is that the contract?

CONNELL: Yeah. *(He notices the Colonel for the first time.)* What's . . .

148. MCU *of the Colonel, looking up at Connell.*

CONNELL *(off)*: . . . he doing here?

ANN *(off)*: Friend of his. They play duets together.

The Colonel smiles crookedly, acknowledging the introduction.

CONNELL *(off)*: Duets?

149. *The camera dollies back from Ann and Connell to reframe John with them in a* MS.

CONNELL: But can we trust him?

ANN: Oh.

JOHN: I trust him.

CONNELL *(sarcastically)*: Oh, you trust him, eh? Well, that's fine. I suppose he trusts you too?

150. MCU *of the Colonel.*

ANN *(off, overlapping the Colonel)*: Oh, stop worrying.

COLONEL *(insulted)*: That's . . .

ANN *(off)*: He's all right.

151. MS, *as 149.*

CONNELL: Okay. But we don't want more than a couple of hundred people in on this thing. *(To John:)* Now the first thing I want is an exact copy of the John Doe letter in your own handwriting.

ANN *(quickly finding the letter)*: I got it already. Here.

CONNELL: That's fine. Now, I want you to sign this agreement. It gives us an exclusive story under your name, day by day, from now until Christmas. On December twenty-sixth, you get one railroad ticket out of town. *(Glancing in the direction of the Colonel, Connell holds up one finger.)* And the *Bulletin* agrees to pay to have your arm fixed. That's what you want, isn't it?

JOHN: Yeah, but it's got to be by Bone-setter Brown.

CONNELL: Okay, Bone-setter Brown goes. Here, sign it. Meanwhile, here's fifty dollars for . . .

152. MCU *of the Colonel. He gestures to John not to sign the contract.*

CONNELL *(off)*: . . . spending money.

153. MCU *of John as he finishes signing.*

CONNELL *(off)*: That's fine. Beany?

154. MLS *of all, as 146. John picks up the money.*
    BEANY *(hurrying to Connell's side)*: Yeah, boss?
    CONNELL: Take charge of him. Get him a suite at the Imperial and hire some bodyguards.
    ANN: Yeah, and some new clothes, Beany.
155. MCU *of John, counting the money with delight. He looks up at the Colonel.*
    BEANY *(off)*: Do you think we better have him deloused?
    CONNELL *(off)*: Yeah, yeah, yeah.
156. MCU *of the Colonel, who signals his concern to John.*
    BEANY *(off)*: Both of them?
    CONNELL *(off)*: Yes, both of them. But don't let him out of your sight.
157. MLS *of Ann, Beany, and Connell, with John, lower right, watching the Colonel.*
    ANN: Hey, Beany, gray suit, huh?
    BEANY: Yeah.
    Beany opens the door.
    CONNELL *(to John and the Colonel, gesturing toward the door)*: Okay, fellows.
158. MCU *of the Colonel, who gathers up the rest of his food.*
159. MLS, *as 146. Track forward as John and the Colonel rise and head for the door.*
    ANN *(shaking his hand as he exits)*: Take it easy, John Doe.
160. *Reverse* MCU *of Ann as she swings on her office door. Connell steps forward to join her.*
    CONNELL: And you! Start pounding that typewriter. Oh, boy, this is terrific! No responsibilities on our part. Just statements from John Doe and we can blast our heads off!
    ANN *(poking Connell in the chest)*: Before you pop too many buttons, don't forget to make out that check for a thousand.
    CONNELL *(grinning through clenched teeth)*: Awww!
    Connell exits to right. Ann leans against the door, smiling smugly.

161. *Dissolve to* LS *of a hotel suite living room. Porters with luggage enter the door, followed by John, the Colonel, Beany, and three bodyguards.*
    BEANY *(directing the bodyguards)*: Okay, fellows. Now let me see. You sit outside the door. Nobody comes in, see. You two fellows sit in here.

162.   MS *of John and the Colonel as they move forward into the room.*
JOHN *(looking around)*: Hey, pretty nifty, huh?
Pan right with John as he moves to a mirror.
COLONEL *(following)*: You ain't gonna get me to stay here.
JOHN *(adjusting his tie and hat)*: Sure you are.
COLONEL: No, sir. That spot under the bridge where we slept last
   night's good enough for me.

163.   MLS, *John and the Colonel to the right as the porters pass.*
PORTER: Say, what'll we do with this baggage?
BEANY *(off)*: Aw, stick 'em in the bedroom.
COLONEL *(grabbing his bag fiercely)*: Gimme mine!

164.   MS, *as 162.*
COLONEL *(to John)*: I ain't staying! You know we were headed for the
   Columbia River country before all this John Doe business came up.
   You remember that, don't you?
JOHN *(turning away from the mirror)*: Sure. I remember. *(Pan left with
   John and the Colonel as they cross the room.)* Say, did your ears pop
   coming up in the elevator? Mine did.
COLONEL: Aw, Long John. I tell you it's no good. You're gonna get
   used to a lot of stuff that's gonna wreck you. Why, that fifty bucks in
   your pocket's beginning to show up on you already.
*They are now in a MCU. Spinning around, John pulls out his harmonica
and plays a riff in response.*
COLONEL: And don't pull that on me either!
JOHN: Stop worrying, Colonel. I'm gonna get my arm fixed out of this.

165.   MLS *of John and the Colonel to the left. In the foreground right, Beany
picks up a box of cigars from a table.*
BEANY: Hey, here's some cigars the boss sent us. *(He offers the box to
   John.)* Have one.
JOHN: Hey, cigars!
John grabs one. Beany offers the box to the Colonel.
COLONEL: Naw.
*A bodyguard, Angelface, rises from a chair in the background and
comes toward John.*

166.   MCU *of John sitting down in a plush chair. Angelface lights John's
cigar. John puffs on it with great satisfaction and Angelface retreats.*
JOHN *(glancing around)*: Say, I'll bet you even the Major Leaguers
   don't rate an outfit like this.

ANGELFACE *(returning with a newspaper)*: Here. Make yourself comfortable.

167. MCU *of the Colonel, watching.*

ANGELFACE *(approaching the Colonel)*: Paper?

COLONEL *(testily)*: I don't read no papers and I don't listen to radios either. I know the world's been shaved by a drunken barber and I don't have to read it. *(He glares at Angelface, who, startled, backs off quickly. Pan with the Colonel as he moves closer to John.)* I've seen guys like you go under before.

168. MCU *of John, as 166. He checks his nails.*

COLONEL *(off)*: Guys that never had a worry. Then they got a hold of some dough and went goofy.

169. MLS *of the Colonel, pointing at a diffident John.*

COLONEL: The first thing that happens to a guy—

BEANY *(interrupting, rising from a seat in the foreground)*: Hey, did you get a load of the bedroom?

JOHN *(suddenly interested)*: No.

John rises. Pan with him and Beany as they head toward the bedroom.

COLONEL *(in pursuit)*: The first thing that happens to a guy like that, he starts wanting to go into restaurants . . .

170. LS *from inside the bedroom as John and Beany enter. The Colonel is on their heels.*

COLONEL: . . . and sit at a table and eat salads, and cupcakes, and tea.

171. MCU *of the Colonel.*

COLONEL: Boy, what that kind of food does to your system!

172. MS *of John. He lowers himself onto the luxurious bed and peeks under the pillows, wide-eyed.*

173. MCU *of the Colonel, as 171.*

COLONEL: The next thing the dope wants is a room. Yessir, a room with steam heat, . . .

174. MLS *of John testing a second bed, as Beany, baffled, looks over at the Colonel.*

COLONEL *(off)*: . . . and curtains and rugs and 'fore you know it, he's all softened up, and . . .

175. MCU *of the Colonel, as 171.*

COLONEL: . . . he can't sleep 'less he has a bed.

176. MLS *as 174. John rises. Pan with him as he approaches the Colonel.*

JOHN: Hey, stop worrying, Colonel. Fifty bucks ain't going to ruin me. *John circles back around the bed.*

COLONEL *(following John)*: I seen plenty of fellows start out with fifty bucks and wind up with a bank account.

BEANY: Hey, what's the matter with a bank account, anyway?

177. MCU *as the Colonel grabs John's arm and turns him around so that John is forced to face him.*

COLONEL: And let me tell you, Long John. When you become a guy with a bank account, they got you. Yessir, they got you! *John jauntily switches the ends of the cigar in his mouth and continues on. Pan right with the Colonel as he passes Beany.*

BEANY: Who's got him?

COLONEL: The Heelots!

BEANY: Who?

JOHN *(off)*: Hey.

178. MLS *from behind the Colonel and Beany with John in the background at the window. They turn in his direction.*

JOHN: There's the City Hall tower I'm supposed to jump off of. It's even higher . . .

179. MCU *the Colonel and Beany.*

JOHN *(off)*: . . . than this.

BEANY *(to the Colonel again)*: Who's got him?

COLONEL: The Heelots!

JOHN *(off)*: Whew!

Suddenly concerned that John may be at risk, Beany dashes to the window. Pan with him to a MS *of John leaning out.*

BEANY *(yanking John back in)*: Hey, wait a minute! You're not supposed to jump till Christmas Eve! Want to get me in a jam?

JOHN *(playfully flicking some ashes in Beany's direction)*: If it's going to get you in a jam, I'll do you a favor. I won't jump.

180. MLS, *as 178. John retreats from the window toward the Colonel. Track with the two of them back into the living room.*

COLONEL: And when they got you, you got no more chance than a road-rabbit.

They stop in a MCU. *Beany comes up from behind.*

BEANY *(to the Colonel)*: Hey. Who'd you say was going to get him?

JOHN: Say, is this one of those places where you ring if you want something?

BEANY *(again interrupted, pointing off to the left)*: Yeah. Just use . . .

181. MLS *of all three with a phone in the foreground right.*

BEANY: . . . the phone.

JOHN *(delighted)*: Boy, I've always wanted to do this.

As John heads for the phone, the Colonel heads for the front door. Pan with Beany in pursuit of the Colonel.

BEANY: Hey, Doc, look. Look, Doc. *(Catching up, he stops the Colonel. Angelface comes up behind Beany as well.)* Gimme that again, will yuh? Who's gonna get him?

COLONEL: The Heelots!

182. CU *of the Colonel over the shoulders of Beany and Angelface.*

BEANY: Who are they?

COLONEL: Listen, sucker. You ever been broke?

BEANY: Sure. Mostly often.

COLONEL: All right. You're walking along, not a nickel in your jeans. You're free as the wind. Nobody bothers you. Hundreds of people pass you by in every line of business: shoes, hats, automobiles, radios, furniture, everything. And they're all nice, lovable people. And they let you alone.

183. MCU *of Beany and Angelface, over the Colonel's shoulder.*

COLONEL: Is that right? *(Beany and Angelface nod in unison, as if hypnotized.)* Then you get hold of some dough, and what happens? *(They shake their head in unison: they don't know.)*

184. CU *of the Colonel, as 182.*

COLONEL: All those nice, sweet, lovable people become Heelots. A lot of heels. They begin creeping up on you—trying to sell you something.

185. MCU *of Beany and Angelface, as 183.*

COLONEL: They've got long claws. And they get a stranglehold on you.

186. CU *of the Colonel, as 182.*

COLONEL: And you squirm, and you duck, and you holler, and you try to push 'em away. But you haven't got a chance. They've got you! First thing you know, you own things. A car, for instance. Now your whole life is messed up with a lot more stuff. You get license fees, and number plates, and gas, and oil, and taxes, and insurance, and identification cards, and letters, . . .

187. MCU *of Beany and Angelface, as 183. They nod with each item the Colonel ticks off.*

COLONEL: . . . and bills, and flat tires, and dents, and traffic tickets,

and motorcycle cops, and courtrooms, and lawyers, and fines, and a
million and one other things. And what happens? *(Beany and Angelface shake their heads.)*

188. CU *of the Colonel, as 182.*
   COLONEL: You're not the free and happy guy you used to be. You gotta
   have money to pay for all those things. So you go after what the other
   fellow's got.

189. MS *of Beany and Angelface over the Colonel's shoulder.*
   COLONEL: And there you are. *(He jabs Beany in the shoulder.)* You're
   a Heelot yourself.
   *The Colonel returns to John; Beany and Angelface stare after him. Then
   Beany starts to turn around.*

190. *Reverse* CU *of Beany as he turns, registering shock as he discovers
   Angelface behind him.*

191. *Reverse* MS, *as 189: Beany recoils in reaction to Angelface.*

192. MS *of John, sitting with the phone to his ear, as the Colonel hovers
   nearby.*

JOHN: You win, Colonel. *(He reaches into his pocket.)* Here, take the fifty. Go out and get rid of it.

COLONEL *(elated)*: You bet I will! Just as fast as I can! I'm gonna get some canned goods, a fishing rod, and the rest I'm gonna give away. *The Colonel races off.*

193. MLS *of Beany and Angelface, as the Colonel darts between them toward the door.*

ANGELFACE *(incredulous)*: Give away?

JOHN *(off, to the Colonel)*: Hey. Hey, get me . . .

194. MS *of John, seated by the phone.*

JOHN: . . . a pitcher's glove. I've got to get some practice.

195. MLS *of Beany and Angelface.*

ANGELFACE *(to Beany)*: Say, he's giving it away. I'm going to get me some of that.

Angelface heads toward the door.

BEANY: Hey, come back here, you Heelot!

Angelface catches himself and retreats.

196. CU *of John on the phone. His call is finally completed.*

JOHN *(to room service)*: Will you send up five hamburgers, with all the trimmings, five chocolate ice cream sodas, and five pieces of apple pie. No, apple, with cheese. Yeah. Thanks.

After hanging up, John is startled to discover a nude female statue on the telephone stand. Very cautiously, he begins to turn it around to face him.

ANN *(off)*: Hello there.

John recoils, as if the statue has spoken, then glances toward the door.

197. LS *as Ann crosses the room, with Eddie (a photographer), Beany, and the bodyguards in tow. John enters from the opposite direction.*

ANN *(sizing John up)*: Well, well. If it isn't the man about town.

198. MS *of John and Ann, with the men behind her.*

EDDIE: All set, Miss Ann.

ANN *(a bit spellbound by John)*: Hmm? Oh, oh, yes. Let's go. *(She glances around the room.)* Er, let's see, we want some action in these pictures.[8]

JOHN: Action?

ANN: Um-hum.

John winds up as if to pitch a baseball.

EDDIE: That's good.

ANN (*turning around to see John's pose*): No, no, no! This man's going to jump off a roof.

JOHN: Oh.

ANN: Oh, here. Wait a minute. Let me comb your hair. (*She pulls a comb out of her purse.*) Sit down.

Ann guides John back to his chair.

199. MS *of John sitting down at Ann's prompting. She combs his hair.*

ANN: There, that's better.

Ann straightens John's bow tie and tucks his shirt into vest. Getting a whiff of her hair, John becomes dreamy-eyed.

200. *Low angle* MS *of Beany, Angelface, and a second bodyguard, intently watching Ann at work.*

201. MS *of John and Ann.*

ANN: You know, he's got a nice face, hasn't he?

202. MS *of the onlookers, as 200.*

ANGELFACE: Yeah. He's pretty.

He chuckles loudly. The other men join in laughing.

203. MCU *of John, over Ann's shoulder. Angered by the teasing, he starts to stand.*

ANN (*to John*): Here. Sit down? (*She turns to Angelface.*) Quiet, Egghead!

204. MS *of onlookers, as 200. They become sober.*

205. *High angle* MS *of John from behind Ann and Eddie.*

ANN (*to John*): All right, now a serious expression.

JOHN (*giggling*): Can't. I'm feeling too good.

ANN: Oh, come on now. This is serious. You're a man disgusted with all of civilization.

JOHN: With all of it?

ANN: Yes, you're sore at the world. Come on now.

JOHN: Oh, crabby guy, huh?

ANN: Yeah.

John tries scowling. Eddie raises his camera.

ANN (*stopping Eddie*): No, no. (*She looks back at John, who strikes another pose.*) No, no. (*She waits as he tries again.*) No, look.

206. MLS *of Ann, with the men behind her.*

ANN (*laughing*): You don't have to *smell* the world.

The men behind burst out laughing.

207. LS *of all.*
     JOHN: Well, all those guys in the bleachers think—
     ANN: Never mind those guys. All right, stand up. *(She adjusts his coat
       again.)* Now, let's see what you look like when you protest.
208. MCU *of John, framed by the back of Ann's head and Eddie's camera.*
     JOHN: Against what?
     ANN: Against anything. Just protest.
     JOHN *(after thinking for a moment)*: You got me.
     Eddie lowers the camera.
     ANN: Oh.
209. MS *of Ann and onlookers, over John's shoulder.*
     ANN: Look, I'm the umpire, and you just cut the heart of the plate with
       your fast one and I called it a ball.
210. MCU *of John, as 208.*
     ANN: What would you do?
     JOHN *(his face transformed)*: Oh, you did, huh?

ANN: Yeah!

JOHN: Why can't you call right, you bonehead . . . *(The camera dollies back as John advances toward Ann.)* . . . pig-eared, lop-eared, pot-bellied . . .

ANN *(overlapping)*: Grab it, Eddie. Grab it!

Eddie's flash goes off.

MONTAGE SEQUENCE #1[9]

211. *Dissolve to the photograph of John on the front page of the newspaper. Above is the headline: "I Protest." (Scored under the sequence to follow is lively music.)*

212. ECU *of John's pointed finger as the photo is raised toward the camera.*

213. *Dissolve to the "I Protest" headline over the photo.*

214. *Dissolve as camera scans down below the photo to another headline: "Against Collapse of Decency in the World."*

215. *Dissolve to high angle* MS *of a stack of papers as one is lifted off the top. Muted calls of "Extra, Extra" are heard.*

216. CU *of the hand in the previous shot lifting the front page into view.*

217. *Dissolve to the "I Protest" headline.*

218. *Dissolve to another headline: "Against Corruption in Local Politics." Then superimpose over this a shot of paper money changing hands.*

219. *Dissolve to matted shot of "I Protest."*

220. *Dissolve to a newspaper as it is flipped over to below the fold. A headline reads: "Against Graft in State Relief."*

221. *Dissolve to canted* CU *of Ann, typing the original John Doe letter furiously, as 37.*

222. *Dissolve to a newspaper as it is flipped to reveal under John's photo the headline: "Against County Hospital Shutting Down to Needy." Then superimpose over this a shot of a couple with a child.*

223. *Dissolve to a flash* CU *of a woman's face.*

224. *Dissolve to blurred shot of* The New Bulletin*'s front page, rising rapidly through the frame.*

225. *Dissolve to* CU *of newspapers being handed out. Calls of "Extra" are again heard, together with the sound of a crowd. (The score becomes increasingly cacophonous.)*

226. *Dissolve to* CU *of a newsboy's hand receiving change.*

227. *Dissolve to* CU *of a money-changer from which coins are dispensed.*

228. *Dissolve to high angle* MS *of man lifting a newspaper off a stack.*
229. *Dissolve to the newspaper banner and "I Protest" headline. It is whipped from view.*
230. *Dissolve to another banner and headline, as 229.*
231. *Dissolve to* CU *of a machine slot into which a hand inserts a coin.*
232. MLS *of* Bulletin's *Circulation Analysis Chart as an animated line graphs a rise in circulation over the summer months. Superimposed over the chart is the money-changer from 227, then a* CU *of circulation figures scrolling downward: 170,000—180,000—190,000.*
233. *Dissolve to* CU *of the animated line, angling upward. Superimposed over this are shots of newspapers and coins exchanging hands.*
234. *Dissolve to low angle* MCU *of a rising stack of newspapers.*
235. *Dissolve to* MS *of the chart; the line angles further upward.*
236. *Dissolve to more circulation figures scrolled over rising stacks of newspapers: 200,000—225,000—250,000—275,000.*
237. *Dissolve to a multiple image of upright newspapers moving leftward across tall stacks of newspapers. The headline on the moving papers reads: "Citizens March on City Hall and State Capitol!"*
238. *Dissolve to low angle* MLS *of placards carried leftward in front of the facade of City Hall. Messages include: "At Last an Honest Voice," "We Want Clean Government," "Why Should John Doe Jump," "We Agree with John Doe."*
239. *Dissolve to low angle* MS *of more placards. Center frame, one reads: "It's Up to You, Mr. Mayor."*
240. *Dissolve to high angle* MLS *of the back of Mayor Lovett as he peers out his office window. Turning around, he finds himself besieged by a sea of protesting citizens. He collapses, disappearing in their midst. (With this the musical score concludes.)*

241. *Governor's office:* MLS *as the Governor speaks to newsmen.*
     GOVERNOR: I don't care whose picture they're publishing. I still say that this John Doe person is a myth. And you can quote me on that. And I'm going to insist on his being produced for questioning. You know as well as I do that this whole thing is being engineered by a vicious man with a vicious purpose—Mr. D. B. Norton.
     As he speaks, the camera tracks forward, ending on a MS *of the Governor.*

242. MS *of a pair of binoculars. D. B. Norton, on horseback, lowers them from his eyes.*
243. *High angle* ELS *of a motorcycle corps performing maneuvers on a field, as Norton, flanked by two uniformed men on horseback, looks on.*
244. *High angle* LS *of the maneuvers.*
245. LS *of the three men on horseback. D.B. exchanges glances with his nephew, Ted Sheldon, to his left.*
246. ECU *of the patch on Ted's uniform sleeve. On it the words, "D. B. Norton Motor Corps" encircle the spokes of a wheel.*
247. *Low angle* MS *of Ted, as he looks out toward the corps and blows his whistle.*
248. *High angle* ELS *of the maneuvers.*
249. *High angle* LS *of the same.*
250. *Low angle* MLS *of Norton, watching. An aide rides up from behind.*
    AIDE: Mr. Connell and Miss Mitchell are at the house, sir.
    D.B.: Oh, they are? All right. *(To the horse:)* Come on.
    He clicks at the horse, and they start off.

251. *Dissolve to* LS *of the interior of Norton's study, panning with D.B., Ann, and Connell as they enter and cross the room.*
    ANN *(a bit breathless, as they walk)*: Personally, I think it's just plain stupidity to drop it now. You should see his fan mail! Thousands! Why, it's going over like a house afire!
    They have now reached D.B.'s desk.
    D.B.: What are you afraid of, Connell? It's doubled our circulation.
    CONNELL: Yeah, but it's got everybody sore.
252. MLS *of the massive back of D.B. as Connell faces him across the desk and Ann stands off to the left.*
    CONNELL: Ads are being pulled. The Governor's starting a libel suit. *(He glances over at Ann.)* What's more they all know John Doe's a phoney and they insist on seeing him.
    ANN *(to Connell)*: Well, what about it? Let them see him! We'll go them one better. They can also hear him. *(She turns to D.B.)* You own a radio station, Mr. Norton. Why not put him on the air?
    CONNELL: Watch out for this dame, D.B. She'll drive you batty.
    ANN: Ohh—
    CONNELL *(to Ann)*: Look, we can't let them get to this bush-league pitcher and start pumping him. Good night! No telling what the screw-

ball might do. *(He turns back to D.B.)* I walked in yesterday. Here he is, standing on a table with a fishing pole, fly-casting. *(He acts out the scene as he speaks.)* Take my advice and get him out of town . . .

253. MLS *of Ann and D.B. over Connell's shoulder.*

CONNELL: . . . before this thing explodes in our faces.

ANN: If you do, Mr. Norton, you're just as dumb a cluck as he is. *(She glances down.)* Excuse me.

CONNELL *(to Ann)*: No, you've got yourself a meal ticket and you hate to let go.

ANN *(eagerly)*: Sure, it's a meal ticket for me. I admit it, but it's also a windfall for somebody like Mr. Norton who's trying to crash national politics. *(She turns to D.B.)* That's what you bought the newspaper for, isn't it? You want to reach a lot of people, don't you? Well, put John Doe on the air and you can reach a hundred and thirty million of them. He can say anything he wants and they'll listen to him. *(Connell is about to interrupt, but she gestures to hold him off.)* All right, we'll forget the Governor, the Mayor, and all small fry like that! This can arouse national interest! If he made a hit around here, he can do it every place else in the country! *(She leans closer to D.B. to deliver her punch line.)* And you'll be pulling the strings, Mr. Norton.

D.B. studies her intently for a moment, then glances at Connell.

D.B.: Go down to the office and arrange for some radio time.

CONNELL: Why, D.B., you're not going to fall for—

D.B. *(cutting Connell off)*: I want it as soon as possible.

D.B. turns his attention to his mail, while Ann smiles triumphantly.

254. MLS *of Connell from behind D.B. Connell picks up his hat and portfolio.*

CONNELL: Okay. I just came in to get warm myself. *(To Ann:)* Come on, let's go.

Connell starts to leave. Ann follows.

D.B. *(off to Ann)*: Er, don't you go. *(Ann and Connell turn back around.)* I want to talk to you.

255. *Low angle* MCU *of D.B. His eyes shift from Ann to Connell.*

256. MCU *of Connell. He registers disdain, then departs.*

257. MS, *panning with Ann as she starts back to the desk.*

D.B. *(off)*: Sit down.

Reaching the desk, she settles into a low chair. On the desk, in the foreground, is a statue of Napoleon on horseback.

258. MS *of D.B. As he sits, a rightward pan reframes him with the statue again in the foreground.*

259. *High angle* MS *of Ann, as 257. She looks around the room self-consciously as she waits for D.B. to speak.*

260. CU *of D.B. He removes his glasses and, cleaning them, squints at Ann.*
     D.B.: Er, this John Doe idea is yours, huh?

261. LS *of D.B. and Ann, separated by the wide expanse of his desk.*
     ANN: Yes, sir.
     D.B. rises. Track forward as he comes closer to Ann.
     D.B.: How much money do you get?
     ANN: Thirty dollars.
     D.B.: Thirty dollars? *(He puts his glasses back on and sits on the edge of the desk, towering over her.)* Well—er—what are you after? I mean, what do you want? A journalistic career?
     ANN *(decisively)*: Money.
     D.B.: Money?

262. *Low angle* MS *of D.B. from over Ann's shoulder.*
     D.B.: Well, I'm glad to hear somebody admit it. Do you suppose you could write a radio speech that would put that fellow over?
     ANN *(leaning forward)*: Oh, I'm sure I can.
     D.B.: Do it, and I'll give you a hundred dollars a week.

263. *High angle* MS *of Ann, over D.B.'s shoulder.*
     ANN: A hundred dollars!
     D.B.: That's only the beginning.

264. *Low angle* MS *of D.B., as 262.*
     D.B.: You play your cards right and you'll never have to worry about money again.

265. *High angle* MS *of Ann, as 263. She and D.B. turn in response to some-one entering the room.*
     D.B.: Oh, I knew it.
     Pan right, anticipating the arrival of Ted Sheldon, and reframing a MLS *of all three.*
     TED: Hello.
     D.B.: Hello. Whenever there's a pretty woman around, er— *(Ted chuckles.)* This is my nephew, Ted Sheldon, Miss Mitchell.
     ANN: How do you do?
     TED: How . . .

266. MLS *of Ted from behind D.B., who is again standing.*
     TED: . . . do you do?
     D.B.: All right, Casanova. *(Ted looks at D.B. expectantly.)* I'll give
     you a break.
267. MS *of D.B. and Ann.*
     D.B.: See that Miss Mitchell gets a car to take her home.
268. MLS *of Ted, as 266.*
     TED *(laughing)*: Always reading my mind, aren't you.
269. MLS *of all three.*
     ANN *(rising, to D.B.)*: Thank you very much for everything.
     Pan right as she crosses the room with Ted.
     D.B. *(off)*: And, Miss Mitchell—
     They turn back around.
270. *Low angle* MS *of D.B., his figure dominating the frame.*
     D.B. *(very firmly)*: I think from now on you'd better work directly
     with me.
271. MLS *of Ann and Ted.*
     ANN *(softly)*: Yes, sir.
     *As she turns back around and exits with Ted, Ann's expression suggests
     that the importance of D.B.'s instruction is not lost on her.*
272. *Low angle* MS *of D.B. He removes his glasses once again as he watches
     them depart. (A somber musical chord is struck on the soundtrack.)
     Fade out.*[10]

273. *Fade in on* MS *of a dog on a couch.*[11] *Track back and pan left to* MS *of
     Ann in the living room of her apartment, at work on the speech. She
     pulls paper out of her typewriter, reads what she has written, and
     crumples it into a ball in frustration. (Playful music is scored under
     shots 273–275.)*
274. LS *of Ann at her desk and the dog on the couch. Ann flings the crumpled
     paper over her shoulder. The dog leaps from the couch and retrieves it.*
275. *High angle* MS *of the dog as it carries the paper to a wastepaper basket
     filled with Ann's discarded efforts. Pan with the dog as it jumps back up
     on the couch.*
276. MLS *of a bedroom door as Ann's younger sisters, Ellen and Irene, dash
     into the living room. Pan left as they sneak up behind Ann and tip her
     chair over backwards. ("Three Blind Mice" is heard on the soundtrack.)*
     ANN *(landing on her back)*: Oh, hey! Hey! I thought you were asleep!

ELLEN: We just wanted to say good night, Sis.

Ellen does a headstand on Ann's stomach, as the dog joins in the roughhousing.

ANN: Oh, oh! Oh, you little brats! You're just stalling. I said good night!

277. MS *of Ann's mother coming out of the kitchen.*

MRS. MITCHELL *(removing her apron)*: Come, come, come, children. It's past your bedtime.

278. LS *of all, as the girls climb off of Ann.*

GIRLS: Oh, all right.

MRS. MITCHELL: Go on.

GIRLS: Come on, pooch! Come on, come on.

Ellen snatches her mother's apron as the girls dash back to their bedroom.

279. MLS *of Ann, stretched out on the floor.*

ANN *(wiping a hand on her pants)*: Stick a fork through me. I'm done. *(She picks up a piece of crumpled paper.)* I'll never get this speech right.

280. MLS *of Mrs. Mitchell as she comes forward, in search of something. Ann remains seated on the floor.*

MRS. MITCHELL: Oh, yes you will, Ann dear. You're very clever.

She circles around Ann, looking about.

ANN: Yeah, I know. What are you looking for?

MRS. MITCHELL: Your purse. I need ten dollars.

ANN: What for? I gave you fifty just the other day.

MRS. MITCHELL *(stopping, looking down at Ann)*: Yes, I know, dear. But Mrs. Burke had her baby yesterday. Nine pounds!

ANN: Hmm.

MRS. MITCHELL: And there wasn't a thing in the house. And then the Community Chest lady came and—

ANN: And the fifty's all gone, huh? Who's the ten for?

MRS. MITCHELL: The Websters.

ANN: The Websters!

MRS. MITCHELL: You remember. *(Ann shrugs.)* Those lovely people your father used to take care of. I thought I'd buy them some groceries. Oh, Ann dear, it's a shame, those poor . . .

ANN: You're marvelous, Ma. You're just like Father used to be. Do you realize a couple of weeks ago we didn't have enough to eat ourselves?

MRS. MITCHELL: Well, yes, I know, dear. But these people are in such need. And we have plenty now.

ANN: If you're thinking of that thousand dollars, forget it! It's practically all gone. We owed everybody in town. *(She rises and heads for her desk.)* Now, you've just got to stop giving all your money away!

MRS. MITCHELL *(slightly wounded)*: Oh, Ann, dear.

ANN *(turning toward her mother)*: Oh, I'm sorry, Ma. *(She embraces her warmly, then tries to explain.)* Oh, don't pay any attention to me. I guess I'm just upset about all this. Gee whiz, here I am with a great opportunity to get somewhere, to give us security for once in our lives, and I'm stuck. If I could put this over, your Mrs. Burke can have six babies.

MRS. MITCHELL: Do you mean this speech you're writing?

ANN: Yeah. I don't know. I, I simply can't get it to jell. I created somebody who's going to give up his life for a principle, hundreds of thousands of people are going to listen to him over the radio. And unless he says something that's, well, that's sensational, it's just no good!

MRS. MITCHELL: Well, honey, of course I don't know what kind of a speech you're trying to write, but judging from the samples I've read, I don't think anybody'll listen.

ANN *(looking at her mother intently)*: What?

MRS. MITCHELL: Darling, there are so many complaining political speeches. People are tired of hearing nothing but doom and despair on the radio. If you're going to have him say anything, why don't you let him say something simple and real, something with hope in it? *(Music softly rises on the soundtrack.)* If your father were alive, he'd know what to say.

ANN *(looking back down at her desk)*: Oh, yes. Father certainly would.

MRS. MITCHELL: Wait a minute—

Pan with Mrs. Mitchell as she crosses room to the study. Ann watches from the foreground.

281. *In the study,* MLS *of Mrs. Mitchell as she slides back the top of a rolltop desk. She gingerly removes a bound volume from a compartment and starts back toward the living room.*

282. MLS, *as the end of 280. Ann watches her mother return. Track back slightly when Mrs. Mitchell reaches Ann's desk and places the volume beside the typewriter.*

MRS. MITCHELL: That's your father's diary, Ann.

ANN: Father's—? I never knew he had a diary.

She sits down, very interested in it.

MRS. MITCHELL: There's enough in it for a hundred speeches, . . .

283. MCU, *of Ann seated, her mother standing beside her.*

MRS. MITCHELL: . . . things people ought to hear nowadays. You be careful of it, won't you dear? It's always helped keep your father alive for me.

Tilt down as Ann lifts her mother's hand and presses it to her cheek.

ANN: You bet I will, Ma.

Fade out.

284. *Fade in on high angle* LS *of the exterior of John's hotel room door. Slowly track in on a guard who is trying to keep a crowd of autograph-seekers at bay.*

GUARD: Wait a minute. John Doe don't want to sign no autographs.

MAN IN CROWD: Well, what does he do all day?

GUARD: What does he do all day? He's writing out his memories.
Sounds of protest are heard from the crowd.
285. *Track back to* MS *of Beany on the telephone, inside the hotel room.*
    BEANY: Sorry, lady. You can't see Mr. Doe. He wants to be alone. No.
    No, he just sits around all day and commutes with himself.
    *He hangs up. The camera pans right with Beany and pulls back as he
    assumes the position of an umpire behind the Colonel, who is playing
    catcher in an imaginary baseball game. ("Take Me Out to the Ball-
    game" is orchestrated in conjunction with the action that follows.)*
286. LS *of John from behind Beany and the Colonel. Angelface sits off to the
    left, watching. John mimes the delivery of a pitch.*
    BEANY: Ball!
287. MS *of the Colonel and Beany. The Colonel glares at Beany, who shrugs.*
288. MCU *of John, who registers frustration as he backs up into a* MLS.
289. MS, *as 287. The Colonel juggles the imaginary ball, then tosses it back
    to John.*

COLONEL: I don't know how you're gonna stand it around here until after Christmas.

290. MLS *of John, who catches the imaginary ball.*
291. LS *of the Colonel and Beany. The Colonel sets himself for another pitch.*

COLONEL: I'll bet you I ain't heard a train whistle in . . .

292. LS *of John and Angelface.*

COLONEL: . . . two weeks.

John picks up an imaginary rosin bag.

293. MCU *of Angelface, eating peanuts as he watches intently.*
294. MLS *of John, who winds up and pitches again.*
295. MCU *of the Colonel and Beany, as 291. The Colonel catches the pitch.*

BEANY: Stee-rike!

296. MCU *of John, who smiles as he backs up into a* MLS.
297. MCU *of Angelface, who grins broadly.*
298. MCU *of the Colonel and Beany, as 291. The Colonel nods his approval. Beany checks the "ball," then returns it to the Colonel.*

COLONEL: I know why you're hanging around.

299. LS *of all, as 286. John positions some imaginary fielders.*

COLONEL *(tossing the "ball" to John)*: You're stuck on a girl.

300. *High angle* MS *of the Colonel, in a catcher's position, giving a hand sign.*
301. MLS *of John, who shakes the sign off.*
302. *High angle* MLS *of the Colonel, who offers another signal.*

COLONEL: That's all a guy needs is to get hooked up with a woman.

303. MLS *of John. Accepting the sign, he goes into a windup.*
304. MCU *of Angelface, watching.*
305. MLS *of John, delivering the pitch, then bolting to his right as if to field a hit.*
306. LS, *of all, as 286. John turns, as if to watch a play at first base.*
307. MLS *of John from the direction he is now facing. He registers dismay.*
308. MCU *of Angelface, who seems to be taking the mock game very seriously.*

ANGELFACE: What was that? A single.

309. MLS *of John, as 307.*

JOHN: First baseman dropped the ball.

310. MCU *of Angelface.*

ANGELFACE *(to the imaginary first baseman)*: Butterfingers! *(Then to John:)* Tough luck, pal.

311. MS *of John, who shrugs it off. He positions himself to pitch without a windup.*
312. MLS *of the Colonel, signaling from his catcher's position.*
    COLONEL: A guy has a woman on his hands, . . .
313. MS *of John, into his windup.*
    COLONEL *(off)*: . . . the first thing he knows his life is balled up with a lot more things. Furniture and . . .
    John suddenly wheels around toward the camera and throws, as if to first base.
314. MLS *of the Colonel and Beany, who looks down toward "first."*
315. MCU *of Angelface, who rises.*
316. MS *of John. He gestures in the direction he has thrown and mouths a verbal response.*
317. MCU *of Angelface.*
    ANGELFACE: Did you get him?
318. MS *of John, who turns toward Angelface and gestures that he got the runner by a wide margin.*
319. LS *of the Colonel and Beany.*
    BEANY *(toward "first")*: You're out!
320. MCU *of Angelface, now all smiles.*
    ANGELFACE *(sitting back down)*: Swell! What's this, the end of the eighth?
    JOHN *(off)*: Ninth.
321. LS *of all, as 286. Beany dusts off the imaginary plate with his hat. John and the Colonel return to their positions.*
322. MLS *of the door to the hall as it is pushed open by the guard.*
    GUARD: Hey, Beany!
323. *High angle* LS *from behind John, toward the Colonel and Beany.*
    GUARD: *(off)*: There's a couple of lugs from the *Chronicle* snooping around out here!
    BEANY *(abandoning his position as umpire)*: Huh? *(He dodges the imaginary pitch John throws.)* Come on, Angelface.
324. MCU *of Angelface, who is disappointed.*
325. LS *looking past John toward the door. John catches a return toss from the Colonel.*
    BEANY *(as he exits)*: Gangway.

GUARD: What's the score, Angelface?

ANGELFACE *(trailing Beany)*: Three to two, our favor.

GUARD: Gee, that's great!

326. CU *of Mike, who has been sitting quietly next to the door, watching John. Opening a newspaper, he checks the door then speaks softly to John.*

MIKE: Hey, you've got a swell form there. Must have been a pretty good pitcher.

327. MLS *of John, who turns toward Mike in the background.*

JOHN: Pretty good? Say, I was just about ready for the major leagues when I chipped a bone in my elbow. I got it pitching a nineteen-inning game!

MIKE: Nineteen?

JOHN: Yep. There was a major league scout there watching me, too. And he came down after the game with a contract. Do you know what? *(Mike shakes his head, no.)* I couldn't lift my arm to sign it. I'll be okay, though, as soon as I get it fixed up.

MIKE *(returning to his newspaper)*: That's too bad.

328. MS *of John, who is disturbed by Mike's remark.*

JOHN: What do you mean, too bad?

329. MCU *of Mike.*

MIKE: Huh? Oh, that you'll never be able to play again.

330. MS *of John, panning with him as he approaches Mike in a* MCU.

JOHN: What are you talking about? I just told you I was going to get a . . .

MIKE *(interrupting, off)*: Well, you know how they are in baseball, if a guy's mixed up in a racket.

JOHN: Racket? What do you mean?

331. MCU *of Mike, his gaze fixed on his newspaper.*

MIKE: Well, I was just thinking about this John Doe business. Why, as soon as it comes out it's all a fake, you'll be washed up in baseball, won't you?

Now Mike looks up at John.

332. MCU *of John.*

JOHN: Y-yeah.

333. MLS *as John crosses to a couch close to Mike.*

JOHN: Doggone it. I never thought of that.

The sound of the Colonel's ocarina can be heard offscreen.

334. MLS *of the Colonel, sprawled across a chair, playing a funeral march on the ocarina.*

335. MLS *of Mike and John, who glances over his shoulder at the Colonel.*
     JOHN: Gosh!
     MIKE: And another thing, what about all the kids . . .

336. *Cut in to* MS *of John and Mike.*
     MIKE: . . . in the country, the kids that idolize ballplayers? What are they going to think about you?
     JOHN *(thinking)*: Yeah. *(Suddenly he rises.)* Hey, Colonel.

337. MLS *of the Colonel, as John hurries over to him. The Colonel switches to "Hi-Diddle-Dee-Dee" on the ocarina.*
     JOHN: Did you hear that? *(The Colonel nods while playing.)* I've got to figure some . . .

338. MCU *of the Colonel.*
     JOHN *(off)*: . . . way out of this thing!
     COLONEL: The elevators are still runnin'.
     He returns to his music.

339. MCU *of Mike.*
     MIKE: I know *one* way . . .

340. MS *of John, who turns back toward Mike.*
     MIKE: . . . you can do it.
     JOHN: How?

341. MLS *of Mike as John returns to kneel on the couch.*
     MIKE: Well, when you get up on the radio, all you have to do is say the whole thing's a frame-up. Make you a hero as sure as you're born.
     JOHN: Yeah, but how am I going to get my arm fixed?
     MIKE: Well, that's a cinch. I know somebody that'll give you five thousand dollars . . .

342. *High angle* MLS *of the Colonel.*
     MIKE: . . . just to get up on the radio and tell the truth.
     COLONEL *(leaping up from his chair)*: Five thousand dollars?

343. MCU *of Mike.*
     MIKE *(to the Colonel)*: Yeah. Five thousand dollars. And he gets it right away. *(Back to John:)* You don't have to wait till Christmas.

344. LS *of all three: Mike in the foreground, the Colonel in the background, and John on the couch in between.*

COLONEL: Look out, Long John, they're closing in on you.

JOHN *(hearing the Colonel, but keeping his eye on Mike)*: Say, who is putting up this dough?

MIKE: Fellow runs the *Chronicle. (He looks surreptitiously toward the door, then removes some papers from inside his jacket.)* Here's the speech you make, and it's all written out for you.

John takes it and sits down on the couch.

COLONEL *(extremely agitated)*: Five thousand dollars.

345. *Cut in to* MS *of the Colonel.*

COLONEL: Holy mackerel! I can see the Heelots comin'. The whole army of them!

He turns away angrily.

346. *High angle* MS *of John, who is looking at the speech. He glances over at Mike.*

MIKE *(off)*: It's on the level.

John returns to the speech.

347. *Dissolve to* MS *of a man nailing to a pole a photo of John with the caption: "Hear John Doe Tonight 9 P.M. WBN."*

348. *Soft horizontal wipe and tilt down along NBC building facade to a similar announcement.*

349. LS *of the NBC building exterior, as traffic passes in front.*

350. MLS *of a receptionist on the phone.*

RECEPTIONIST: No, I'm sorry, . . .

351. *Cut in to* CU *of receptionist.*

RECEPTIONIST: . . . tickets for the broadcast are all gone. Phone the *Bulletin.*

352. *Track into* CU *of a switchboard operator on the line.*

OPERATOR: Sorry. No more tickets left.

353. *Dissolve to high angle* LS *of the broadcasting station's hallway. From around the corner in the distance, Beany leads a phalanx of policemen who are helping John and the Colonel make their way through the crowd.*

354. *High angle, telephoto* MLS, *panning with John and the Colonel.*

355. LS *of an interior office, with Ann in the foreground by a desk. Beany enters the door, followed by John, the policemen, and a cluster of photographers.*

BEANY: Here he is.

Track forward with Ann as she rushes to greet John.

ANN: Hello, John. All set for the big night? *(He doesn't respond.)* Swell!

BEANY *(grabbing John's arm to position him for the photographers)*: Turn around.

1ST PHOTOGRAPHER: One moment.

BEANY *(to John)*: Now stand still.

2ND PHOTOGRAPHER: Hold it, Mr. Doe.

3RD PHOTOGRAPHER: Big smile, Mr. Doe.

They take a round of pictures.

1ST PHOTOGRAPHER: That's swell.

ANN: Okay, Beany, take them out.

1ST PHOTOGRAPHER *(to Ann)*: Come on, Miss. I just want to get another one—

Ann and Beany usher the photographers out. She returns to John.

ANN: Now, look, John. Here's the speech. It's in caps and double-spaced. . . .

356. *Cut in to* MS *of Ann and John.*

ANN: . . . You won't have any trouble reading it. *(She hands him the speech.)* Not nervous, are you?

JOHN *(clearly uncomfortable)*: No.

ANN: Of course not! He wouldn't be.

JOHN: Who?

ANN: John Doe. *(She points to the speech.)* The one in there.

BEANY (returning from the door, to John): Hey, don't let your knees rattle. It picks up on the mike.

ANN: Oh, Beany! *(She pulls John away. Beany departs.)* You needn't be nervous, John. All you have to remember is to be sincere.

357. MS *of the door, as a man pokes his head in.*

MAN: Pick up the phone, Miss Mitchell.

358. MS *of Ann and John. Pan left with Ann as she heads for the phone.*

MAN *(off)*: It's for you.

ANN: Okay.

359. MS *of John, alone, nervously toying with the script.*

ANN *(off)*: Hello? Yes, Mother. Oh, thank you, darling.

360. MS *of the door, as Mrs. Brewster barges in, followed by an entourage of older women.*

MRS. BREWSTER *(heading toward John)*: Oh, there he is, the poor, dear man!

361.   LS *of all, as Mrs. Brewster crosses the room to John.*

MRS. BREWSTER: Oh, good luck to you, . . .

362.   MLS *as she reaches him and grasps his hand. He backs away.*

MRS. BREWSTER: . . . Mr. Doe. We want you to know that we're all for you.

363.   LS, *as 361. Finished with her phone call, Ann rushes to John's aid.*

ANN: Sorry, ladies. Mr. Doe can't be bothered now . . .

MRS. BREWSTER *(overlapping with the voice of Ann)*: The girls all decided . . .

364.   MS *of door, as Mike enters.*

ANN *(overlapping, off)*: He's got to make a speech now, and . . .

MRS. BREWSTER *(overlapping, off)*: . . . that you're not going to jump off any roof at all.

365.   LS *of all. Mike slips around the women as Ann ushers them out.*

MRS. BREWSTER *(to Ann)*: Oh, stop it!

366.   MS *of John as Mike joins him. The voices of the women can be heard in the distance.*

MIKE: Have you got the speech I gave you?

JOHN *(taking it from his pocket)*: Yeah.

MIKE: Now, look. *(He shows John an envelope filled with cash.)* I'll give this money to the Colonel just as soon as you get started. We'll have a car waiting at the side entrance for you.

JOHN: Okay.

367.   LS *panning with Ann as she comes over to John and Mike.*

ANN *(walking, to Mike)*: How'd you get in here?

She comes up beside the two men in a MS.

MIKE: Huh? Oh, I just came in to wish him luck.

ANN *(gesturing toward the door)*: Come on, out. Out! *(Mike goes. Ann turns to John.)* Mother says good luck, too. John, . . .

368.   *High angle* CU *of Ann from behind John.*

ANN: . . . when you read that speech, please, please believe every word of it. He turned out to be a wonderful person, John.

369.   *Low angle* CU *of John from behind Ann.*

JOHN: Who?

ANN: John Doe, the one in the speech.

JOHN: Oh.

ANN: You know something? I've actually fallen in love with him.

John looks at her, a bit dazed.

370. LS *of Ann and John as Connell bursts through the door in the background, followed by photographers and a woman in a bathing suit. The woman wears a banner announcing her as "Miss Average Girl."*

CONNELL: All right, there he is, sister. Now, come on, plenty of oomph!

ANN *(startled)*: What's the idea?

"Miss Average Girl" throws her arms around John; flashbulbs go off.

CONNELL: No, no, no, no. That's too much. No, no, not so much. Come on.

371. MLS *of Connell repositioning "Miss Average Girl" and John for the photographers in the foreground, while Ann watches off to the right. Connell places John's arm more discreetly around the bathing beauty.*

ANN: Oh, this is no time for cheap publicity, . . .

372. MLS *of Connell from behind Ann.*

ANN: . . . Mr. Connell!

CONNELL *(pointing at John with his pencil)*: Listen, if that guy lays an egg, I want to get something out of it. I'm getting a *Jane* Doe ready!

373. LS, *as 370. Ann tries to get this new group to leave.*

ANN *(to the photographers)*: Oh, come on, will you fellows. Give me a chance. I have to— *("Miss Average Girl" walks past her.)* That's fine, honey. You, go ahead.

374. Telephoto MS *of Ann pushing everyone out. Amid the confusion at the doorway stands the Colonel.*

COLONEL *(calling to John)*: How're you doin'?

375. MS *of Connell, checking his notes.*

CONNELL: All right, Beany. Bring 'em in!

376. MS *of the Colonel in the doorway. A male and female midget make their way around opposite sides of him as they enter the room. The Colonel jumps back in fright.*

COLONEL: Holy smoke! A half a Heelot!

377. MLS *of the midgets as they cross the room toward John, with Beany and more photographers right behind.*

BEANY: There you are, boss, just like you ordered. Symbols of little people.

378. MS *of John. Studying the midgets for a moment, he smiles at them shyly.*

CONNELL *(off)*: Okay. Get them up.

379. MLS *of John and the midgets from behind the photographers. Beany lifts a midget into each of John's arms.*

    ANN *(rushing over to Connell)*: This is ridiculous, Mr. Connell! Come on, give me a chance. The man's on the air in—

    Flashbulbs pop. Ann turns to the photographers.

    ANN *(herding them toward the door)*: No, come on, come on. That's right.

    Beany lifts the midget man out of John's arm.

380. MS *of John as the midget woman makes eyes at him. Beany tries to help her down, but she hangs on to John.*

    ANN *(off, to photographers)*: Afterwards, you can get all the pictures you want. Come on, that's right.

381. *High angle* MLS *of the midget man.*

    MIDGET MAN *(to his partner)*: Come on, snooks. You'd better bail out.

    Ann, at the door behind him, spins around.

382. MS *of John and midget woman.*
MIDGET WOMAN *(coyly)*: Say good-bye, Mr. Doe.
John says nothing as Beany lifts her down.
383. LS *of all, as Ann hurries over from the door.*
ANN *(exasperated)*: Beany!
BEANY *(guiding the midgets out)*: All right. All right.
384. MS *of John, checking his coat pockets to make sure nothing is missing.*
385. LS *of all. A man pokes his head in the door.*
MAN: Better get ready. One minute to go.
ANN *(racing to the desk in the foreground)*: Wow! One minute to go,
and the score's nothing to nothing. *(Track in on Ann as she gets a
comb from the drawer and turns to comb John's hair.)* Now please,
John. You won't let me down, will you? *(John is silent. She takes his
face in the palms of her hands.)* Will you?
386. *High angle* CU *of Ann, from behind John. Her expression of concern
gives way to a radiant smile.*
ANN: Of course you won't. If you just think of yourself as the real John
Doe. Listen, everything in that speech are things a certain man believed in.
387. *Low angle* CU *of John, from behind Ann. She brushes off his shoulders.*
ANN: He was my father, John. And when he talked, people listened.
(John stiffens.) And they'll listen to you, too. Funny, . . .
388. *High angle* CU *of Ann, as 386.*
ANN: . . . you know what my mother said the other night? She said to
look into your eyes. That I'd see Father there.[12]
389. *Low angle* CU *of John, as 387. He looks at Ann gravely, then glances
down.*
390. MS *of the door, as the studio director looks in. Behind him photogra-
phers stand ready.*
DIRECTOR: Hey, what do you say?
ANN *(off)*: Okay. We're coming. *(To John:)* Come on.
*Ann moves into the shot, with John in tow. She pauses at the door to
give him a final word.*
ANN: Now listen, John, you're a pitcher. Now get in there and pitch.
391. *Low angle* CU *of John as Ann leans forward to kiss him on the cheek.
He smiles weakly.*
ANN: Good luck.

MALE VOICE #1 *(off)*: Give him room. Let him through.

392. MS, *as 390. John and Ann exit into the crowded hallway.*

MALE VOICE #2 *(off)*: Come on.

393. *High angle* LS, *tracking with John and Ann as they are led through a double line of policemen. As they enter the studio, the camera tracks along an exterior wall to a window through which they can be seen in the distance. John appears lost; Ann takes his arm.*

394. MLS *inside studio, as Ann pulls John into* MS *near the microphone. The Colonel and Mike are now behind them.*

395. *Low angle* MCU *of John. The microphone, adjusted by the director, suddenly rises up in the frame, and John appears stricken.*

396. MS, *as end of 394. The director continues to work with the microphone. The Colonel steps forward and tugs at John's sleeve.*

COLONEL: Hey, let's get out of here. There's the door right there.

DIRECTOR *(to the Colonel)*: Hey, what are you doing here?

COLONEL: That's what I'd like to know!

DIRECTOR *(whispering)*: Come on, out, out.
JOHN: Say, he's a friend of mine.
ANN *(to the director)*: Never mind. Let him alone.
Pan left with Colonel as he is led away by staff member and Mike.
ANN *(off)*: He's all right.

397. MS *of Ann and John at the microphone lectern, with the director to the right.*
ANN: I'll be right over there pulling for you.
She exits left. Hesitating briefly, John tries to follow but is stopped by the director. Ann returns to John's side.
ANN *(whispering as she repositions him at the lectern)*: No, John. Over here.
She leaves again. John grabs the lectern to steady himself.

398. CU *of the studio clock: in thirty seconds it will be nine o'clock. A "Stand By" sign lights up.*

399. MS *of John at the lectern, with the director further back to the right.*
DIRECTOR *(to the orchestra)*: Stand by.

400. LS *of the stage curtain from the perspective of the studio audience. As the curtain parts, the audience applauds. A photographer rushes forward to snap pictures of John, who stands center stage in front of an orchestra.*

401. LS *of the audience from the perspective of the stage. Across the back of auditorium is a large sign: "MEET JOHN DOE TO-NIGHT." Applause continues.*

402. MLS *side view of John at the lectern. The director comes forward to cue the audience to be silent.*

403. MS *of Connell seated at a side table with Ann and Beany standing beyond. Ann is clearly excited.*

404. MLS, *as 402. The director gives animated hand signals. Photographers come into view and take pictures of John.*

405. MLS *of Mike at the side door passing the envelope of money to the Colonel.*

406. MS *of John as the director, watching the clock, raises his arm. John glances in the direction of the Colonel.*

407. MLS, *as 405. The Colonel signals to John that he has the money.*

408. MCU *of John at the lectern. He takes out of his coat pocket the speech Mike had given him.*

409. MS *of Mike and the Colonel at the door. Mike gives an "OK" sign to someone in the audience.*
410. MS *of Spencer of the* Chronicle, *who gets Mike's message.*
    SPENCER *(leaning over to an aide)*: Phone the *Chronicle.* Tell them to start getting those extras out.
411. MCU *of John nervously looking over the speech. He glances over at Ann.*
412. MCU *of Ann. Smiling, she shakes her clasped hands in a gesture of encouragement.*
413. MCU *of John examining the two speeches. He swallows hard.*
414. MLS *of the control room through a pane of glass. A man with his eyes fixed on his watch holds his hand high in the air.*
415. CU *of the clock: a few seconds before nine o'clock. The "On the Air" sign lights up.*
416. MS *of John and the director. When the director's hand falls, the band plays a loud fanfare, startling John. The director cues an announcer offscreen left.*
417. MCU *of the announcer at a second microphone. Ann is visible in the background beneath the clock.*
    ANNOUNCER: And good evening, ladies and gentlemen.
418. MS *of John and the director, listening. John is visibly nervous.*
    ANNOUNCER *(off)*: This is Kenneth Frey, speaking for *The New Bulletin.* Tonight we give you something entirely . . .
419. *High angle* MS *of Spencer, who smiles in anticipation of the speech.*
    ANNOUNCER *(off)*: . . . new and different. Standing beside me . . .
420. MS, *as 418.*
    ANNOUNCER *(off)*: . . . is the young man who has declared publicly that on Christmas Eve he intends to commit suicide, . . .
    John looks toward Ann.
421. CU *of Ann, who is smiling back.*
    ANNOUNCER *(off)*: . . . giving as his reason, quote:
422. MS, *as 418.*
    ANNOUNCER *(off)*: . . . "I protest against the state of civilization." End quote. *(The director raises his hand. John begins to look panicked.)* Ladies and gentlemen, *The New Bulletin* takes pleasure in presenting the man who is fast becoming the most talked-up person in the whole country. John Doe!
    The director drops his hand, and the orchestra bursts forth with "For He's a Jolly Good Fellow." He cues the audience to stand and cheer.

423. LS *of audience from behind the director, announcer, and John, as the people rise and applaud.*
424. MS *of Ann, Connell, and Beany at the side table. Ann pokes Connell to get him to applaud with the rest of them.*
425. MS *of John and the director. When the song ends, the director signals for John to begin. Silent, he glances over at Ann.*
426. MS, *as 424. Realizing something is wrong, Ann heads toward John.*
427. MS *of John and the director, who is trying to get John to speak. Pan left and reframe Ann and John as she reaches him. She lifts her speech off the lectern and places it in his hand. Looking at it, he leans toward the mike and clasps its stand.*

   JOHN *(reading the speech)*: Ladies and gentlemen, . . .[13]
   The announcer reaches over and lowers John's hand on the mike stand.
   JOHN: . . . I am the man you all know as John Doe. *(Seeing that he is all right, Ann departs. Pan right, reframing John with the director. John clears his throat.)* I took that name because it seems to describe . . .
   Leaning too close to the mike, John is pulled back by the director. John clears his throat.

428. MS *of Ann at the table. Crossing fingers on both hands, she sits down.*
   JOHN *(off)*: Because it seems to describe . . .
429. MS *of John, alone at the mike.*
   JOHN: . . . the average man, and that's me. *(His voice breaks to a higher register. The audience laughs. He recovers the proper pitch.)* And that's me.
430. MS *of Mike and the Colonel, who realizes John is not going to deliver Mike's speech. Grinning, he hands the envelope of money back to Mike. Perturbed, Mike heads toward Spencer.*
   JOHN *(off)*: Well, it *was* me . . .
431. MS *side view of John with Ann, Connell, and Beany in the background.*
   JOHN *(his hand trembling)*: . . . before I said I was going to jump off the City Hall roof at midnight on Christmas Eve. Now, I guess I'm not average anymore. Now, I'm getting all . . .
432. MS *of Spencer, very agitated, as Mike rushes up to him and hands him the envelope.*
   JOHN *(off)*: . . . sorts of attention, from big shots, too.
   MIKE *(whispering)*: We've been double-crossed!
   JOHN *(off)*: The Mayor . . .

SPENCER *(whispering)*: We have!

JOHN *(off)*: . . . and the Governor, for instance.

433. MS *of John.*

JOHN: They don't like those articles I've been writing.

SPENCER *(interrupting, off)*: You're an imposter, young fellow!

434. MS *of Spencer, on his feet.*

SPENCER: That's a pack of lies you're telling!

435. MCU *of John, who seems paralyzed.*

436. *High angle* LS *of Spencer amid an audience who is beginning to buzz.*

SPENCER: Who wrote that speech for you?

437. MS *of Ann and Connell, rising to their feet, with Beany behind them. Connell gives a signal to the police force.*

438. *High angle* MLS *of the audience as the police head toward Spencer.*

439. MS *of Ann and Connell, as 437.*

CONNELL: Beany, get that guy!

440. MLS *side view of John, who is watching the scene in the audience.*

441. MLS *of the Colonel at the door. He waves to John.*

442. MS *of John. His eye is caught by the Colonel.*

443. MLS *of the Colonel. He swings open the door to suggest that they might still escape.*

444. MS *of John. He looks back out at the audience.*

445. *High angle* LS *of Spencer as the policeman escort him out.*

446. *Norton's study:* MS *of D.B., seated to the left, and Ted, standing to the right, as they listen to the radio broadcast.*

D.B.: Spencer!

ANNOUNCER *(over D.B.'s radio)*: Ladies and gentlemen, the disturbance you just heard was caused by someone in the audience who tried to heckle Mr. Doe.

447. *The studio:* LS *of the stage from the audience.*

ANNOUNCER: The speech will continue.

448. MS *of John and the director, who taps John on the arm and gestures for him to resume.*

JOHN: Well, people like the Governor— *(he laughs, then ad libs)* people like the Governor and that fellow there can, can stop worrying. I'm not going to talk . . .

449. MS *of Ann and Connell.*

JOHN *(off)*: . . . about them. *(Relieved, Ann elbows Connell playfully, and they both sit down.)* I'm going to talk about us, the average guys, the John Does.

450. LS *of audience from behind John.*

JOHN: If anybody should ask you what the average John Doe is like, you couldn't tell him, because he's a . . .

451. *High angle* LS *of the audience.*

JOHN *(off):* . . . million and one things. He's Mr. . . .

452. *High angle* MLS *of the audience.*

JOHN *(off):* . . . Big and Mr. Small. He's simple . . .

453. LS *of the stage from the audience.*

JOHN: . . . and he's wise. He's inherently honest, but he's got a streak of larceny in his heart.

454. MS *of John.*

JOHN: He seldom walks up to a public telephone without shoving his finger into the slot to see if somebody left a nickel there.

455. *High angle* LS *of the audience, which is moved to laugh by John's description.*

456. MS *of John. He looks around edgily, as if trapped by the role in which he has been cast. He spies the Colonel.*

457. MS *of the Colonel, who repeats his invitation to escape through the swinging door.*

458. MS *of John. He turns to the next page of the speech.*

459. CU *of Connell. He rubs his eye and glances over toward Ann.*

JOHN *(off):* He's the man the ads are written for.

460. MS *side view of John with Ann, Connell, and Beany in the background.*

JOHN: He's the fellow everybody sells things to. He's the Joe Doakes, the world's greatest stooge and the world's greatest strength.

John accidentally flips the mike over with his thumb. The announcer quickly steps forward and fixes it. He places John's hand lower on the mike stand, and glares at John, annoyed. John clears his throat.

461. CU *of Connell, glancing around as the audience responds to the scene on stage with light laughter.*

JOHN *(off):* Yes, sir.

462. MS *of John.*

JOHN: Yes sir, we're a great family, the John Does. We are the meek who are, who are supposed to inherit the earth. You'll find us everywhere. We raise the crops, we dig the mines, work the factories, keep the books, fly the planes, and drive the buses. And when a cop yells, "Stand back there, you!" he means us, the John Does.

463. *Norton's study:* MS *of D.B. and Ted, listening to the radio.*
TED: Well, what kind of a speech is that? Didn't you read it?
D.B. quiets Ted with a gesture of his hand.

464. *The studio:* CU *of Connell, his head resting on his fist.*
JOHN (*off*): We've existed since time began. We built the pyramids, we saw Christ crucified, pulled the oars for Roman emperors, sailed the boats for Columbus, . . .
Connell's eyes register greater interest in the speech.

465. MS *of John.*
JOHN: . . . retreated from Moscow with Napoleon, and froze with Washington at Valley Forge.

466. CU *of Connell. Now very attentive to the speech, he glances in the direction of its author, Ann.*
JOHN (*off*): Yes, sir, . . .

467. CU *of Ann. Absorbed, she mouths the words John speaks.*
JOHN (*off*): We've been in there dodging left hooks . . .

468. CU *of Connell. He looks back at John.*
JOHN: (*off*): . . . since before history began to walk. In our . . .

469. MS *of John.*
JOHN: . . . struggle for freedom we've hit the canvas many a time, but we always bounced back, . . .

470. *High angle* LS, *panning over the audience.*
JOHN (*off*): . . . because we're the people, and we're tough!

471. MS *of John. He looks up as the audience applauds his last remark.*

472. MS *of the Colonel, who has been pacing at the door. He stops and leans against the wall.*
JOHN: (*off*): They've started a lot of talk about free people going soft, . . .

473. MS *of John.*
JOHN: . . . that we can't take it. That's a lot of hooey. (*He begins to gain momentum.*) A free people can beat the world at anything, from war to tiddledywinks, if we all pull in the same direction!
The audience applauds. John turns to the next page with new assurance.

474. MS *of the Colonel. Frustrated but resigned, he settles back against the wall.*

475. MS *of John.*

> JOHN: I know a lot of you are saying, "What can I do? I'm just a little punk. I don't count." Well, you're dead wrong! The little punks have always counted because in the long run the character of a country is the sum total of the character of its little punks.

He has looked up to deliver this last statement directly to the audience.

476. *High angle* MS *of the audience as it bursts into applause.*
477. *Norton's study: low angle* CU *of D.B., who is listening intently.*
478. MLS *of Norton's servants, gathered around a radio in the pantry, applauding along with the studio audience.*
479. LS *of Norton from the foyer. He rises from his chair and comes toward the foreground. Pan right with him as he crosses to the pantry door.*

> JOHN (*off, from the radio in the pantry*): But we've all got to get in there and pitch. We can't win the ballgame unless we have teamwork. (*D.B. pushes open the pantry door; inside the servants are engrossed by the broadcast.*) And that's where every John Doe comes in. It's up to him to get together with his teammate. (*Letting the door swing closed, D.B. turns around into a* ECU. *He is thinking.*) And your teammate, my friends, is the guy next door to you. Your neighbor. He's a terribly important guy, that guy next door. (*D.B. smiles. Track back and pan with him as he returns to the study.*) You're going to need him and he's going to need you—so look him up. If he's sick, call on him. If he's hungry, feed him. If he's out of a job, find him one.

480. *The studio:* MLS *through the control room window where everyone is listening to the speech.*

> JOHN (*off*): To most of you, your neighbor is a stranger, . . .

481. MS *of John.*

> JOHN: . . . a guy with a barking dog and high fence around him. Now you can't be a stranger to any guy that's on your own team. So tear down the fence that separates you, tear down the fence, and you'll tear down a lot of hates and prejudices. Tear down all the fences in the country . . .

482. LS *of the audience from behind John.*

> JOHN: . . . and you'll *really* have teamwork!

The audience applauds.

483. MS *of the Colonel. Bored, he idly sews a button on his coat.*
484. *Track into* CU *of the studio clock: it is 9:07.*

485. *Dissolve (with a sound bridge of applause) to the clock a short while later: it is 9:15.*

     JOHN *(off)*: I know a lot of you are saying to yourselves, . . .

486. MS *of John.*

     JOHN: . . . "He's asking for a miracle to happen. He's expecting people to change all of a sudden." Well, you're wrong.

487. *Norton's study:* MS *of D.B. and Ted listening to the radio.*

     JOHN *(over the radio)*: It's no miracle. It's no miracle because . . .

488. *Low angle* MS *of Ted, who looks at D.B. quizzically.*

     JOHN *(off, over the radio)*: . . . I see it happen once . . .

489. *Low angle* CU *of D.B. Smiling smugly, he waves Ted off.*

     JOHN *(off, over the radio)*: . . . every year. And so do you, . . .

490. MS *of John.*

     JOHN: . . . at Christmas time. There's something swell about the spirit of Christmas, to see what it does to people, all kinds of people.

491. *High angle* MLS *of the audience.*

     JOHN *(off)*: Now, why can't that spirit, that same warm . . .

492. *High angle* MLS *of another section of the audience.*

     JOHN *(off)*: . . . Christmas spirit last the whole year around?

493. MS *of John.*

     JOHN: Gosh, if it ever did, if each and every John Doe would make that spirit last three hundred and sixty-five days out of the year, we'd develop such a strength, we'd create such a tidal wave of good will, that no human force could stand against it.

494. CU *of Connell, who is clearly surprised by John's performance.*

     JOHN *(off)*: Yes, sir, my friends, the meek . . .

     Pan left to Ann as Connell glances her way. She appears deeply moved.

495. MS *of John.*

     JOHN: . . . can only inherit the earth when the John Does start loving their neighbors. You'd better start right now. Don't wait till the game is called on account of darkness. Wake up, John Doe, you're the hope of the world.

     Ending the speech on a quiet note, John looks up at the audience. There is a pregnant silence.

496. *High angle* LS *of the hushed audience.*

497. CU *of Ann as she gazes at John.*

498. LS *of the stage from the audience. Ann gets up from the table and hurries over toward John. The audience begins to buzz.*

499. MS *of John as Ann comes up beside him and embraces him.*
     ANN: John! You were wonderful!
     Applause breaks out in the audience.
500. ELS *of the stage from the rear of the auditorium. In the foreground, spectators rise to their feet, cheering wildly.*
501. MLS *of John, from behind, as he is mobbed from all sides.*
502. MS *of John and Ann. He pulls her arms from around his neck and exits to the left.*
503. MLS, *panning with John as he makes his way through the crowd.*
504. *High angle* MLS *from above John as he approaches the Colonel.*
505. *High angle* MS *from above John as he reaches the Colonel.*
     JOHN: Let's get out of here.
     COLONEL: Now you're talking!
     They pass through the door, pursued by the crowd.
506. *Exterior* LS *as John and the Colonel come out of the studio to confront another crowd.*
507. *High angle* MLS *from behind John and the Colonel. Bystanders ask for autographs as John and the Colonel cut a path through the crowd.*
     COLONEL: Gangway, you Heelots!
508. *Dissolve to* ELS *of a camp John and the Colonel have set up under a bridge by a stream. Moonlight reflects off the water. The Colonel carries wood for the fire as they settle down at the campsite.*
509. LS *as they sit down, John to the right against the base of the bridge, the Colonel to the left by the fire.*
     COLONEL: I knew you'd wake up sooner or later. Boy, am I glad we got out of that mess.
510. MS *of John, lit by the fire. He wears his ball glove on his left hand.*
     JOHN *(bitterly)*: I had that five thousand bucks sewed up. Could have been on my way to old Doc Brown. *(He imitates Ann.)* "You're a pitcher, John," she said. "Now go in there and pitch."
511. LS, *as 509.*
     JOHN: What a sucker!
     COLONEL: Yeah, she's a Heelot just like the rest of them. It's lucky you got away from her.
     JOHN: What was I doing up there making a speech anyway? Me? Huh? Gee, the more I think about it the more I could—
     COLONEL *(cutting John off)*: Huh! Tear down all the fences!
512. *High angle* MLS *of the Colonel.*

COLONEL: Why if you tore one picket off of your neighbor's fence, he'd sue you!

513. MS *of John, as 510, cupping his right hand to hold the imaginary money.*
JOHN: Five thousand bucks. Had it right in my hands! [14]

514. *Soft wipe left to Norton's study.* MS *of D.B. on the telephone, with Ted hovering nearby and a teletype machine clacking in the foreground.*
D.B.: What do you mean, he ran away? Well, go after him! Find him! That man is terrific!

515. *Dissolve to the interior of a train boxcar, with a sound bridge from the clacking teletype to the clack of the wheels on the track. Silhouetted in the open boxcar door, against a night sky, are John, seated to the left, and the Colonel, standing to the right.*

516. MS *profile of John as he looks out at the passing scene.*

517. CU *of the Colonel's feet, shuffling in rhythm with the sound of the wheels.*
COLONEL *(off)*: Columbia River, here we come.

518. MS *of John, as 516. He pulls out his harmonica and plays a riff.*

519. MS *of the Colonel, seen from behind. He looks over at John.*

520. LS *as 515. The Colonel sits down on the other side of the open door and vocalizes a percussive sound in rhythm with the train.*

521. MS *profile view of the Colonel.*

522. MS *of John, as 516. He conducts the Colonel with his hand.*

523. LS, *as 515. They segue into "Hi-Diddle-Dee-Dee" on their instruments.*

524. MS *from behind the Colonel as he gets back onto his feet.*

525. LS, *as 515. The Colonel dances, his bow legs bending in silhouette. Fade out.* [15]

526. *Fade in on* LS *inside of Dan's Beanery: a cash register and customer are in the foreground; young people jitterbug to jukebox music in the middleground; John and the Colonel can be seen approaching through a window in the background. Track with them as they enter and walk past some pinball machines and the dancers. John does a few steps to the music.*
COLONEL: Jitterbuggers.
JOHN: Yeah. *(Putting down their bags, they find two seats at the counter.)* Say, how much money we got left?
COLONEL: Four bits.

JOHN: Better make it doughnuts, huh?

COLONEL: Yeah.

The Colonel taps the counter in time to the music. Swinging around on their stools to watch the dancers, they take out their instruments and play along.

527. MS *of Dan cooking on the grill, with the dancers visible in the background.*

528. MCU *of John and the Colonel as Dan approaches from the background, stepping lively to the music. Reaching them, he drums on the counter.*

DAN: What'll it be, gents?

JOHN *(turning back around, measuring with his hands)*: Have you got a couple of steaks about that big and about that thick?

COLONEL *(turning also)*: Y-yeah. With hash brown potatoes and tomatoes and, and apple pie and ice cream and coffee and—

DAN *(skeptical)*: And doughnuts! I know. Hey, Ma! *(He points to the John and the Colonel.)* Sinkers, a pair.

MA *(off)*: Sinkers, a pair, coming up.

Dan goes to the coffee urn, still bopping to the music.

COLONEL *(to John)*: Glad he took the "t" out of that.

John swings back around. Something catches his eye.

529. LS *through the restaurant window, panning with a truck. It carries a large signboard that reads: "Join the John Doe Club."*

530. MS *of John and the Colonel from Dan's side of the counter. The truck passes by in the background.*

JOHN *(to the Colonel)*: Hey, look!

COLONEL *(turning toward the window)*: "Join the John Doe . . .

531. MS *of Dan at the coffee urn.*

COLONEL *(off)*: . . . Club."

JOHN *(off)*: John Doe Club?

Dan stares hard in the direction of John, then reaches behind the urn.

532. MCU *of Dan as he pulls out the local newspaper. John's picture is on the front page, beneath a headline that reads: "John Doe Radio Talk Big Sensation!" Looking toward the counter, Dan mouths "John Doe," then checks the photo again.*

533. MS *of John and the Colonel as they turn back toward Dan.*

COLONEL: Uh-oh.

534. MCU *of John and the Colonel, as 528. Dan comes back toward them.*

DAN *(his gaze fixed on John)*: Are you John Doe?

COLONEL: Who?

DAN *(again checking the paper)*: John Doe.

COLONEL: Aww, you need glasses, buddy.

DAN *(showing the paper to John)*: Ah! But gee, it's the spitting image of John Doe.

COLONEL: Yeah, but his name is Willoughby.

DAN *(dismissing the Colonel with a hand gesture)*: Aww!

JOHN: Long John Willoughby. I'm a baseball player.

John holds up his baseball glove.

COLONEL: Sure.

DAN *(unpersuaded)*: Ohhh, no. I'd know that voice anywhere. You can't kid me. You're John Doe. Hey, Ma!

535. LS *of the counter through the kitchen window. Ma appears in the foreground as Dan hurries over from the counter.*

DAN *(pointing at his customer)*: Ma! That's John Doe!

MA: John Doe!

DAN: Yeah. Sitting right there, big as life.

CUSTOMER *(approaching the counter)*: Who'd you say it was?

DAN *(to the customer)*: John Doe! The big guy there! Picture's in the paper!

John is surrounded at once by other customers.

536. LS *looking down the counter toward the front door. Track forward with John and the Colonel as they attempt to beat a hasty retreat, then panning left as they pass outside the window with the customers in pursuit. The camera comes to rest on Dan, who has crossed left to a telephone to place a call.*

DAN: Hey, operator. Dan's Beanery. Look, call everybody in town. John Doe was just in my place. Yeah. He ordered doughnuts.

537. *Dissolve to* ELS, *panning left along a city street, ending on a distant view of the Millville City Hall. Townspeople race toward the building in search of John Doe.*

538. LS *of City Hall. A throng has gathered at the steps, and more people are arriving.*

539. *High angle* MLS *of the crowd, as Mayor Hawkins makes his way down the front hallway to halt the forward movement of the townspeople.*

MAYOR HAWKINS: I know, you're all anxious to see John Doe. We're all neighbors, but my office is packed like a sardine box.

WOMAN: What does John Doe look like, Mr. Mayor?

The camera slowly cranes down in on the Mayor.

MAYOR: Oh, he's one of the great, big outdoor-type men. *(His attention is drawn to a man in front.)* No, you can't see him. You didn't vote for me the last time. Shame on you! *(He turns to someone else.)* What are you doing there? Get off my front porch anyhow! *(He turns to a nearby policeman.)* Mr. Norton come yet? Oh, I wonder where he's at. What's keeping him? He should have been here fifteen minutes ago. *(A siren is heard in the distance.)* Oh. There he comes now.

540. LS *of the street, panning rapidly to the left with an arriving limousine.*

541. *High angle* MLS, *as 539. Everyone turns toward the street.*

MAYOR: Now, everybody on your dignity. Don't do anything to disgrace us. This is a little town, but we got to show off.

542. LS *of the street, from above the heads of the Mayor and the townspeople on the City Hall steps. The limousine pulls up front.*

543. MCU *of D.B. and Ann inside the limousine. Ann stops D.B. as he prepares to exit.*

ANN: Better let me talk to him.

D.B.: All right, but present it to him as a great cause for the common man.

544. LS, *as 542, rising upward as D.B. and Ann emerge from the limousine.*

MAYOR HAWKINS: Ah! Here he comes! Give him room down there! Give him room, folks! Come on now!

545. *High angle* MLS, *as 539.*

MAYOR HAWKINS: Here he comes. Here he comes. Here comes Mr. Norton. How do you do, Mr. Norton! I'm Mayor Hawkins. Hey, Mr. Norton!

D.B. pays no attention as he hurries past. One of his policemen pushes the mayor aside. Mayor Hawkins tries to catch up.

MILLVILLE POLICEMAN *(to Mayor)*: Come back here!

MAYOR HAWKINS: Let me go, you darn fool! I'm the Mayor! *(He heads back down the hallway.)* Mr. Norton! Mr. Norton!

546. *High angle* LS *of Norton and Ann from inside City Hall as they walk toward the Mayor's office.*

MAYOR HAWKINS: Mr. Norton, I'm Mayor Hawkins. Your office telephoned to me to hold him.

D.B.: Well, that's fine. How is he?

MAYOR HAWKINS: Oh, he's fine. He's right in my office there. *(Pan*

left with them from what is now a high angle MLS.*)* You know, this is
a great honor having John Doe here. And you too. Haven't had so
much excitement since the old City Hall burned down.

547. *High angle* LS *from inside the Mayor's outer office, panning leftward as*
they enter and cross the room.

MAYOR HAWKINS: People were so excited, they nearly tore his clothes
off. *(He calls to his secretary as they pass by.)* Oh, Matilda, darling,
phone the newspapers, tell them Mr. Norton is here. *(He turns his*
attention back to D.B.) Step right inside, Mr. Norton—my office.

548. *High angle* LS *from inside the office, panning left as they cross to*
the desk.

MAYOR HAWKINS: Very comfortable here, Mr. Norton. Just had it air-
conditioned. Gangway, please. Make room for Mr. Norton. Gangway,
gangway. *(They reach John, who is sitting behind the desk.)* Here he
is, Mr. Norton, well taken care of.

549. *John stands up into a* MCU; *a portrait of Lincoln is on the wall behind*
him.

MAYOR HAWKINS *(off)*: The neighbors are serving him a light lunch.

550. MCU *of Ann, with D.B. to the left and Mayor Hawkins to the right.*

ANN *(smiling)*: Hello, John.

551. MCU *of John, over Ann's shoulder. He grins sheepishly.*

JOHN: Hello.

D.B. *(off)*: Oh, . . .

552. MCU, *as 550.*

D.B. *(removing his hat)*: . . . Mr. Mayor, if you don't mind, we'd like
to talk to him alone.

MAYOR HAWKINS: Why, certainly, certainly. All right, everybody . . .

553. *High angle* LS *of everyone at the desk.*

MAYOR HAWKINS: . . . clear out. Everybody quickly now. Come on.
Come on. *(Pan right to the door as the townspeople exit.)* Come on.
That's it. That's it. That's it. All right. That's it. *(He tries to usher his*
wife out the door, but she resists.) Don't argue with me here. Wait till
I get home.

MAYOR'S WIFE: Don't you push me around like that! Even though I'm
your wife, you can't push me around . . .

MAYOR HAWKINS: Ohhh.

554. MLS *of John from behind D.B.'s back. The Colonel stands to the left of John. On the wall are portraits of Lincoln and Washington, and a War Relief poster.*

JOHN: Look, Mr. Norton. I think you've got a lot of nerve having those people hold . . .

555. MCU *of D.B.*

JOHN *(off)*: . . . us here.

D.B.: There's nobody holding you here, Mr. Doe.

556. MS *of John on the left, D.B. on the right, with Ann between.*

D.B.: It's only natural that people—

JOHN *(interrupting)*: Well, if there's nobody holding us here, let's get going. *(Pan left with John as he joins the Colonel.)* Incidentally, my name isn't Doe. It's Willoughby.

ANN *(hurrying over to him, clasping the lapels of his coat)*: Look, John. Something terribly important's happened.

557. MCU *of John and Ann.*

ANN: They're forming John Doe clubs. We know of eight already and they say that there's going . . .

JOHN: John Doe clubs? What for?

ANN: Uh-huh. To carry out the principles you talked about in your radio speech.

558. MS *of John between Ann and the Colonel. John pulls away from her.*

JOHN: I don't care what they're forming. I'm on my way and I don't like the idea of being stopped either.

The last remark is aimed at D.B., who has just stepped forward.

ANN *(again clasping John's coat)*: Oh, but you don't know how big this thing is. You should see the thousands of telegrams we've received, and what they're saying about *you*.

JOHN *(wearily)*: Look, it started as a circulation stunt, didn't it?

ANN: Oh—

JOHN: Well, you got your circulation. Now, why don't you let me alone?

ANN: Oh, it started as a circulation stunt, but it isn't anymore. *(She glances over at D.B.)* Mr. Norton wants to get back of it and sponsor John Doe clubs all over the country. He wants to send you on a lecture tour.

JOHN: Me?

ANN: Uh-huh.

D.B.: Why, certainly. With your ability to influence people, it might grow into a glorious movement.

JOHN *(to D.B.)*: Say, let's get something straight here. I don't want any part of this thing. If you've got an idea I'm going around lecturing to people, why, you're crazy. *(To Ann:)* Baseball's my racket, and I'm sticking to it.

559. LS *of all, from behind D.B.*

JOHN *(picking up his bags)*: Come on, Colonel. Let's get out of here.

ANN: John!

Pan left with John as he starts to the door, the Colonel in tow. When he gets there he discovers a crowd of people pressing to get into the office, while the Mayor tries to hold them back.

MAYOR HAWKINS: Please! Please! I . . .

560. MS *of the Mayor at the door.*

MAYOR HAWKINS: . . . just got rid of one crowd!

WOMAN: But please, Mr. Mayor. *(She looks over in John's direction.)* Tell him the John Doe Club wants . . .

561. MLS *of John, flanked by the Colonel on the left, Ann and D.B. on the right.*

WOMAN: . . . to talk to him.

D.B.: Let them in, Mr. Mayor. Let them come in.

562. MLS *angled view of the group at the door, as the Mayor backs up.*

MAYOR HAWKINS: Okay, folks, but remember your manners. No stampeding. Walk slow, like you do when you come to pay your taxes.

563. LS *of all. The club members enter slowly, quietly, shyly. For a moment, everyone waits. Then Bert, a man in a soda jerk's uniform, is nudged forward by his wife.*

BERT: Okay.

564. MLS *of the club members as Bert moves to the foreground. On the wall behind them is Red Cross insignia beneath the single word, "JOIN!"*

BERT: All right, give me a chance.

WOMAN *(making room for him)*: Come right in.

BERT *(clearing his throat, grinning sheepishly)*: Uh, my name's Bert Hansen, Mr. Doe. I'm the head soda jerker at Schwabacher's Drug Store.

565. MS *of Bert, from a three-quarters angle, with his wife at his elbow and the club members behind him.*

> BERT: Well, sir, you see, me and my wife, we heard your broadcast, and we got quite a bang out of it, especially my wife. Kept me up half the night saying, "That man's right, honey."

566. MCU *of John, with the Colonel standing behind to the left. Intrigued, but wary, he glances over at Mrs. Hansen.*

> BERT (off): "The trouble with the world is, nobody gives a hoot about his neighbor. That's why everybody in town's . . .

567. MCU *of Ann and D.B., who watch what is unfolding between John and the townspeople with great interest. They exchange knowing glances.*

> BERT *(off):* . . . sore and cranky at each other." And I kept saying, "Well, that's fine, but how's a guy going to . . .

568. MLS, *as 564.*

> BERT: . . . go around loving the kind of neighbors we got?" Old Sourpuss, for instance? *(The club members laugh.)* You see, Sourpuss Smithers is a guy lives all alone next door to us. He's a cranky old man that runs a second-hand furniture store. We hadn't spoken to him for years. I always figured that he was an ornery old gent that hated the world cause he was always slamming his garage door and playing the radio so loud he kept half the neighbors up. *(More laughing.)* Well, anyway, the next morning I'm out watering the lawn and I look over and there's Sourpuss on the other side of the hedge straightening out a dent in his fender. And, er, my wife yells to me out of the window. She says, "Go on. Speak to him, Bert."

569. *High angle* MLS *of John, with the Colonel to left, and Ann and D.B. to the right, from behind Bert.*

> BERT: And, I figured, well, heck, I can't lose anything. *(Seeing that John is listening intently, the Colonel retreats to a chair and sits down.)* So I yelled over to him, "Good morning, Mr. Smithers." *(Pan right to reframe John, Ann, and D.B.)* He went right on pounding his fender. Was I burned.

570. MLS, *as 566.*

> BERT: So I turned around to give my wife a dirty look, and she said, "Louder, louder. He didn't hear you." So, in a voice you could have heard in the next county, I yelled, "Good morning, Mr. Smithers!"

571. *High angle* MLS *of the Colonel resting in the chair. Laughter from the*

club members greets Bert's remark, but the Colonel reacts with disgust.

BERT *(off)*: Well, sir, . . .

572. MLS, *as 566.*

BERT: . . . you could have knocked me over with a feather. Old Sourpuss turned around, surprised like, and he put on a big smile, came over and took my hand like an old lodge brother, and he said, "Good morning, Hansen.

573. MCU *of John, between portraits of Lincoln and Washington.*

BERT *(off)*: "I've been wanting to talk to you for years, only I thought you didn't like me." And then he started chatting away like a happy little kid, and he got so excited his eyes begin watering up.

Listening intently, John smiles slightly, sympathetically.

574. MLS, *as 564.*

BERT: Well, Mr. Doe, before we got through, I found out Smithers is a swell egg, only he's pretty deaf, and that accounts for all the noises.

575. *High angle* MLS, *as end of 569.*

BERT: And he says it's a shame how little we know about our neighbors, and then he got an idea, and he said, "How's about inviting everybody some place where we can all get together and know each other a little better?"

576. MLS, *as 564.*

BERT: Well, I'm feeling so good by this time, I'm ripe for anything. So Smithers goes around the neighborhood inviting everybody to a meeting at the school house, and I tell everybody that comes in the store, including Mr. Schwabacher, my boss. *(The people around Bert laugh.)* Oh, I'm talking too much. *(But the others urge him to go on.)* Well, I'll be doggoned if over forty people don't show up. Course, none of us . . .

577. MCU *of Ann and D.B. Ann smiles at D.B.; he nods and sighs in relief.*

BERT *(off)*: . . . knew what to do, but we sure got a kick out of seeing how glad everybody . . .

Ann glances over at John.

578. MCU *of John. He again smiles slightly.*

BERT *(off)*: . . . was just to say hello to one another.

579. MCU *of Ann and D.B. Ann looks from John back to Bert, on whom D.B.'s eyes are fixed.*

MRS. HANSEN *(off)*: Tell him about making Sourpuss . . .

580. MS *of Bert at a three-quarters angle, with the rest of the club members behind him, including his wife at his elbow.*
    MRS. HANSEN: . . . chairman, honey.
    BERT: Oh, yeah. We made Sourpuss chairman and decided to call ourselves the John Doe Club. And, say, incidentally, this is my wife. Come here, honey. *(She steps forward.)* This is my wife, Mr. Doe.

581. MCU *of John. He nods shyly.*
    MRS. HANSEN *(off)*: How do you do, Mr. Doe. Er, . . .

582. MLS, *as 564.*
    MRS. HANSEN *(pointing behind Bert)*: . . . Sourpuss is here, too.

583. CU *of Sourpuss, a hand cupped to his ear.*
    BERT *(off)*: Oh, is he?
    Smiling, Sourpuss steps forward.

584. MLS, *as 564. Sourpuss emerges from the crowd to stand beside Bert.*
    BERT: This is Sourpuss—Er, excuse me—Mr. Smithers, Mr. Doe.
    SOURPUSS: Th-that's all right. If you didn't call me Sourpuss, it wouldn't feel natural.

585. *High angle* MLS *of the Colonel in the chair. As the club members again laugh, he looks down, bored, and scratches his stubbly beard.*
    BERT *(off)*: Well, anyway . . .

586. *High angle* MLS, *as 569. John is smiling more warmly.*
    BERT: . . . I, I guess nearly everybody in the neighborhood came, except the Delaneys.

587. MS, *of Bert at three-quarters angle, with his wife to the right and Sourpuss to the left.*
    BERT: The Delaneys live in a big house, with an iron fence around it, and they always keep their blinds drawn. And we always figured that he was just an old miser that sat back counting his money, so why bother about inviting him? Until, er, Grimes, the milkman . . .

588. MCU *of John, who looks from his hat in his hands.*
    BERT *(off)*: . . . spoke up and he said, er, "Say, . . .

589. MS, *as 587.*
    BERT: . . . you've got the Delaneys all wrong." And then he tells us about how they cancelled their milk last week, and how when he found a note in the bottle he got kind of curious like, and he sort of peeked in under the blinds and found the house was empty. "If you ask me," he says, "they're starving."

SOURPUSS: Old man Delaney has been bringing his furniture over to my place at night, one piece at a time, and selling it.

590. *High angle* MLS, *as 569. John looks back down at his hat.*

BERT: Yeah. And, well, sir, a half a dozen of us ran over there to fetch them, and we got them to the meeting . . .

591. MS, *as 587.*

BERT: . . . and what a reception they got. Everybody shook hands with them, and made a fuss over them, and well, finally Mr. and Mrs. Delaney just sat right down and cried.

592. MCU *of John.*

SOURPUSS (*off*): And then we started to find out about a lot of other people.

John looks up again. His eyes have moistened.

BERT (*off*): Yeah, sure.

593. MLS, *as 564.*

BERT: Er, you know Grubbel, for instance.

MRS. HANSEN: Grubbel's here. See?
Pan right as she points in his direction.
BERT: Yeah. That's, . . .
594. CU *of Grubbel. His face is weather-beaten; his eyes are sad.*
     BERT *(off):* . . . that's him. Of course, you don't know Grubbel, but he's
     the man that everybody figured was the worst no-account in the neigh-
     borhood . . . *(Grubbel looks down)* . . . because he, he was living
     like a hermit and nobody'd have anything to do with him. Er, that is,
     until Murphy the postman told us the truth. "Why, Grubbel," . . .
595. MCU *of John. Looking at Grubbel, John appears pained.*
     BERT *(off):* . . . he says, "he lives out of garbage cans . . .
596. CU *of Grubbel.*
     BERT *(off):* . . . because he won't take charity. Because it'd ruin his
     self-respect," he says.
     Grubbel looks up squarely at John.
597. MLS, *as 564.*

MRS. HANSEN: Just like you said on the radio, Mr. Doe.

SOURPUSS: Well, sir, . . .

598. MCU *of John. He looks away, as if the scene before him is too much to take in.*

SOURPUSS *(off):* . . . about a dozen families got together and gave Grubbel a job watering their lawns. Isn't that wonderful?

599. MS, *as 587.*

SOURPUSS: And then we found jobs for six other people, and they've all gone off relief.

BERT: Yeah. Er, and my boss, Mr. Schwabacher, made a job in his warehouse for old man Delaney—

MRS. HANSEN: And he gave you that five-dollar raise.

BERT: Yeah. Wasn't that swell?

600. *High angle* MLS *of the Colonel in the chair. As the club members laugh, he waves his hand at them dismissively.*

MAYOR HAWKINS *(off):* Why, Bert, I, . . .

601. MLS, *as 564. The Mayor has come over to speak to Bert.*

MAYOR HAWKINS: . . . I feel slighted. I'd like to join, but nobody asked me.

SOURPUSS: I-I'm sorry, Mayor, but we voted that no politician could join.

MRS. HANSEN: Just the John Does of the neighborhood, 'cause you know how politicians are.

The others laugh. Embarrassed, she leans her forehead on Bert's shoulder.

MAYOR HAWKINS *(retreating, chastened):* Yeah, yeah.

BERT *(to John):* Well, er, the reason we wanted to tell you this, Mr. Doe, was to, to give you an idea what you started. And from where I'm sitting, I, I don't see any sense in you jumping off any building.

602. MCU *of John. He appears very grave.*

SOURPUSS *(and others, off):* No! No!

BERT *(off):* Well, . . .

603. MLS, *as 564.*

BERT: . . . thank you for listening. *(Pan left as Bert steps forward with an outstretched hand and shakes John's.)* Goodbye, Mr. Doe. You're a wonderful man, and it strikes me you can be mighty useful walking around for a while.

In the background others nod in agreement. Pan right with Bert as he returns to the group.

CLUB MEMBERS *(as they turn to leave)*: Bye. Goodbye, Mr. Doe. *They depart silently.*

604. MS *of John, with Ann and D.B. in the background right. Silent, they watch the club members depart.*

605. MS *of the doorway as the group files out. Pan left with an old couple who, against the flow of the departing club members, make their way over to John, ending on a high angle MS of them with John to the left.*
    MRS. DELANEY: I'm Mrs. Delaney, Mr. Doe. And God bless you, my boy.
    She reaches for his hand and gently kisses it.

606. *Low angle CU of John, who appears deeply moved.*

607. *High angle CU of Mrs. Delaney. She looks up at John, smiling, eyes beaming. Then she slowly backs away.*

608. *High angle MS of Mrs. Delaney and her husband, with John to left, as Mr. Delaney stops briefly in front of John. The old man nods and smiles.*

609. *MLS of the Delaneys as they exit. Pan right as they approach the door. The Mayor pats Mrs. Delaney on the back, helping her out.*

610. *Low angle CU of John. He is thinking.*

611. LS *of side view of John, to right, Ann and D.B. behind him, and the Colonel in the chair seated at the far left. John turns around.*

612. MLS *of John as he turns. Seeing Ann and D.B., he backs away.*
    JOHN: Gee whiz. I'm all mixed up.

613. MS *of John. Pacing, he comes forward into a MCU.*
    JOHN: I don't get it. *(He points toward the door.)* Look, . . .

614. MCU *of Ann and D.B., watching John's every move.*
    JOHN *(off)*: . . . all those swell people think I'm going to jump off a building or something. *(D.B. glances back and forth between Ann and John.)* I never had any such idea.

615. MS *of John.*
    JOHN: Gosh, a fellow'd have to be a mighty fine example himself to go around telling other people how to— *(The camera has panned right to include Ann and D.B.)* Say, look what happened the other night was on account of Miss Mitchell, here. She wrote the stuff.

ANN *(stepping forward toward John)*: Don't you see what a
   wonderful . . .

616. *High angle* MLS *of the Colonel in the chair. He appears concerned.*
   ANN *(off)*: . . . thing this can be?

617. CU *of Ann and John.*
   ANN *(seductively)*: But we need *you*, John.
   COLONEL *(off)*: You're hooked!

618. *High angle* MLS *of the Colonel, who is now sitting upright.*
   COLONEL: I can see that right now. They got you. Well, I'm through.

619. LS *of all. Pan right with the Colonel as he rises, grabs his bag, and
   heads toward the door. Suddenly, he starts back toward John.*

620. MCU *of Ann and John as the Colonel returns. D.B. watches from the
   background.*
   COLONEL: For three years I've been trying to get up to the Columbia
      River country. First, it was your glass arm. Then it was the radio.
      And now it's the John Doe Clubs. Well, I ain't waiting another minute.

621. LS, *as 619, again panning right with the Colonel as he departs.*

622. *High angle* MLS *on the other side of the door, where the club members
   are hovering.*
   COLONEL *(exiting through the door)*: Gangway, you Heelots!
   He pushes his way through the crowd.
   CLUB MEMBERS: Ohhh.

623. *High angle* MCU *as John appears at the door. He strains to see over the
   crowd.*
   JOHN *(calling)*: Hey, Colonel! Wait a minute! Hey! Colonel!

624. *Dissolve to* MLS *of D.B. seated behind a desk in his headquarters. On
   the wall behind him is a large map of the United States with flags marking
   the location of John Doe Clubs. In front of D.B.'s desk stands Charlie, a
   promoter.*
   D.B.: I want you personally to go along with John Doe and Miss Mitchell
      and handle the press and the radio.
   CHARLIE: Me?
   D.B.: Yes. I don't want to take any chances. *(He turns to someone off
      screen.)* And, Johnson?
   JOHNSON *(moving into foreground left)*: Yes, D.B.?

D.B.: Your crew will do the mop-up job. They'll follow John Doe into every town, see that the clubs are properly organized and the charters issued.

JOHNSON: Right.

D.B. *(to both, pointing to the map)*: There are only eight flags up there now. I want to see that map covered before we get through.

The camera tilts up and tracks forward until the map fills the frame.[16]

MONTAGE SEQUENCE #2[17]

(A medley of familiar songs are scored under this sequence: "Oh Tannenbaum!" [625–631], "Nothing Could Be Finer Than to Be in Carolina" [634–637], "My Darling Clementine" [639–640], "Chicago" [644–646], "The Farmer in the Dell" [647–649], "California, Here I Come" [650–655], "East Side, West Side" [656–658], "Yankee Doodle" [665–667], and "I've Been Working on the Railroad" [673–677].)

625. *Dissolve to* LS *of airplane, panning right as it takes off.*

626. *Dissolve to aerial view of a map of midwestern states, panning eastward.*

627. *Dissolve to* CU *of John inside a plane, peering out of the window.*

628. *Dissolve to* MCU *of Ann, over John's shoulder, sitting in a plane seat opposite him. She is typing. He leans forward; she looks up and smiles.*

629. *Dissolve to the sky. Superimposed over the sky, a banner emerges from the background reading: "John Doe Coming."*

630. *Dissolve to* MLS *of John, smiling as he steps down out of a plane to off screen cheers. A photographer takes his picture.*

631. *Dissolve to high angle* MS *of people cheering.*

632. *Dissolve to* MS *of revolving searchlights at night.*

633. *Dissolve to low angle* LS *of a banner, stretched above a street, illuminated by searchlights against a night sky. It reads: "John Doe To-Night."*

634. *Dissolve to a double image of John's "I Protest" newsphoto moving from the background into* CU, *superimposed over a* LS *of a crowd entering an auditorium. Then superimposed over both is a brief low angle* MLS *of John at a microphone with Ann at a distance behind.*

635. *Low angle* LS *of a hand-painted John Doe Club sign.*

636. *Dissolve to low angle* MLS *of another club sign across the front of a building, with people at second story windows above it.*

637. *Dissolve to low angle* MS *of a third club sign on an exterior wall.*

638. *Soft wipe leftward to a low angle* LS *of a train as it approaches the camera.*
639. *Dissolve to low angle* MCU *of John speaking and gesturing.*
640. *Dissolve to low angle* MLS *of a group of mineworkers listening.*
641. *Soft wipe upward to low angle* LS *of the John Doe Club sign over a porch.*
642. *Soft upward wipe to a low angle* LS *of another club sign.*
643. *Soft upward wipe to a low angle* MS *of a club plaque on the front of an urban building.*
644. *Soft upward wipe to a* CU *of Illinois and Indiana on the headquarters map. There are a few scattered flags. Dissolve in many more flags until the map is covered.*
645. *Dissolve to a double image: a* MS *of a cascade of John Doe buttons superimposed over* LS *of an urban skyline, tracking left. Dissolve to* CU *of the buttons falling over the same backdrop.*
646. *Dissolve to a double image: a* CU *of the buttons at rest superimposed over a rightward traveling shot through the country. Above a photo of John, the buttons read: "Be a Better Neighbor." The buttons are then replaced by a* MCU *of hands typing over the same backdrop.*
647. *Dissolve to low angle* MCU *of John delivering a speech.*
648. *Dissolve to* MLS *of a group of farmers listening and nodding.*
649. MS *of the same group of farmers, who applaud.*
650. CU *of Pennsylvania, New York, and New England on the headquarters map. By way of a dissolve, the field of a few scattered flags gives way to many.*
651. LS *of train arriving in a station, awaited by a cheering crowd in the foreground.*
652. *Dissolve to a low angle* MCU *of a "Welcome John Doe" banner moving rightward through the frame.*
653. *Dissolve to high angle* MLS *of a marching band.*
654. *Dissolve to aerial* ELS *of a parade moving down a city street.*
655. *Dissolve to high angle* MLS, *moving rightward over an excited crowd.*
656. *Dissolve to a double image: a* MS *of three copies of* Time *magazine are spread out and superimposed over a* LS *of the city. On the cover of the magazine is a photo of John.*
657. *Dissolve to a double image: a* MS *of the magazines over a* LS *of the city; one issue is lifted to reveal John's photo on the cover below.*

658. *Dissolve to a double image: an* ECU *of the caption under the photo—*
     "Man of the Hour (National Affairs)"—superimposed over an aerial
     ELS *of Wall Street. The former image fades, leaving only the latter.*
659. *Dissolve to high angle* LS *of a conference table around which a group*
     of men are gathered. Standing at the far end is a business leader.
     LEADER: This has been growing like wildfire! If they made demands,
       I'd understand it.
660. *Low angle* MLS *of the same figure.*
     LEADER: But the John Does ask for nothing.
661. *While the man is speaking, dissolve to tracking shot in on a door marked*
     "Relief Administrator."
662. *Dissolve to low angle* MLS *of the Relief Administrator, from behind*
     a second figure in shadow, to whom the administrator speaks across
     his desk.
     RELIEF ADMINISTRATOR: People are going off relief.
663. CU *of the administrator.*

RELIEF ADMINISTRATOR: If this keeps up, I'll be out of a job!

664. *While he is speaking, dissolve to low angle* ELS *of the Capitol Building in Washington, D.C.*

665. *Dissolve to* MS *of three men at the steps of the Capitol. The man in the center points at the newspaper and speaks to his colleagues.*

LEGISLATOR: As soon as he gets strong enough, we'll find out what John Doe wants.

666. MCU *of the man who is speaking.*

LEGISLATOR: Thirty every Thursday! Sixty at sixty! Who knows what?

667. *Dissolve to tracking shot in on a sign for Democratic Headquarters.*

668. *Dissolve to low angle* MLS *of man leaning over the desk of his superior, who is seated in the foreground.*

DEMOCRAT: I'm sorry, boss. They just won't let anybody talk politics to them. It's crazy.

669. *While he is speaking, dissolve to tracking shot in on a sign for Republican Headquarters.*

670. *Dissolve to high angle* LS *of a man behind his desk, surrounded by aides in the foreground.*

REPUBLICAN *(slapping a newspaper on his desk)*: We've got to get to them.

671. CU *of the man who is speaking, as he leans forward.*

REPUBLICAN: They represent millions of voters!

672. *Dissolve to low angle* MS *of John moving up to a cluster of radio microphones, smiling broadly. Cheering is heard off screen.*

673. *Dissolve to high angle* LS *of an audience as people stand and applaud.*

674. *Dissolve to aerial view of a map of eastern and midwestern states, from the northern to southern borders. A field of John Doe Club placards rise up and are superimposed on the map through a series of dissolves.*

675. *Dissolve to aerial view of another section of the map, further west. The placards again rise up.*

676. *Dissolve to aerial view of a third section of the map, the far west. More placards rise up.*

677. *Dissolve to* LS *of the headquarters map, covered with flags.*

D.B. *(off)*: I tell you, ladies and gentlemen, this thing has been nothing short of a prairie fire. *(As the camera begins to pull back, D.B. comes into view, standing behind his desk.)* We've received so many applications for charters to the John Doe clubs, we haven't been able to take care of them.

MAYOR LOVETT *(off)*: I'd hate to have that many pins stuck in me.

There is laughter as the camera continues on back, tracking past rows of people who are listening to D.B. Mayor Lovett sits up front.

D.B.: This John Doe convention is a natural.[18] It's going to put our city on the map. Why, over twenty-four John Doe clubs are sending delegates. Can you imagine that?

The camera has come to rest in a wide angle ELS *from the back of the room.*

678. *Three-quarter angle* MLS *of D.B. Beyond him sit Connell and Ted Sheldon.*

D.B. *(turning to Mayor Lovett)*: You, Mr. Mayor, will be the official host. You will make the arrangements for decorating the city.

679. *High angle* MS *of Mayor Lovett seated in a chair.*

D.B. *(off)*: Parades and reception for John Doe when he gets home! And don't wear your high hat.

MAYOR LOVETT *(disappointed)*: No high hat?

D.B. *(off)*: No high hat. And from you, Connell, . . .

680. MLS, *as 678*.

　　D.B. *(shaking a finger at Connell)*: . . . I want a special John Doe edition every day . . .

681. MS *of Connell, arms folded across his chest. He nods.*

　　D.B. *(off)*: . . . until the convention is over.

682. *Frontal* LS *of D.B. from the audience.*

　　D.B.: And now, if you will please, just step into the outer office, and look your prettiest because there are photographers there to take pictures of this committee.

　　MAYOR *(rising with the others)*: Don't worry, D.B. Everything will be taken care of.

　　D.B.: I'm sure.

　　Pan left with the group as they depart.

　　COMMITTEE WOMAN *(amid the chatter of the others)*: Isn't it all too wonderful!

683. MS *of Connell, frowning.*

　　PHOTOGRAPHER: *(off)*: Oh, Mr. Mayor, would you step down in the front row, please? *(Connell rises from his chair and heads toward D.B.)* Will you ladies get close to him? That's it.

684. MLS, *as 678. Connell comes over to D.B.'s desk as Ted, still seated in the background, watches on.*

　　CONNELL: Well, I don't get it.

　　D.B.: Get what?

　　CONNELL: Look, D.B., I'm supposed to know my way around. This John Doe movement has cost you a fortune. Now, this convention's going to cost plenty.

　　D.B.: Well?

　　CONNELL: Well, I'm stuck with two and two, and I'm a sucker if I can make four out of it. Where do *you* come in?

685. MS *of D.B. from behind Connell's shoulder. D.B. removes his glasses and begins to clean them methodically with his handkerchief.*

　　D.B.: I'll have the satisfaction of knowing that my money has been spent for a worthy cause.

686. MS *of Connell from behind D.B.'s shoulder.*

　　CONNELL: I see. I'd better stick to running the paper, huh?

687. MS *of D.B., as 685.*

D.B.: I think maybe you better had.

688. MLS, *as 678. Pan left with Connell as he turns and leaves.*

D.B.: And Connell, I'd like to have the John Doe contract, all the receipts for the money we have advanced him, and the letter Miss Mitchell wrote, for which I gave her a thousand dollars.

CONNELL *(who has come back toward the desk)*: Yes. Sure.

Connell exits left.

689. *Dissolve to* MLS *of a hotel living room door as Charlie enters.*[19]

CHARLIE: Well, we leave for the airport in half an hour. *(Pan right with him as he crosses the room.)* Is that Johnny Boy's room? I'd better hustle him up.

Ann, packing up her papers at a desk, comes into view.

ANN *(soberly)*: He'll be ready on time. He's packing now.

CHARLIE: Ah, good.

690. MS *of Charlie and Ann as he reaches the desk. He shows her a magazine.*

CHARLIE: Did you see his picture on the cover of *Time?*

ANN *(without enthusiasm)*: Yeah.

CHARLIE *(folding the magazine and putting it in his pocket)*: I've got to give you credit, Annie Girl. I've handled a good many big promotions in my time, everything from the World's Fair to a Channel swimmer, but this one has certainly got me spinning.

He opens a Coca-Cola. Pan with Ann as she crosses left to her bedroom.

CHARLIE *(off)*: And now a John Doe convention. Wow! *(Framed by the bedroom door, Ann pauses before her open luggage, seemingly distracted.)* Hey, . . .

691. MLS *of Charlie, pouring his drink.*

CHARLIE: . . . if you could only get him to jump off the City Hall roof on Christmas Eve, . . .

692. *Ann moves back toward the living room, and leans in* MCU *on the doorframe.*

CHARLIE *(off)*: . . . I'd guarantee you half a million people there.

ANN *(troubled)*: Charlie?

CHARLIE *(off)*: Huh?

ANN: What do you make of him?

693. MLS *of Charlie. He nods toward John's room.*

CHARLIE: Who, Johnny Boy? *(Pan left as he puts his drink on the desk and crosses the room toward Ann.)* Well, I don't know what angle you want, but I'll give it to you quick. *(He moves into a* MS *with Ann.)* Number one, he's got great yokel appeal, but he's a nice guy. *(Ann smiles.)* Number two, he's beginning to believe he really wrote that original suicide letter that you made up.

694. MCU *of Ann over Charlie's shoulder.*
CHARLIE: Number three, he thinks you're Joan of Arc or something.
ANN *(looking down)*: Yeah, I know.
CHARLIE: Number four—well, you know what number four is. He's nuts about you. *(Ann glances up sharply.)* Yeah, it's running out of his ears.
ANN: You left out number five. We're all heels, me especially.
She heads back into her bedroom.
CHARLIE: Holy smoke.

695. MS *of Ann and Charlie. A knock is heard on John's door.*
ANN *(spinning around)*: Come in.

696. MS *of John's door, as he exits carrying his luggage. Pan left with John as he crosses to Charlie and Ann in* MLS.
JOHN: I'm all packed.
CHARLIE: Good.

697. MS *of Ann and Charlie.*
CHARLIE: I'll go and get Beany Boy.
Pan right with Charlie as he heads for the front door. John comes into view from the other direction as he approaches Ann's room.
JOHN *(waving to Charlie)*: Okay, Charlie Boy.
CHARLIE: Huh?
Realizing that John is joking, Charlie laughs and exits. John turns toward Ann's room.

698. LS *of Ann through the doorway to her room as she folds clothes. John steps into the foreground and leans against the doorframe to the right. He watches here for a moment.*
JOHN: Can I help you pack?
ANN *(glancing briefly at John)*: No, thank you.

699. MS *profile of Ann as she continues to fold her clothes in silence.*

700. LS, *as 698. John looks about.*
JOHN: Do you care if I sit down, out here?
ANN: No.

Ann watches John settle into a chair at the doorway, then she crosses to a second suitcase on the left and gathers more clothes.

JOHN: You know, I had a crazy dream last night. *(He pauses.)* It was about you.

ANN (looking over at John): About me?

JOHN: Yeah. Sure was crazy. I dreamt I was your father. *(Ann stares for a second, then returns to her packing.)* There was, there was something that I was trying to stop you from doing. So, er, so I got up out of bed . . . *(Ann looks over again.)* . . . and I walked right through the wall here, right straight into your room. *(John laughs; Ann returns back to the first suitcase.)* Huh, you know how dreams are. And, and, and there you were in bed. But you, you were a little girl, you know, about ten. And very pretty, too. So, I, I shook you, and the moment you opened your eyes, you hopped out of bed, and started running like the devil, in your nightgown. *(Ann looks over.)* You ran right out the window there. And you ran out over the tops of buildings and roofs and everything for miles. And I was chasing you.

(After briefly glancing out the window, Ann returns to packing.) And, and, all the time you were running, you kept growing bigger and bigger and bigger, and pretty soon you were as big as you are now. *(Ann looks over, briefly.)* You know—grown up. And all the time I kept, I kept asking myself, "What am I chasing her for?" And I didn't know. Huh, isn't that a hot one? *(Again, she briefly looks over.)* Well, anyway, you ran into some place, and then I ran in after you and, . . .

701. MS *of Ann, packing.*

JOHN *(off)*: . . . and when I got there, there you were getting married.
Ann looks up, startled by the turn John's story has taken.

702. MLS *of John, seated low, boyish and awkward.*

JOHN: And the nightgown had changed into a beautiful wedding gown.

703. MCU *of Ann, still watching him intently.*

JOHN *(off)*: You sure looked pretty, too. *(John laughs; Ann turns back away.)* And then I knew what it was I was trying to stop you from doing.

704. MS *of John.*

JOHN: Dreams are sure crazy, aren't they? *(Ann doesn't respond.)* Well, would you like to know who it was you were marrying?

705. MCU *of Ann. She turns back toward John.*

ANN *(with forced humor)*: Oh, a tall, handsome Ubangi, I suppose.
Pan left with Ann as she moves over to the second suitcase.

JOHN *(off)*: No, not that bad. It was that fellow that sends you flowers every day. Er, what's his name? Mr. Norton's nephew.

ANN *(softly)*: Ted Sheldon.

JOHN *(off)*: Yeah, that's the one.

706. MCU *of John.*

JOHN: But here's the funniest part of it all. I was the fellow up there . . .

707. LS, *as 698.*

JOHN: . . . doing the marrying. You know, the justice of the peace or something.

ANN *(with interest)*: You were? I thought you were chasing me.

JOHN: Well, yes, I was. But I was your father then, see? But the real me, John Doe, er, that is, Long John Willoughby . . . *(Ann returns to her first suitcase)* . . . I was the fellow up there with the book. You know what I mean?

ANN *(while packing)*: I guess so. Then what happened?

708. MLS *of John.*
    JOHN: Well, I took you across my knee and I started spanking you.
709. MS *of Ann, who is amused.*
    JOHN *(off)*: That is, *I* didn't do it. *(Still smiling, Ann goes back to the
    dresser.)* I mean, I did do it, but it, it, wasn't me. You see, I was your
    father then. Huh, well, I laid you across my knee and I said, "Annie!"
    She looks over, startled.
710. MLS *of John.*
    JOHN: "I won't allow you to marry a man that's . . . *(John slaps his
    thigh)* . . . that's just rich, or that has his secretary send you . . .
    (slap) . . . flowers. The man you marry has got to swim . . .
    (slap) . . . rivers for you! . . . *(Beany appears in the doorframe
    behind John, without John knowing)* . . . He's got to climb . . .
    (slap) . . . high mountains for you! He's got to . . . *(slap)* . . . slay
    dragons for you!"
711. MCU *of Ann, panning right as she returns to the first suitcase.*
    JOHN *(off)*: "He's got to perform wonderful . . . *(slap)* . . . deeds for
    you! Yes, sir!"
712. MLS *of John, seated, with Beany watching over John's shoulder.*
    JOHN: And all the time, er, the guy up there, you know, with the book,
    me, just stood there nodding his head.
713. LS *of Ann, framed by John, seated right, and Beany, standing left.*
    JOHN: And he said, "Go to it, Pop . . . *(Ann glances over, briefly)* . . .
    whack her one for me because that's just the way I feel about it, too."
    So he says, "Come on down here and whack her yourself! *(Again
    Ann looks over.)* So I came down and I, I . . . *(slap)* . . . whacked
    you a good one, . . .
714. MLS, *as 712.*
    JOHN *(becoming a bit giddy)*: . . . see? And then he whacked you . . .
    (slap) . . . and I whacked you . . . *(slap)* . . . another one, and we
    both started . . . *(slap, slap, slap)* . . . whacking you like—
    BEANY *(having paid close attention to each slap)*: Well, if you're
    through whacking her, come on, let's get going.
    *Startled to discover that Beany has been listening and watching, John is
    immediately deflated.*
715. MCU *of Ann, smiling broadly.*
    BEANY *(to porters, off)*: Okay, fellows, right in here.

716. LS, *as 713. Beany leads three porters into Ann's room as she quickly*
     puts on her coat.
     BEANY *(to John)*: You go out the side entrance, there's a bunch of
     autograph-seekers out front.
717. MS *of John, who slowly rises.*
     BEANY *(off)*: We'll be down with the bags in a minute. *(Ann hurries*
     past John on the way out. Beany, calls to the porters.) Come on.
     Don't make a government project out of this.
     John exits with the porters and Beany.

718. *Dissolve to* MLS *from behind an airport lunch counter as Beany joins*
     Charlie, who is seated to the left, eating. It is nighttime.
     CHARLIE: Hi, Beany.
     BEANY *(wearily)*: When does our plane take off again?
     CHARLIE: Couple of minutes.
719. MS *of John and Ann seated at nearby table. The music of "Begin the*
     Beguine" can be heard from the jukebox behind them.
     JOHN: H-How many people do you think we've talked to already.
     O-outside radio, I mean?
     ANN *(softly, eyes cast downward)*: Oh, I don't know. About three hun-
     dred thousand.
     JOHN: Three hundred thousand? . . .
720. MCU *of John with Ann's face in profile at right.*
     JOHN: . . . What makes them do it, Ann? What makes them come and
     listen, and, and get up their John Doe clubs the way they do?
721. MCU *of Ann with John's face in profile at left.*
     JOHN: I've been trying to figure it out.
     ANN: Look, John. What we're handing them are platitudes. Things
     they've heard a million times: "Love thy neighbor," "clouds have
     silver linings," . . .
722. MCU *of John, as 720.*
     ANN: . . . "turn the other cheek." It's just a—
     JOHN *(interrupting)*: Yeah, I heard them a million times, too, but—
     (He suddenly looks at Ann as if struck by a revelation.) There you
     are. Maybe they're like me, just beginning to get an idea what those
     things mean. You know, I never thought much about people before.
     They were always just somebody to fill up the bleachers. The only
     time I worried about them was if they—is when they didn't come in

to see me pitch. You know, lately I've been watching them while I
talked to them.

723. MCU *of Ann, as 721. She looks at him with concern.*

JOHN: I could see something in their faces. I could feel that they were
hungry for something. Do you know what I mean? Maybe that's why
they came. Maybe they're just lonely and wanted somebody to say
hello to. *(Ann looks away.)* I know how they feel. I've been lonely
and hungry for something practically all my life.

There is an awkward silence.

MAN *(call to passengers, off)*: All aboard, folks!

Ann and John rise to go.[20]

724. *Soft leftward wipe to* LS, *tracking left with D.B., Ann, and Ted Sheldon
as they walk through Norton's opulently appointed dining room, chatting.*

ANN: Yeah. That's true. *(They stop at the dining table, where Ann notes
a fur coat on the back of what she thought was her chair.)* Oh, somebody else sitting here?

D.B.: No, no, no. That's your seat.

TED: And this is your coat.

Lifting it off the chair, he puts the coat around Ann's shoulders.

ANN: Mine?

D.B.: A little token of appreciation.

ANN: Oh!

*Pan left with Ann as she walks over to a dining room mirror and ad-
mires herself.*

725. MCU *of Ann as she turns around, excited. Pan right with Ann as she
comes back toward the table.*

ANN: Oh, it's beautiful, D.B.

726. MLS *of Ann, between D.B. and Ted.*

ANN: Well, I don't quite know what to say.

D.B.: Well, don't say anything at all. Just sit down.

ANN *(admiring her coat)*: Oh.

Ted helps her into her seat. Ann notices a jewelry box on her plate.

D.B.: Go ahead. Open it, open it.

*As Ann reaches toward the box, Ted circles around to the other side of
the table.*

727. CU *of the box, as Ann opens it to discover a diamond bracelet.*

ANN *(off)*: Oh!

728. *Track left slightly to frame Ann, seated in* MS *left, and D.B., at the end of the table right.*

ANN: Oh, it's lovely.

729. MS *of Ted, standing on the opposite side of the table near an ornate candelabra.*

TED: And a new contract goes with it.

730. MS *of Ann, over D.B.'s shoulder. Playing with the bracelet, she eyes him warily.*

ANN: Well. Come on, spring it. You've got something on your mind.

731. *D.B. and Ann, as end of 728. D.B. laughs.*

ANN: Must be stupendous.

D.B. laughs still more heartily.

D.B. *(to Ted)*: You know, that's what I like about her. Right to the point. *(He snaps his fingers.)* Like that! *(Again he laughs, and removes his glasses to clean them with his handkerchief.)* All right, practical Annie, here it is.

732. MCU *of D.B., squinting without his glasses.*

D.B.: Tomorrow night, before a crowd of fifteen thousand people and talking over a nationwide radio hookup, John Doe will . . . *(He breathes on a lens of his glasses.)* . . . announce the formation of a third party.

733. MS *of Ann, as 730.*

ANN: A third party?

D.B. *(breathing again on a lens)*: Yes. The John Doe Party. *(Ann glances in the direction of Ted, then stares again at D.B.)* Devoted entirely to the interests of all the John Does all over the country. Which practically means . . . *(He breathes on his glasses a third time.)* . . . 90 percent of the voters. He will also announce the third party's candidate for the presidency.

734. MCU *of D.B. He puts his glasses back on.*

D.B.: A man whom he personally recommends. A great humanitarian. The best friend the John Does have.

735. MCU *of Ann.*

ANN *(leaning forward, whispering)*: Mr. D. B. Norton!²¹

736. MCU *of D.B.*

D.B.: Yes.

737. MCU *of Ann. She leans back, the bracelet wrapped around her fingers.*

ANN: Wow!
Fade out.

738. *Fade in on* LS *of the front of a ballpark at night, as people stream through the gates.*[22] *Three searchlights are aimed high into the sky. Across the front of the stadium is a gigantic banner welcoming John Doe clubs to the convention. The sound of "The Battle Hymn of the Republic" can be heard.*
739. *A closer view of the front gates.*
740. *High angle* LS *from under the stadium seats, tracking left with the conventioneers as they make their way into the ballpark.*
741. *High angle* ELS *of the ballfield, with a central platform illuminated by a ring of lights. The seats appear filled. At the conclusion of the song, there is loud cheering.*
742. LS *inside a radio booth, high above the ballfield. Three radio announcers, viewed from the rear, stand looking out the windows at the scene below as technicians work around them.*[23]
743. *High angle* ELS *of the convention, from behind the NBC announcer on the far left.*
    NBC ANNOUNCER: And although the opening of the convention is hours off, the delegates are already pouring into the ballpark by the droves, with lunch baskets, banners, and petitions asking John Doe not to jump off any roof.
    The crowd below begins to sing "Take Me Out to the Ballgame." The camera tracks right to Knox Manning at the CBS mike in the center.
    KNOX MANNING (*his voice overlapping that of the NBC announcer*): But no matter how you look at it, it is still a phenomenal movement. These John Does, or the hoi polloi as you've heard people call them, have been laughed at and ridiculed, but here they are, gay and happy, having traveled thousands of miles, their expenses paid by their neighbors, to come here to pay homage to their hero, John Doe.
    The camera tracks further to the right, coming to rest on the third announcer, John B. Hughes.
    JOHN B. HUGHES (*overlapping Manning's address*): And in these days of wars and bombings, it's a hopeful sign that a simple idea like this can sweep the country, an idea based on friendliness, on giving and not taking, on helping your neighbor and asking nothing in return. And

if a thing like this can happen, don't let any of your grumbling friends
tell you that humanity is falling apart. This is John B. Hughes,
signing off now and returning you to our main studio until nine o'clock,
when the convention will officially open.

The song comes to an end.

744. MLS *of Mrs. Mitchell* [24] *answering the front door of her new apartment.*
John appears on the other side, with a package bulging from beneath
his wet raincoat.

MRS. MITCHELL: Oh, John. Come in.

JOHN *(entering)*: Say, I'm kind of— it's raining out a little.

MRS. MITCHELL *(taking his hat)*: That's all right.

745. MS *of the dog sitting upright on the couch, wagging its tail.*

MRS. MITCHELL *(off)*: It's good to see you. Sit down.

746. LS *of John as Mrs. Mitchell takes his hat.*

JOHN: Thanks.

Pan left with John as he crosses to the couch and Mrs. Mitchell sets his
hat on a side table. Patting the dog, John sits down; Mrs. Mitchell
crosses to a chair opposite. A fire burns in a fireplace in the background.

747. MLS *of John. He pulls a large, gift-wrapped package from under his*
coat, and hands it to Mrs. Mitchell.

JOHN: It's for Ann.

MRS. MITCHELL *(off)*: Oh, how nice. Thank you very much.

JOHN: Flowers.

748. MS *of Mrs. Mitchell, with the box in her lap.*

MRS. MITCHELL: I'm terribly sorry she isn't here.

749. LS *of them both, favoring John.*

JOHN: She isn't?

MRS. MITCHELL: No, she just left. I'm surprised you didn't run into
   her. She went over to Mr. Norton's house.

JOHN: Oh.

MRS. MITCHELL: Did you want to see her about something important?

JOHN: Yeah. I, er, well—no. It'll wait. *(He laughs nervously.)* Say,
   he's a nice man, isn't he? Mr. Norton, I mean. He's, er, he's done an
   awful lot for the . . .

John gestures a completion to his thought, then, swallowing hard,
scratches the dog. Mrs. Mitchell toys with the ribbon on the box.

750. MLS *of John and the dog. He looks at his coat.*

JOHN *(rising)*: Say, my coat's pretty wet. I, I'm afraid I . . .

751. MS *of the dog, who looks at where John was sitting.*

JOHN *(off)*: . . . might have wet the couch a little.

The dog jumps off the couch and hides underneath, behind John's legs, looking out sheepishly.

752. LS *of John, standing across from Mrs. Mitchell.*

JOHN: Well, I guess I'll see her at the convention later.

MRS. MITCHELL *(rising)*: Yes, of course. I'll see that she gets the flowers.

JOHN: Thanks. *(He reaches for her hand and shakes it.)* Good night, Mrs. Mitchell.

MRS. MITCHELL: Good night, John.

Pan right with John as he heads toward the door, pausing to pick up his hat on the way. Suddenly, he turns around.

JOHN: Say, Mrs. Mitchell. *(Pan left with John as he retraces his steps back to her. He plays nervously with his hat.)* I, er, I'm kind of glad Ann isn't here. You see, I, I came over here hoping to see her alone, and kind of hoping I wouldn't, too. You know what I mean? There was something I wanted to talk to her about. But, well, I can wait, I guess. Good night.

MRS. MITCHELL: Good night, John.

Pan right as John heads back toward the door. Again, he stops and turns. Pan left as he returns to Mrs. Mitchell a second time.

JOHN *(impulsively)*: Say, look, Mrs. Mitchell, have you ever been married? Oh, sure you have. Gosh, that's pretty silly. Well, I guess you must think I'm kind of batty. *(He laughs. She smiles warmly, but says nothing.)* Well, I guess I'd better be going at that.

Pan right a third time as John walks toward the door. When he reaches it, he is stopped by the sound of Mrs. Mitchell's voice.

MRS. MITCHELL *(off)*: John. *(He pivots around. She arrives in a MLS with John by the door.)* My husband said, "I love you. Will you marry me?"

JOHN: He did? *(She nods.)* What happened?

MRS. MITCHELL: I married him.

753. *Low angle* MCU *of John from over Mrs. Mitchell's shoulder.*

JOHN *(excited)*: Yeah, that's what I mean, see? It was easy as all that, huh?

MRS. MITCHELL: Uh-huh.

JOHN: Yeah, yeah, but look, Mrs. Mitchell. You know, I, I love Ann, and it's going to be awfully hard for me to say it, because, well, you know, she's so wonderful . . .

754. *High angle* MCU *of Mrs. Mitchell over John's shoulder.*

JOHN: . . . and, well, the best I ever was was a bush-league pitcher.

755. *Low angle* MCU *of John, as 753.*

JOHN: And you know, I think she's in love with another man, the one she made up. You know, the real John Doe. Well, that's, that's pretty tough competition. I bet you he'd know how to say it all right. And me, I, I get up to it and around it and in back of it, but, but I never get right to it. Do you know what I mean? So the only chance I've got is, well if somebody could kind of give her a warning, . . .

756. *High angle* MCU *of Mrs. Mitchell, as 754.*

JOHN . . . sort of, sort of prepare her for the shock.

MRS. MITCHELL: You mean you'd like me to do it, . . .

757. *Low angle* MCU *of John, as 753.*

MRS. MITCHELL: . . . huh?

JOHN: Well, I was thinking that—yeah, you know, sort of break the ice.

MRS. MITCHELL *(nodding)*: Course I will, John.

JOHN *(grinning)*: Well, er, thank you, Mrs. Mitchell. Hey, you're okay. *He leans forward and kisses her gingerly on the cheek, then quickly exits. Mrs. Mitchell closes the door behind him, then turns around, lost in thought.*

758. *Cut to* LS *of front door to the Mitchell's apartment building. In the foreground are Beany and some uniformed bodyguards, standing wait under a protective awning in the rain. John's car is at the curb.*

BEANY: This John Doe meeting is going to be one of the biggest things that ever happened.

BODYGUARD: Is that so?

John comes down the front steps in high spirits, winding up as if to pitch a baseball.

BEANY: Why, they're coming from all over. Trains, boxcars, wagons— *(He notices John just at the moment that John pretends to deliver a pitch.)* Look out!

Beany and the bodyguards duck.

JOHN: Hello . . .

759. *Telephoto* MLS *from the same perspective as 758.*

JOHN: . . . bodyguards! Hey, had your dinner yet?

BODYGUARD: Not yet.

BEANY: Oh, that's all right.

JOHN: Well, look, no. Go ahead and have your dinner, I'll—

760. MS *of Connell standing by a taxi in the rain.*

CONNELL: Wait a minute, John.

Connell pays the taxi driver. Pan left with him as walks toward John, an unsteady gait betraying his intoxication.

JOHN *(off, cheerfully)*: Hello, Mr. Connell.

Reaching the group under the awning, Connell is framed in MCU with John and Beany.

CONNELL: How are you, John. *(He steadies himself.)* John, I want to have a little talk with you.

761. MS *of the three from another angle. Connell teeters backwards. Amused, John grabs Connell's coat and pulls him upright.*

CONNELL: What's, what's the matter? Are you falling? Come here.

Connell starts to lead John off.

BEANY *(protesting)*: Hey, boss.

CONNELL: Oh, quiet, quiet, quiet. *(He returns to John. Track left with them as Connell talks. Beany and the bodyguards follow.)* Say, tell me something. Did you, did you read that speech you're gonna make tonight?

JOHN: No, I never read the speeches before I make them. I get more of a kick out of it that way.

CONNELL: Uh-huh. Just exactly what I thought. Beany, go down to the office, tell Pop to give you the speech. There's a copy on my desk.

BEANY: Gee whiz, boss. You know Mr. Norton told me not to leave him, not even for a minute.

CONNELL: Go on, go on, go on, go on. We'll be at Jim's Bar up the street.

762. *Dissolve to MLS of the neon sign for Jim's Bar.*

763. *Dissolve to interior LS of John and Connell seated at a table in the middle of the bar. A bartender serves them drinks in shot glasses.*

CONNELL: You're a nice guy, John. I like you. You're gentle. *(Track forward as Connell continues.)* I always like gentle people. Me? I'm, I'm hard. Hard and tough. *(The camera comes to rest with the two in MS, John seen in profile.)* I got no use for hard people.

764. MS *of John, with Connell in* MCU *profile to right.*

    CONNELL: Gotta be gentle to suit me. *(Connell tries to light a bent cigarette. The flame never touches the cigarette, but he does not seem to notice.)* Like you, for instance.

    Connell downs a stiff drink from his shot glass.

765. MS *of John and Connell, as end of 763.*

    CONNELL: Yep, I'm hard. But you wanna know something? I've got a weakness. You'd never guess what, would you? Well, I have. Wanna know what it is? *(John watches him closely, but doesn't respond.)* "The Star-Spangled Banner." Screwy, huh? Well, maybe it is. But play "The Star-Spangled Banner" and I'm a sucker for it. It always gets me right here. *(He points to his stomach.)* You know what I mean?

    JOHN: Yeah. *(John points to the back of his neck.)* It gets me right back here.

    CONNELL *(leaning to see)*: Oh, back there, huh? Well, every man to . . .

766. MS, *as 764.*

    CONNELL: . . . his own taste. *(Connell strikes a match and tries to light his bent cigarette, again missing his target.)* You, you weren't old enough, . . .

767. MCU *of Connell with John in profile and shadow to the left.*

    CONNELL: . . . you weren't old enough for the world war, were you? *(He rubs his eye and scratches the side of his face.)* No, no, of course not. No, you, you must have been just a kid. I was. I was just ripe. And raring to go. *(He pours the contents of John's shot glass into his own.)* Know what my old man did when I joined up? He joined up too. Got to be a sergeant. And here's the kicker for you. We were in the same outfit. Funny, huh? Hmm? *(He lifts the shot glass to his lips. His look grows distant.)* He was killed, John. I saw him get it. *(Pause.)* I was right there and I saw it with my own eyes.

768. MS, *as 764. John appears about to say something, but instead he looks down, as does Connell.*

    CONNELL: Me? I came out of it without a scratch.

769. MCU, *as 767. Connell looks over at John.*

    CONNELL: That is, except for my ulcers. *(He bolts down the contents of the shot glass, and shivers in response.)* I should be drinking milk, you know. This stuff is poison. *(Calling to the bartender:)* Hey, Tubby!

    TUBBY *(hurrying over to the table)*: Yes, Mr. Connell.

CONNELL *(lifting his empty glass)*: Whaddya say, huh?

TUBBY: All right.

The bartender departs with the glass.

CONNELL *(to John)*: Yep, I'm a sucker for this country. I'm a sucker for "The Star-Spangled Banner" and I'm a sucker for this country. *(He taps on the table with his finger for emphasis.)* I *like* what we got here. I like it. *(The bartender returns with a drink.)* A guy can *say* what he wants, and *do* what he wants, without having a bayonet shoved through his belly. And that's all right, isn't it?

JOHN: You betcha.

CONNELL *(nodding decisively)*: There now. And we don't want anybody coming around changing it, do we?

JOHN: No, sir.

CONNELL: No, sir. And when they do I get mad. I get b-boiling mad. And right now, John, I'm sizzling. I get mad for a lot of other guys besides myself. I get mad for a guy named Washington. And a guy named Jefferson. And Lincoln. Lighthouses, John, lighthouses in a foggy world.[25] You know what I mean.

JOHN *(softly)*: Yeah, you bet.

CONNELL *(staring directly at John)*: Uh-huh. Listen, pal. This, this fifth column stuff is pretty rotten, isn't it?

JOHN: Yeah, it certainly is.

CONNELL: And you'd feel like an awful sucker if you found yourself marching right in the middle of it, wouldn't you? *(John says nothing. Connell points at him.)* Y-y-you! Of course, you wouldn't know it because you're gentle. But that's what you're doing. You're mixed up with a skunk, my boy.

770. MS, *as 764.*

CONNELL: A no-good, dangerous skunk.

John appears puzzled. Connell fumbles with his matches.

JOHN: Say, you're not talking about Mr. Norton, are you?

CONNELL: I'm not talking about his grandfather's pet poodle!

Connell again tries to light his bent cigarette and misses.

JOHN: You must be wrong, Mr. Connell. He's been marvelous about the John Doe clubs.

771. MCU, *as 767.*

CONNELL *(sarcastically)*: Yeah? *(He laughs.)* Say, you're sold on the John Doe idea, aren't you?

JOHN: Sure.

CONNELL: Yeah, sure. I don't blame you. So am I. It's a beautiful miracle, a miracle that could only happen right here in the good old U.S.A. And I think it's terrific. What do you think of that? Me, hard-boiled Connell. I think it's plenty terrific. All right, now supposing a certain unmentionable worm, whose initials are D.B., was trying to use that to shove his way into the White House. So he could put the screws on, so he could turn out the lights in those lighthouses.

772. MS, *as 764.*

CONNELL: What would you say about that? Huh?

JOHN *(resolute)*: Nobody's going to do that, Mr. Connell. They can't use the John Doe clubs for politics. That's the main idea.

CONNELL: Is that so? Then what's a big political boss like Hammett doing in town? And a labor leader like Bennett? And a lot of other big shots who are up at D.B.'s house right now?

773. MCU, *as 767.*

CONNELL: Wolves, John. Wolves waiting to cut up the John Does. *(He snorts knowingly.)* Wait till you get a gander at that speech you're going to make tonight.

774. MS, *as 764.*

JOHN: You're all wet. Miss Mitchell writes those speeches, and nobody can make her write that kind of stuff.

CONNELL *(sarcastically)*: They can't, huh? Who do you think writes them? My Aunt Emma? *(John puzzlement begins to turn to anger.)* Ehhta, I *know* she writes them. And gets a big bonus for doing them, too. A mink coat and a diamond bracelet. Don't write 'em! Why that gold-grabbing dame would double-cross her own mother for a handful of Chinese yen!

JOHN *(outraged)*: Shut up!

775. MCU, *as 767. Rising to his feet, John grabs Connell's jacket and yanks him up out of his seat as well.*

JOHN: If you weren't drunk, I'd—

776. MLS *of Beany as he enters the front door.*

BEANY *(to Connell)*: Hey, boss.

Beany hurries in the direction of Connell's table.

777. MCU *of John gripping Connell violently. Beany appears in the background between them.*

BEANY: Here's the speech, boss. *(John grabs it. Beany realizes something odd is afoot.)* Hey!

CONNELL *(the bent cigarette dangling from his lips)*: Go on and read it, John, and then start socking.

John bolts for the door, speech in hand.

BEANY *(in pursuit)*: Hey, wait a minute, Mr. Doe!

Lowering himself into his chair, Connell is seen from a high angle MS.

CONNELL: Tubby?

TUBBY *(hurrying to his side)*: Yes, sir?

CONNELL: Better bring me a glass of milk.

(Tubby hurries off to fill the order.)

CONNELL *(after attempting to draw on his unlit cigarette)*: I, I'm smoking too much.

He grinds the cigarette in an ashtray, then looks over toward the bar.[26]

778. *Soft leftward wipe to high angle* ELS *of D. B. Norton's dining room. At the far end stands D.B. Seated at the near end is Ted Sheldon. Along the*

sides are prominent men of industry, media, and politics—D.B.'s cabal—
and Ann Mitchell, seated at a far corner next to D.B.
D.B. *(on the telephone)*: Yes, Charlie. You've got everything all set?
Fine. John Doe been taken care of? Good. How many people . . .

779. MLS *of four men on D.B.'s right, including Hammett, Bennett, and*
Barrington. They appear self-satisfied as they listen in.
D.B. *(off)*: . . . you think will be there? Fifteen thousand? Oh . . .

780. *Mirror image* MLS *of the other side of the table, with Weston and others*
beside an elegantly dressed Ann. She appears troubled.
D.B. *(off)*: . . . my, that's fine. Now, listen, Charlie, as soon as John
Doe stops talking . . .

781. *High angle* LS *of the group from Ted's end of the table toward D.B.*
D.B.: . . . about me, I want you to start that demonstration. And make
it a big one, . . .

782. MS *of Ted, leaning back, smoking a cigarette.*
D.B. *(off)*: . . . you understand?
TED *(confidently)*: Don't worry about that, D.B. My boys are there.

783. *Low angle* MLS *of D.B., framed by Ann and Weston.*
TED *(off)*: They'll take care of it.
D.B. *(still on the phone)*: What? Yes, I'll be there fifteen minutes after I
get your call.

784. MLS *of interior of front door, opened by the butler to reveal the figure*
of John. Uniformed guards are visible in the background.
BUTLER: Why, Mr. Doe.
JOHN *(moving forward into* MCU*)*: Where are they?
BUTLER: In the dining room, sir.
Pan left with John as he strides toward the dining room.

785. *High angle* ELS, *as 778. Removing his glasses to clean them with his*
handkerchief, D.B. speaks to those present.
D.B.: Well, gentlemen, I think we're about ready to throw that great big
bombshell.

786. *Frontal* MLS *of John as he approaches the dining room from the foyer.*
A VOICE *(among others from the dining room, off)*: Yeah, well, it's
about time.
John comes to stop at the entranceway.
D.B. *(off)*: Even a conservative estimate shows that we can count . . .

787. ELS *of the dining room table, exclusive of the far end with D.B., from behind John.*

> D.B. *(off)*: . . . on anywhere between ten and twenty million John Doe votes.

788. MLS *of the men on a D.B.'s right, facing him as he speaks from the background. He puts his glasses back on.*

> D.B.: Now, add to that the labor vote that Mr. Bennett will throw in, and the votes controlled by Mr. Hammett, and the rest of you gentlemen in your own territories, and . . .

789. *High angle* MS *of Ann. She looks in the direction of D.B., disturbed.*

> D.B.: . . . nothing can stop us.
>
> HAMMETT *(off)*: As I said before, I'm with you, . . .
>
> *Ann glances across at Hammett.*

790. *High angle* MS *of Hammett and Bennett.*

> HAMMETT: . . . providing you can guarantee the John Doe . . .

791. *High angle* MS *of Ann, glancing back and forth between Hammett and D.B.*

> HAMMETT *(off)*: . . . vote.
>
> D.B. *(off)*: Don't worry about that.
>
> BENNETT *(off)*: You can count on me on one condition.

792. *High angle* MS *of Hammett and Bennett.*

> BENNETT *(tapping his cigar on his chest)*: Little Bennett's got to be taken care of.

793. MLS *of John in the entranceway.*

> D.B. *(off)*: Didn't I tell you that everybody in this room would be taken care of?

794. LS *of the butler in the foyer, summoning the other servants to come and listen.*

> D.B. *(off)*: My agreement with you gentlemen stands.
>
> BARRINGTON *(off)*: I'm with you, D.B. But I . . .

795. *High angle* MLS *of Barrington.*

> BARRINGTON: . . . still think it's a very daring thing we're attempting.

796. MLS *profile of D.B. with Ann and Weston watching in the background.*

> D.B.: These are daring times, Mr. Barrington. We're coming to a new order of things. There's too much talk been going in this country.

797. MLS *of John in the entranceway, with the servants visible in the distance. Sounds of agreement can be heard from the group in the dining room.*

D.B. *(off)*: Too many concessions have been made!

VOICE *(off)*: True.

798. MLS *of D.B., as 796.*

D.B.: What the American people need is an iron hand!

799. MLS *of the men at D.B.'s right.*

GROUP: You're right. That's true.

800. MLS *of the three men on the other side.*

GROUP: Absolutely right. You're quite right, D.B.

801. *High angle* MS *of Ann, eyes darting from the others back to D.B.*

D.B. *(off)*: Discipline!

VOICES *(off)*: Quite right. Quite true.

802. *Low angle* MLS *of D.B., as 783.*

D.B.: And now— *(He turns toward Ann.)* May I offer a little toast to Miss Ann Mitchell, . . .

803. *High angle* MS *of Ann, who appears somewhat alarmed.*

D.B. *(off)*: . . . the . . .

804. MLS *of John in the entranceway.*

D.B. *(off)*: . . . brilliant and beautiful lady who is responsible for all this.

805. ELS *of the dining room table from John's point of view. D.B. lifts his glass. The men all rise.*

GROUP: To Miss Mitchell!

806. *High angle* MS *of Ann. She leans forward toward D.B.*

ANN *(softly)*: Mr. Norton, I'd like to talk to you alone for a minute.

807. MLS *of Ann, surrounded by the men at D.B.'s end of the table.*

D.B. *(chortling)*: Oh, oh. Miss Mitchell has something to say to us.

GROUP: Well, that's fine. Speech! Go ahead and say it. Speech! *The men clap as they sit down.*

808. MLS *of John in the entranceway, taking in the scene.*

809. MS *of Ann from a new angle. Spotting John, she rises.*

D.B. *(off)*: Hello?

810. MLS *of Ann, D.B., and others, from across the table. Ann starts around the table toward John.*

811. LS *of the servants, who back up slightly as if to keep out of anyone's sight.*

812. LS *of Ann quickly making her way around the table. Pan left with her as she moves into* MS *with John. He removes his hat.*

ANN: John, I'm so glad to see you. I, I was terribly worried.

JOHN *(showing her a copy of the speech)*: Did you write this?

ANN: Yes, I did, John. But I, I had no idea what was going on.

813. MS *of John from behind Ann's shoulder.*
     JOHN *(smiling skeptically)*: You didn't?
     ANN: No.
     JOHN *(looking down at her wrist)*: That's a swell bracelet you're wearing.
     He moves on past her. She turns around into a frontal MS, *and watches him gravely.*

814. LS *of John, tracking briefly with him as he moves toward the table, Ann on his heels.*
     D.B. *(off)*: John? Why aren't you at the convention?
     Track right with John as he slowly and silently makes his way along the length of the table, staring at each man as he passes by. Ann splits off and circles around the other side of the table, crossing in the foreground to her seat. D.B. stares at her for a moment, then back at John.[27]
     D.B.: Is there anything wrong?
     JOHN: No, no. Nothing's wrong. Everything's fine.

815. MLS *of John and D.B. from behind Ann.*
     JOHN *(to all)*: So there's going to be a new order of things, huh? Every-
     body's going to cut himself a nice, fat slice of the John Does, hey?
     (There is rumbling from the group. John turns to D.B.) You forgot
     one detail, Mr. Big Shot. You forgot me, . . .

816. MS *of Ann, listening intently.*
     JOHN *(off)*: . . . the prize stooge of the world.

817. MLS, *as 815.*
     JOHN: Why, if you or anybody else thinks he's going to use the John
     Doe clubs for his own rotten purpose, he's going to have to do it over
     my dead body!
     There is more rumbling from the group.
     D.B.: Now, hold on a minute, young man. Hold on. That's rather big
     talk. I started the John Doe clubs with my money and I'll decide
     whether or not they're being properly used.

818. MS *of John and D.B.*
     JOHN: No, you won't. You're through deciding anything. And what's
     more, I'm going down to that convention and I'm going to tell those
     people exactly what you and all your fine feathered friends here are
     trying to cook up for them. *(He looks over at Ann.)* And I'm going to
     say it in my *own* words this time.

819. MS *of Ann, watching to see what will happen.*

820. LS *from the far end of the table. John tears up the speech and flings it*

across the table toward Ann. Pan left with him as he starts to exit.
GROUP *(amid general uproar)*: My! He'll ruin us, D.B.!
As John approaches the end of the table, Ted intercepts him in MS.
TED *(with bravado)*: Wait a minute, wait a minute, fella.
John pushes away the hand with which Ted restrains him.

821. MS *of John and Ted from another angle.*
TED: My uncle wants to talk to you.
D.B. approaches John from behind.
D.B.: Listen to me, my son. *(John spins around.)* Before you lose your head completely, may I remind you that I picked you up out of the gutter and I can throw you right back there again!

822. MCU *of all three from an angle favoring D.B.*
D.B.: You've got a nerve accusing people of things! These gentlemen and I know what's the best for the John Does of America, regardless of what tramps like you think!

823. MCU *of John from over D.B.'s shoulder. Ted watches from behind John.*
D.B.: Get off that righteous horse of yours and come to your senses. You're the fake! We believe in what we're doing! You're the one that was paid the thirty pieces of silver! Have you forgotten that! Well, I haven't! *(John looks away, disturbed.)* You're a fake, John Doe, and I can prove it!

824. MCU, *as 822.*
D.B.: You're the big hero that's supposed to jump off tall buildings and things. Do you remember? What do you suppose your precious John Does will say when they find out that you never had any intention of doing it? That you were being paid to say so? You're lucky if they don't run you out of the country!

825. LS *of Ann standing beside Weston, watching, as the scene she witnesses is reflected in the dining room mirror on the wall behind her.*
D.B. *(off)*: With the newspapers and the radio stations that these gentlemen control . . .

826. MCU, *as 824.*
D.B.: . . . we can kill the John Doe movement deader than a doornail, and we'll do it, too, the moment you step out of line! *(John is dumbstruck. Behind him, Ted smiles.)* Now, if you still want to go to that convention and shoot your trap off, you go ahead and do it.

827. *High angle* ELS *from Ann's side of the table. D.B. and Ted return to their*

chair at opposite ends. Ann circles back around, pausing behind Ted.

JOHN *(after thinking for a moment)*: You mean to tell me you'd try to kill the John Doe movement if you can't use it to get what you want?

D.B. *(puffing on his cigar)*: You bet your bottom dollar we would.

828. MLS *of John.*

JOHN *(contemptuously)*: Well, that certainly is a new low. I guess I've seen everything now. *(Pan left as he steps over to Ted's end of the table and throws his hat on it.)* You sit there back of your big cigars and think of deliberately . . .

829. MLS *of the men at D.B.'s right, their faces turned toward John.*

JOHN *(off)*: . . . killing an idea that's made millions of people a little bit happier!

830. MCU *of John.*

JOHN: An idea that's brought thousands of them here from all over the country, by bus and by freight, in jalopies and on foot, . . .

831. MS *of D.B. His comportment registers utter disdain.*

JOHN *(off)*: . . . so they could pass on to each other their own simple, little experiences.

832. MCU *of Ann. Her eyes are bright.*

JOHN *(off)*: Why, look. I'm just a mug and I know it. But I'm beginning to understand a lot of things.²⁸

833. MCU *of John.*

JOHN: Why, your type's as old as history. If you can't lay your dirty fingers on a decent idea and twist it and squeeze it and stuff it into your own pocket, you slap it down! Like dogs, if you can't eat something, you bury it!

834. MLS, *as 829. Grumbling can be heard from the group.*

JOHN *(off)*: Why, this is the one worthwhile thing that's come along—

835. MCU *of John.*

JOHN: People are finally finding out that the guy next door isn't a bad egg. That's simple, isn't it?

836. MCU *of Ann.*

JOHN *(off)*: And yet a thing like that gets a chance of spreading till it touches every last doggone human being in the world, and you talk about, about killing it.

837. MLS *of John, Ted, and Ann.*

JOHN: Well, when this fire dies down, what's going to be left? More misery, more hunger, and more hate. And what's to prevent that from starting all over again? Nobody knows the answer to that one, and certainly not you, with those slimy, bollixed up theories you've got! The John Doe idea may be the answer, though! It may be the one thing capable of saving this cockeyed world! Yet you sit back there on your fat hulks and tell me you'll kill it if you can't use it! *(He points at the group.)* Well you go ahead and try! You couldn't do it in a million years, with all your radio stations and all your power! Because it's bigger than whether I'm a fake! It's bigger than your ambitions! And its bigger . . .

838. MCU *of Ann, who has grown increasingly excited.*
JOHN: . . . than all the bracelets and fur coats in the world!
Pan right with Ann and she runs around to reach John.
ANN: You bet it is, John!

839. MLS *of John, Ann, and Ted.*
JOHN: And that's exactly what I'm going to tell . . .

840. LS *of the servants in the foyer, listening.*
JOHN: . . . those people.
The servants applaud.

841. MLS *of John, Ann, and Ted from a new angle. Pan left as John, grabbing his hat, starts to leave. Ted lunges after him, spinning John around by his coat.*
TED: Wait a minute, you ungrateful rat! My uncle's been too good to—
Before he can finish, John slugs Ted in the jaw. With the blow, dramatic music is set off on the soundtrack and continues over the remainder of the scene. Ted collapses. John races off.

842. MLS, *as 829. The men rise.*
BENNETT: He's getting away!

843. MCU *of D.B. He blows a shrill whistle.*

844. MLS *of Ann, as she races out of the room.*
ANN: John!

845. MLS *of D.B. at one phone, Hammett at another, with commotion about.*
D.B.: Get me the *Bulletin!*

846. MLS *of the interior front door as uniformed troopers pour into the house.*

847. LS *of John hurrying through the foyer, with Ann in pursuit. Troopers moving in the opposite direction pass them by.*

ANN *(running to catch up)*: John!

848. MS *of Barrington.*

     BARRINGTON: I've always told you, D.B., . . .

849. MLS *of Ted being helped to his feet as troopers enter from the foyer.*

     BARRINGTON *(off)*: . . . you're playing with dynamite!

850. MCU *of D.B. at the telephone.*

     D.B. *(to the troopers)*: Don't let that girl get away!

851. MLS *of the butler and others, as Ted is helped off. Troopers rush back out again.*

852. MLS *of the cabal, gathered at D.B.'s end of the table.*

     WESTON: Before he gets through tonight, he'll ruin us all!

     BENNETT: You've got to stop him, D.B.!

     D.B.: I'll stop him. I'll stop him cold. Don't worry, I've been ready for this.

853. *Exterior* MLS *tracking rightward with John as he strides along the walkway toward his car, with Ann on his heels.*

     ANN *(pleading)*: John! Oh, John, please listen to me! *(She comes up alongside of him.)* Please! I can explain everything, John. *(He forces his way past her to get into the car.)* I didn't know what they were going to do! Let me go . . .

854. MS *of John climbing into the car, viewed from the opposite side.*

     ANN: . . . with you, John! *(He closes the door on her.)* John, please!

     JOHN: Go ahead, driver. Ballpark.

     ANN *(pounding on John's window)*: Please, let me explain it to you, John! Please let me go with you! Please! John! *(The car drives off, leaving her behind.)* Oh!

     Several troopers arrive on the scene and grab Ann.

     TROOPER: Mr. Norton wants to see you.

855. MS *of D.B. on the phone, with Hammett on a second phone in the background. Others crowd around. The air is thick with smoke.*

     D.B.: Listen to me, Mayor Lovett, you do as I say. I want them both arrested. You tell the police department to pick up Connell. I've got the girl here.

     HAMMETT *(to D.B.)*: I've got the *Bulletin*.

     D.B. *(still on the phone)*: I don't care what you charge them with. If you're worried, let them go in the morning, but keep them in jail overnight. *(He hangs up and grabs the other receiver from Hammett.)* Hello, *Bulletin*? Put Pop Dwyer on.

856. *Dissolve to high angle* ELS *of the ballfield with the platform illuminated in the rain. The crowd is singing "Oh, Susanna!"*
857. CU *of the sign marking the delegation from Texas.*
858. CU *of the sign marking the delegation from Ohio.*
859. CU *of the sign marking the delegation from Wisconsin.*
860. MLS *of the platform where last-minute adjustments are being made.*
861. *High angle* ELS *of the platform from the upper deck. Pan left past a pillar to the crowd in the grandstands.*
862. MS *of the Colonel sitting alone. He looks over his shoulder at the crowd behind.*
863. *Low angle* LS *of the platform; in front microphones have been arranged for the evening speeches. Pan right to* MCU *of singing delegates.*
864. *High angle* LS *of the crowd, singing and dancing to the music.*
865. *High angle* LS, *panning left with John as makes his way through the crowd toward the platform.*
866. *High angle* ELS, *panning left with John as he reaches the platform. Climbing the steps, he is recognized and welcomed by supporters.*
867. ELS *of the platform with the crowd in the foreground. Spotting John, they stand and cheer.*
868. ELS *of the platform from another angle. More of the crowd rises; their cheering drowns out the music.*
869. ELS *side view of the grandstand as the crowd stands and cheers.*
870. *High angle* ELS, *as 856. Cheering continues.*
871. *Low angle* LS *of the platform. John is mobbed by well-wishers.*
872. MS *of Bert and Sourpuss, warmly greeting John on the platform.*
873. *High angle* LS *of a sea of umbrellas. Flashbulbs go off as the cheering continues.*
874. MCU *of John as he comes forward to the microphones. He raises his hand as if to quiet the crowd. More flashbulbs go off.*
     MAN #1 *(off)*: Three cheers for . . .
875. *Low angle* MCU *of the man who is calling for the cheers. A woman stands beside him.*
     MAN #1: . . . John Doe!
876. MS *of a man who answers this call (as do others offscreen).*
     MAN #2: Hooray!

877. *High angle* ELS, *as 856.*
     CROWD: Hooray!
878. *Low angle* MLS *tracking along the rows of delegates.*
     CROWD: Hooray!
879. MLS *of the Colonel; he remains seated and silent amidst the hoopla.*
880. *Low angle* MLS *of the band on the platform. They raise their instruments.*
881. MCU *of John at the microphone. He raises his arms to request quiet, but the band suddenly begins to play "My Country 'Tis of Thee."*
     CROWD *(singing along, off):* My Coun- . . .
882. *High angle* ELS, *as 856.*
     CROWD: . . . -try 'tis of . . .
883. MS *of John, looking out at the crowd in a daze.*
     CROWD *(off):* . . . thee, sweet . . .
884. ELS *of the platform from the upper deck.*
     CROWD: . . . land of . . .
885. LS *side view of the grandstand.*
     CROWD: . . . liberty, . . .
886. *Low angle* MLS, *tracking along rows of delegates.*
     CROWD: . . . of thee I sing . . .
887. MS *of John. He now mouths the lyrics along with the crowd.*
     CROWD *(off):* . . . land where my fathers died, land of the pilgrim's pride, . . .
888. MS *of Bert and Sourpuss, their voices audible among the others.*
     CROWD: . . . from every mountainside, . . .
889. MS *of John, numbly mouthing the words.*
     CROWD *(off):* . . . let freedom ring!
890. *High angle* ELS *of the crowd as they cheer once again.*
891. MCU *of John as he steps forward to the microphones again. He wipes his face with his hands.*
     JOHN: Ladies and gentlemen—
     Pan right and reframe as a minister steps up beside John.
     MINISTER: One moment, John. We begin with a short prayer.
892. *Low angle* MLS *side view of platform as John steps back from the mikes.*
     MINISTER *(to the crowd):* Quiet, please.
893. MCU *of the minister, with John in the background left.*
     MINISTER: Ladies and gentlemen, . . .
894. MCU *of John, looking about anxiously.*
     MINISTER *(off):* . . . let us have a moment of silent prayer for the John

Does all over the world, . . .
895. MCU, *as 893.*
   MINISTER: . . . many of whom are homeless and hungry. Rise, please.
896. *High angle* ELS *of the platform, as people stand.*
   MINISTER: Everybody rise.
897. ELS *side view of the grandstand. People rise; men remove their hats.*
898. CU *of the minister. He bows his head.*
899. MCU *of John. Gathering his coat at his neck, he lowers his head.*
900. *High angle* LS, *craning down from the platform and tracking right along a sea of umbrellas, shiny in the rain. There is complete silence.*
901. *High angle* LS *of the front of the ballpark. The silence is suddenly punctured by the sound of the engines of delivery trucks, filled with newsboys, arriving from both directions.*
902. *High angle* LS *of the same scene from a slightly closer position. More trucks arrive. The boys begin to clamor out of the trucks.*
903. MLS *of the newsboys, racing to enter the ballpark.*
   NEWSBOYS *(shouting):* Extra, extra. Read all about it.
904. *High angle* ELS *from the rafters under the grandstands, panning left with the newsboys as they pour into the stadium. Their voices resound.*
905. MLS *from the floor under the grandstand. The newsboys pass out papers as they move toward the ballfield.*
906. *Telephoto* MS *of the horde of newsboys, heading toward the camera. The front page of the* Bulletin *is visible as one passes. The headline reads: "JOHN DOE A FAKE!"*
907. LS *of the newsboys climbing stairs to the grandstand.*
908. LS *of the crowd in the grandstand, turning to see the source of the sudden commotion.*
909. MCU *of the minister with John behind. They both look up.*
910. MLS *of row of delegates, under umbrellas, looking around.*
911. MS *of the back of John B. Hughes, at the radio booth window. A man next to him surveys the scene below through binoculars.*
   JOHN B. HUGHES *(into the broadcast mike):* Newsboys! Hundreds of yelling newsboys are swarming into the park like locusts.
   MALE VOICE *(off):* They're yelling, "John Doe's a fake!"
   HUGHES *(to this offscreen assistant):* Fake?
912. *High angle* ELS *of the platform from a side view. A newsboy delivers a paper to someone on the platform.*
913. *Low angle* MS, *panning over the faces of delegates, as the clamoring*

newsboys distribute copies of the paper.

914. *High angle* MLS *of a newsboy climbing the stairs toward the camera, with a newspaper headline prominent.*

915. MCU *of John. His eyes dart about anxiously.*

916. MS *of the Colonel, who receives a wet copy of the paper. He looks over his shoulder at the others as they read theirs.*

917. *Low angle* MCU *of woman with man who had first cheered John Doe in 875.*

   MAN #1 *(reading)*: "Federal investigation urged by Chamber of Commerce." [29]

918. MS *of Sourpuss and Bert.*

   SOURPUSS: How could he be a fake?
   BERT: It must be some kind of a gag.
   SOURPUSS *(unable to understand Bert)*: A what?
   BERT: A gag. *(Sourpuss still can't hear.)* A gag!

919. *Low angle* LS *of the stairs to the platform. John is handed a copy of the* Bulletin.

920. *High angle* ELS *of a limousine, accompanied by the sound of sirens, as it speeds past a concession stand inside the stadium. A second car follows.*

921. LS *of the limousine as it races around a curve. In the foreground a trooper drags a drunk with a balloon off to the side.*

922. LS *of the limousine from a different angle. It is now followed by a string of cars.*

923. MLS *of the limousine as it comes to a halt and Ted steps out.*

   TED *(calling to cars behind)*: Come on, come on, step on it!

924. MLS *of uniformed guards emerging from the next car, the door of which is marked "D. B. Norton's Troopers." The men hurry forward.*

   TED *(off)*: Step on it! Step on it!

925. MLS *of Ted as the troopers reach him. There is the sound of sirens and shrill whistles.*

   TED: You all know your places, now let's get going! Wait for the signal. *Pan left with Ted as he heads for the ballfield, passing the drunk with the balloon.*

   DRUNK: Hey, mister?

926. MCU *of Ted as he turns toward the drunk.*

   DRUNK: Will you autograph my balloon?
   TED: Sure!

He punctures the balloon with the tip of his cigar, then continues on through the gate to the field.

927. MLS *of D.B. surrounded by troopers near the limousine. Pan left with him as he follows Ted's route on through the gate.*
TROOPER: Gangway!

928. *High angle, telephoto* LS *of Ted in the ballpark. Positioning himself on a walkway, he waves the troopers on down toward the platform.*

929. MCU *of John at the microphone, a copy of the* Bulletin *in his hand.*
JOHN *(straining to be heard above the noise of the crowd)*: Ladies and gentlemen! This is exactly what . . .

930. *High angle, telephoto* MLS *of D.B. catching up with Ted amid the crowd. Pan left as the two head for the platform.*
JOHN *(his voice reverberating in the ballpark, off)*: . . . I came down here to tell you about tonight. Please, if you'll all just be quiet for a few minutes I can explain this whole thing to you.

931. *High angle* ELS, *panning left with D.B. and his entourage through the crowd, up the steps of the platform toward John.*
JOHN *(growing desperate)*: As you all know, this paper is published by a man by the name of D. B. Norton—

932. MCU *of John as troopers, reaching him, pull him away from the mike.*
TROOPERS' VOICES: D. B. Norton! Stand back!

933. *High angle* LS *of D.B., seen from the side, as he advances to the open mike.*
D.B. *(to the crowd)*: Wait a minute, everybody! Wait a minute!

934. MCU *of a row of delegates, looking up from the newspapers.*

935. MCU *of the Colonel, who also looks up.*
D.B. *(off)*: Wait a minute, ladies and gentlemen!

936. MCU *of another cluster of delegates with newspapers.*

937. LS *of D.B. at the microphone.*
D.B.: My name is D. B. Norton.

938. MCU *of Bert and Sourpuss. Bert is agitated and perplexed.*
D.B. *(off)*: You all know me.

939. *Telephoto* CU *of D.B., his black hat slanted downward, at the CBS mike.*
D.B.: I accuse this man of being a faker! We've been taken for a lot of suckers, and I'm the biggest of the lot! I spent a fortune backing this man in what I believed to be a sincere and worthy cause, just as you all did! And now I find out it's nothing but a cheap racket, cooked up

by him and two of my employees for the sole purpose of collecting
dues from John Does all over the country!
*John breaks away from the troopers in the background and returns to
the mike.*

JOHN: That's a lie!

D.B.: It's not a lie!

940. MCU *of D.B. and John.*

D.B.: Nickels and dimes! To stuff into their own pockets! You can read
all about it in the newspapers there!

JOHN: That's a lie! *(He grabs D.B. by the coat.)* Listen, don't believe
what he says—

D.B. *(overlapping)*: Let go of me! *(Troopers pull John off.)* This man
had no intention of jumping off of the top of a building! *(John makes
his way back to the mike.)* He was paid to say so! *(He turns to John.)*
Do you deny that?

JOHN: That's got nothing to do with it!

D.B.: Did—were you paid for it, or weren't you?

JOHN: Yes. I was paid. But the—

D.B. *(interrupting)*: And what about the suicide note? You didn't write that, either!

JOHN: What difference does that make?

D.B.: Did you write it, or didn't you?

JOHN: *No,* I didn't write it, but—

D.B.: Ah, you . . .

941. MCU *of Bert and Sourpuss, listening.*

D.B. *(off):* . . . bet your life you didn't! You look in your papers, ladies and gentlemen, and you'll find Miss Mitchell's signed confession that she was the one who wrote it!

Bert opens up the paper; Sourpuss looks on.

JOHN *(off):* Listen, folks, it's a fact . . .

Bert and Sourpuss look over toward John.

942. MCU *of John and D.B.*

JOHN: . . . that I didn't write the letter, but this whole thing started—

D.B. *(overlapping):* There, you see, he admits it! You're a fake, John Doe!

943. MCU *of Bert and Sourpuss.*

D.B. *(off):* And for what you've done to all these good people, . . .

944. MCU *of D.B. and John.*

D.B.: . . . they ought to run you out of the country! And I hope they do it! *D.B. stalks off the platform, his troopers in tow, leaving John alone at the mike.*

945. *Low angle* MLS *of a row of delegates, waiting in silence.*

946. MS *of another row, under umbrellas, also waiting.*

947. *High angle* LS *of the Kansas delegation, looking upward, facing the camera.*

948. MS *of another row. They too are watching.*

949. *High angle* LS *of another group facing the camera. Everyone is silent.*

950. ELS *side view of the grandstand.*

MALE VOICE *(calling out from the crowd):* Speak up, John!

951. MCU *of John at the mike.*

MALE VOICE *(off):* We believe you!

JOHN: Please, listen, folks!

952. MLS *of a group of troopers, pulling up wires for the public address system under the platform.*

     JOHN *(off, the sound of voice distorted by feedback)*: Now that he's through . . .

953. MS *of two of the troopers, with an exposed wire in their hands.*

     JOHN *(off)*: . . . shooting off his face, . . .

954. CU *of the troopers' hand.*

     JOHN *(off)*: . . . I've got a couple of things to tell you about—
     They split the cable with wire cutters. John's mike immediately goes dead.

955. *High angle* MLS *of Ted's back as he stands amid the crowd.*

     TED *(to the troopers)*: Come on! The rest of you get in here and riot! Break this crowd up! Come on!

956. *Low angle* MS *of the NBC radio announcer at his mike in the booth.*

     NBC ANNOUNCER: I'm sorry, folks, but we can't hear him anymore. Something's gone wrong with the loudspeakers.

957. MCU *of man and woman from 875. A trooper comes up from behind them.*

     TROOPER #1 *(cupping his hands to his mouth and shouting)*: John Doe's a fake! Booo!

958. CU *of John.*

     JOHN: They, they can't . . .

959. MS *of John, looking around for help.*

     JOHN: . . . hear me!

960. *Low angle* MCU *of another trooper, as the crowd grows restless.*

     TROOPER #2: Booo!

961. MS *of John. He grabs a microphone.*

     JOHN: This thing's not working. *(There are more boos from the crowd.)* Ladies and gentlemen!

962. *High angle* LS *of the Kansas delegation. People are booing John.*

963. *Low angle* MS *of a row of delegates; a trooper in front leads the booing. Brief pan left as he turns around to face the group.*

964. MS *of John, bewildered as he listens to boos and catcalls.*

965. MCU *of Bert, who appears crushed, and Sourpuss, who stares at John.*

966. MS *of a trio of supporters on the platform, all staring blankly.*

967. ELS *side view of the grandstand. The crowd boos and waves newspapers.*

968. MCU *of John, his mouth slightly agape at the scene before him.*

969. *High angle* LS *of the Wisconsin delegation. A paper is tossed toward the platform as the fury of the crowd mounts.*

970. MS *of John. Papers fly through the air. John abandons the microphones to speak to former supporters on the platform.*

971. MCU *of John's back as he turns to them.*
    JOHN: This thing's bigger than whether . . .

972. MCU, *panning right over a line of them, including the minister.*
    JOHN: . . . I'm a fake.[30]
    No one responds.

973. MCU, *panning left with John as he walks over to Bert and Sourpuss.*
    JOHN: Look, Bert, you believe me, don't you?
    BERT *(sarcastically)*: Sure, I believe you. *(He pulls a roll of paper out from his coat.)* Walking my legs off digging up five thousand signatures for a phoney. *(He crumbles up the petition.)* Well, there you are, Mr. Doe! Five thousand names asking you not to . . .

974. MS *of Bert, Sourpuss, and John.*
    BERT *(throwing the petition at John)*: . . . jump off any roof!
    Turning to go, Bert is stopped by Sourpuss.
    SOURPUSS: It makes no difference, Bert. The idea's still good. We don't have to give up our club.
    In the background, departing club members beckon Bert to join them.
    BERT *(bitterly)*: Yeah? Well, you can have it!
    Pulling away from Sourpuss, Bert exits.

975. MCU *of John to the right, Sourpuss watching Bert leave on the left. Pan right with John as he moves into* MCU, *looking out at the crowd, the sound of whose frenzy has grown into a roar.*

976. *The radio booth: low angle* MS *of the CBS announcer, assisted by a man with binoculars.*
    CBS ANNOUNCER: They're starting to throw things!

977. MS *of the back of the two men in the booth, looking down on the scene below.*
    CBS ANNOUNCER: Somebody's going to get hurt!

978. *Police station office interior:* CU *of a radio on a desk with an officer's cap to the side.*
    CBS ANNOUNCER *(over the radio)*: I'm afraid it'll be John Doe! *(Tilt up to, and shift focus on, Ann in* MS, *seated beyond. Leaning forward, she bites her lower lip.)* Listen to that mob.

979.   MCU *of Connell, slouched in a chair, hat cocked at an angle on his head. He glances over at Ann.*
980.   MS *of Ann. Suddenly she leaps from her seat.*

ANN *(racing toward the door)*: I've got to go to him!

Pan left: Ann is stopped at the door by two officers as Connell watches from the left.

OFFICER: Sorry, lady. I can't let you out.

ANN *(struggling)*: Oh, let me go! I want to see him! *(Pan left and pull back as she crosses the room to a supervisory officer at the desk. Over the radio, one can hear the roar of the mob at the ballpark.)*
Oh, please, please let me go! They're crucifying him![31] I can help him!

DESK OFFICER: Sorry, sister. We got orders to hold you.

ANN *(shouting)*: Orders from who? Can't they see it's a frame-up?

Behind her, Mrs. Mitchell enters through the door and hurries over to Ann.

MRS. MITCHELL: Ann, darling!

Pan right as Ann turns and embraces her mother.

ANN *(sobbing in her mother's arms)*: Oh, Mother! They won't let me go! They won't let me go!

Connell reaches over and touches Ann to comfort her.
981.   *The ballpark:* ELS *of the platform from a crowd on the verge of riot.*
982.   CU *of John, newspapers flying around him.*

JOHN *(trying to be heard, to no avail)*: Listen, folks! You've got to listen to me, everybody!
983.   *Low angle* MCU *of the man and woman of 875.*

MAN #1 *(to John)*: Back to the jungle, you hobo!
984.   *Low angle* MLS *of a row of delegates.*

MAN #2: Just another racket!
985.   CU *of John.*

JOHN: Stick to your clubs!
986.   *Low angle* MS *of a man and a woman under umbrellas.*

MAN #3 *(shouting)*: We've been fed baloney so long we're getting used to it!
987.   MLS *of John, alone on a deserted platform. He lets go of a microphone stand he has been holding.*
988.   *High angle* ELS *of the platform from the grandstand. People hurl newspapers through the air.*

989. ELS *side view of the grandstand. Loud booing persists.*
990. MS *of the Colonel, an expression of concern on his face. He is struck from behind by a paper and flings it aside in disgust.*
991. CU *of John.*
> JOHN *(pleading)*: The idea is still good! *(A damp newspaper strikes him in the face.)* Believe me, folks!
992. *High angle* LS *of the crowd, facing the camera, tossing papers and shouting.*
993. MCU *of an angry woman. Reaching into a bag, she pulls out a tomato. Pan right as she hands it to the man next to her.*
994. CU *of John.*
> JOHN *(desperately)*: Listen, John Does! You're the hope of the world! *A tomato strikes him squarely on the forehead. He stands still, dazed.*
995. MS *of the Colonel. He turns around to toss another airborne newspaper back at the crowd behind him, then leaves his seat.*
996. *High angle, telephoto* MS, *panning with the Colonel as he makes his way to the platform and walks up the steps.*
997. MS *of John as the Colonel reaches his side. Gesturing contemptuously at the crowd, he leads John toward the stairs.*
998. *Low angle* LS *of the side of the platform. Police arrive on the scene to help rescue John as he and the Colonel descend the stairs.*
999. *High angle* ELS *of the platform from the grandstand.*
1000. *High angle* MLS *of John, propped up by the Colonel and surrounded by police, staggering toward an exit in the rain. He is bombarded by the crowd.*
1001. *High angle* ELS *of the same.*
1002. *High angle, telephoto* MS *of John and the Colonel as they make their way through the angry mob. John's face is battered and bruised.*
1003. *High angle* MLS *of John, moving along a railing. People in the crowd pelt him at close range.*
1004. *The radio booth:* MS *of the back of John B. Hughes, broadcasting as he surveys the scene below.*
> JOHN B. HUGHES: The police finally manage to get him out of the park! If that boy isn't hurt, it'll be a miracle!
1005. *Police station office interior:* CU *of the radio.*
> JOHN B. HUGHES *(over the radio)*: Well, ladies and gentlemen, this certainly looks like the end of the John Doe movement.
> *Pan left and pull back as the desk officer reaches over and switches the*

radio off. In MLS *in the background sits Connell, who lifts a small bottle of milk, as if in a toast.*

CONNELL: Well, boys, you can chalk up another one to the Pontius Pilates.

Pan right and track into CU *of Ann leaning against her mother's shoulder. (An ominous chord is struck on the soundtrack, followed by gentle music.)*

ANN *(weeping)*: I should have been there. I could have helped him. He was so all alone.

1006. *Dissolve to* MS *of Bert driving his car home, with Sourpuss in the front seat beside him.*[32]

SOURPUSS *(soberly)*: A lot of us are going to be mighty ashamed of ourselves after tonight. We certainly didn't give that man much of a chance.

Without responding, Bert stares straight ahead at the road.

1007. *Dissolve to* MLS *of the Colonel*[33] *seated by a campfire at his and John's old spot under the bridge. He takes a drink from a tin can. Pan right to* MCU *of John, lying on his back, a pained look on his face.*

COLONEL *(off)*: Have some more, coffee, Long John?

JOHN *(shaking his head)*: No thanks, Colonel.

John stares off into the distance.

1008. MLS *of the Colonel, as the beginning of 1007. Watching John with concern, he takes another drink.*

MONTAGE SEQUENCE #3[34]

1009. ECU *of fragments of a* Bulletin *headline: "JOHN DOE" / swish pan/ "PROVEN/swish pan/ "FAKER!" / swish pan/ "CLUBS DISBANDING" [in smaller type].*

(Each fragment is matched by a dissonant brass chord, along a descending tonal scale.)

1010. *Flash superimposition, over the end of 1009, of what appears to be the silhouettes of two figures at a window.*

1011. *Dissolve to high angle* MLS *of a flyer with John's photo on it floating down a stream of rainwater along a curb and disappearing down a sewer. (Agitated music.)*

1012. *Dissolve to multiple image:* CU *of John, against a black backdrop, walking toward the camera, superimposed over concentric rings of*

rippling water. *(Somber, rhythmic music is scored under the remainder of the sequence.)*

1013. *Multiple image:* ELS *of John walking toward the camera against a black backdrop; in reverse motion newspapers then unfold from a crumpled state, and rise to fill the frame, superimposed over the diminutive figure of John. Large-scale headlines read: "FAKER" and "MOVEMENT PROVEN TO BE HOAX."*

1014. *Dissolve to* MS *of John walking toward the camera, his hand covering half of his face. A series of faces in* CU *then are matted in to the left and right of him, alternating in sequence from side to side as these figures verbally taunt him.*

WOMAN #1 *(superimposed over the end of 1013, on the left)*: Faker.

MAN #1 *(on the right)*: Racketeer.

MAN #2 *(on the left)*: Liar.

MAN #3 *(on the right)*: Cheat.

MAN #4 *(on the left)*: Imposter.

1015. *Dissolve to multiple image:* CU *of John walking, with rings of water, as 1012. Two more figures, slightly smaller in scale, are matted in sequentially, after the fashion of 1014.*

MAN #5 *(on the right)*: Why don't you jump?

WOMAN #6 *(on the left, sarcastically)*: Christmas Eve at midnight! *She laughs mockingly.*

1016. *Superimpose* CU *of John over flashback of Bert shaking hands with him in Millville (603).*

BERT: Goodbye, Mr. Doe. You're a wonderful man. *Fade out flashback image.*

1017. *Superimpose* CU *of John over flashback of Mr. and Mrs. Delaney bidding him farewell (605).*

MRS. DELANEY: God bless you, my boy. *She kisses John's hand. Fade out flashback image.*

1018. *Superimpose* CU *of John over flashback of Ann's pep talk before his first speech (similar to 390–391).*

ANN: Now get in there and pitch. *She kisses his cheek.*

1019. *Superimpose* CU *of John over: a)* MS *of Ann typing, and b)* ECU *of the word "FAKE" in bold letters. He lifts his hand to cover a side of his face again.*

1020. *Superimpose* CU *of John over flashback of John's confrontation with D.B. and Ted in Norton's dining room (similar to 823–824).*

D.B.: You're a fake, John Doe, and I can prove it!

1021. *Superimpose over* CU *of John a series of high angle views of John amid the hostile crowd at the ballpark (similar to 1000–1103).*

D.B. *(voiceover)*: You're the big hero that's supposed to jump off tall buildings and things.

1022. *Dissolve to* CU *of John's feet and tilt up as he walks alone down a rain-slick city sidewalk at night, off into* LS.

D.B. *(voiceover)*: You remember? What do you suppose your precious John Does will say when they find out you never had any intention of doing it, that you were being paid to say so?

WOMAN #2 *(voiceover, as end of 1015)*: Christmas Eve at midnight! *Again we hear her mocking laughter.*

1023. *Dissolve to* ELS *of the city at night, with snow gently falling. To the right is City Hall, brightly lit against the night sky; to the left, a hotel sign slowly blinks off and on. The mocking laughter from the previous sequence gives way to the singing of "Silent Night."*

1024. *Dissolve to* LS *of D.B. at home on Christmas Eve. Dressed in dinner clothes, he stands beside a towering, ornately decorated Christmas tree and checks his wristwatch. The singing of "Silent Night" continues.*

1025. MS *of D.B., checking his watch. Branches of the tinsel-ladened tree fill the foreground. A butler arrives with a liqueur on a tray.*
BUTLER: Merry Christmas, sir.
D.B. *(his attention momentarily averted)*: Oh. Merry Christmas.
Pulling out some money and placing it on the butler's tray, D.B. gestures off to the left, then takes the drink. The butler departs and D.B. walks leftward; the camera tracks in the same direction around the tree to a frosted window. Outside, carolers conclude the singing of "Silent Night" as D.B. arrives at the window and the butler appears at the door with the money. Through the window, the carolers can be heard thanking first the butler, then D.B.

1026. *Exterior* MCU *of D.B. through the window.*
CAROLERS *(off)*: Merry Christmas! Merry Christmas! Happy New Year![35]
D.B. solemnly looks down at his watch.

1027. CU *of D.B.'s watch: it's 10:50.[36]*

1028. *Interior of a police station:* MS *of a sergeant on the phone, his card game with a policeman on the other side of the desk having been interrupted.*
DESK SERGEANT: Who? John Doe? Is that screwball still around?
POLICEMAN: Aw, that dame's been calling all day.
DESK SERGEANT *(still on the phone)*: Sure, sure, I know. Yeah. At midnight, huh? *(He laughs.)* Okay, lady. We'll have the place surrounded with nets.

1029. *Interior of Ann's bedroom:* MS *of Ann in bed as she angrily hangs up the phone.*
ANN: They're laughing at me!
Pan right to MCU *profile of Ann's mother, seated at the foot of the bed. She glances up to the left. Pan left and tilt up to low angle* MCU *of a doctor, his face in shadow. He checks a thermometer and shakes his head.*

1030. MS *of Ann, with her mother in profile to right.*
DOCTOR *(off)*: You're a sick girl, Ann. You'd better take it easy.
Meanwhile Ann has located another number and is dialing again.
MRS. MITCHELL: Whom are you calling now? You called that number not ten minutes ago.
ANN *(paying no attention)*: Hello, Mr. Connell? Have you seen him yet? Have you—

1031. *Low angle* MCU *of Connell in a phone booth, his face in shadow.*
CONNELL: Now listen, Ann, he can't possibly get in without our seeing him. I'm watching the side door and the Colonel's out front, so stop worrying.

1032. *High angle* MS *of Ann on the phone in her bedroom.*
ANN *(sighing)*: Oh. Thank you.
She hangs up, and looks down in frustration. Her mother reaches over to comfort her. Ann suddenly has an idea; pan right as she jumps out of bed and runs to her closet.
MRS. MITCHELL *(racing over to her daughter)*: Why, Ann!
DOCTOR *(off)*: Ann, don't be foolish!

1033. *Exterior of Bert's car:* [37] MS *through the windshield as Bert drives through snow at night, his wife beside him, Sourpuss beside her, and other members of the Millville John Doe Club in the back.*

1034. MS: *Bert, Mrs. Hansen, and Sourpuss, angled from the driver's side.*
BERT *(as he drives)*: If this isn't the craziest, the battiest, the looniest wild goose chase I ever heard of—
MRS. HANSEN: Oh, shut up, Bert. Sourpuss is right.
BERT: Yeah? Well, if he is, I'm a banana split.
SOURPUSS: That man is going to be on that roof. Don't ask me how I know. I just know. And you know it as well as I do.
BERT: Sure, sure. I'd like to believe in fairy tales, but a guy that's a fake isn't going to jump off any roof.
MRS. HANSEN: I don't think he was any fake, not with that face. And, anyway, what he stood for wasn't a fake.
BERT: Okay, honey, okay.

1035. *Dissolve to* ELS *of City Hall, as 1023. Snow falls in silence.*
1036. *Interior grillwork of the City Hall front door:* MS *of Ann as she enters.*
1037. MS *of a janitor, seated on the floor by a wash bucket, smoking a cigar.*

Pan left slightly to LS *of Ann approaching from the front door. As she passes, the janitor hides his cigar.*

1038. ELS *of a cavernous lobby as Ann runs to the elevators. In the fore-ground right the dwarfed figure of the Colonel can be seen at the base of the stairs.*

1039. LS *of the Colonel at the stairs, his eyes on the elevator.*

COLONEL: Elevators ain't . . .

1040. MLS *of Ann over the Colonel's shoulder.*

COLONEL: . . . running.

ANN *(her face brightening at the sight of him)*: Colonel!

COLONEL: You shouldn't have gotten out of bed, Miss.

She hurries over to him.

ANN *(now in* MCU *)*: Has he been here?

COLONEL: No.

ANN: Have you seen him?

COLONEL: I ain't seen him for a week.

ANN: Where's Connell?

COLONEL: He's watching the other door.

ANN: Oh. Gee, you're swell! *(She returns to an elevator, then realizes she can't use it.)* Ohh!

Ann takes note of the stairway.

1041. MLS *of Ann and the Colonel, panning right with her as she bolts for the stairs.*

COLONEL *(grabbing Ann's arm)*: No sense in going up there. I been here for hours. He ain't here!

ANN *(pulling away)*: Let me go, will you!

1042. *High angle* LS *of Ann and the Colonel from the next landing up, pan-ning with her as she begins her ascent.*

COLONEL *(remaining at the bottom)*: Now, that's crazy. It's fourteen floors!

Ann continues upward, moving out of view.

1043. MS *of the janitor, who watches the scene at the stairs.*

1044. MLS *of the Colonel. Turning back around, he notices something.*

1045. LS *of the interior front door as D.B. enters with an entourage, includ-ing Bennett, Hammett, Weston, and Mayor Lovett.*

1046. MS *of the janitor. Hearing the men approach, he hides his cigar in the cap on his head.*

1047. ELS *of the front door, with the janitor in the lower right foreground. D.B.'s group comes forward, passing the janitor as he busily scrubs the floor.*

1048. ELS, *as 1038. The men arrive at the elevators.*

1049. MS *of the Colonel, peering around the corner of the stair wall.*

1050. MLS *of D.B.'s group. Mayor Lovett unlocks an elevator and they enter.*

1051. MS *of the Colonel, who is quizzical.*

1052. MS *of the janitor, again watching the scene. Suddenly, painfully, he is reminded of the lit cigar in his hat. Retrieving it, he sticks it back in his mouth.*

1053. *Dissolve to* MS *of the fourteenth-floor directory. Pan right to* LS *of the elevators as they open and D.B.'s group steps out.*
    MAYOR LOVETT: This is as far as the elevator goes. We've got to walk up to the tower.

1054. LS *of Mayor Lovett leading the entourage down the hall toward the stairs.*[38]

1055. *Dissolve to low angle* MLS *behind the group, panning with them as they climb the stairs.*

1056. *Exterior of the City Hall roof: high angle* MLS *of D.B. and the others as they emerge through a door on the right. Pan left as they slowly advance toward the parapet, looking for John.*

1057. *High angle* LS *of the group as they fan out.*

1058. *Track leftward along a side parapet, following the men in* LS, *then moving on past them to an* ELS *of the lights of the city.*

1059. *High angle* LS *(closer than 1057) of the men at the ledge, searching in all directions.*

1060. *Aerial* ELS *of the city below. Lights illuminate the falling snow.*

1061. LS *of a clock tower: it's 11:52. A distant bell chimes.*

1062. *High angle* LS, *as 1059.*

1063. MLS *of the men in shadow by the parapet.*[39]
    BENNETT *(breaking the silence)*: The tramp is probably full of Christmas cheer and asleep in some flophouse.
    MAYOR LOVETT: Let's go. I've got to decorate my tree.

1064. *The stairway: high angle* MLS *of Ann, panning with her as she climbs higher.*

1065. *Dissolve to* CU *of clock: it's 12:00. Bells begin to peal about the city.*

1066. MLS *of the men, as 1063. (Bells continue to peal, as they will through-*

out the remainder of this scene.)

D.B.: Well, I give up. I don't know what gave us the idea that he, he'd attempt anything like this.

WESTON: I guess you're right. I'm afraid the joke's on us. Let's go.

D.B.: I hope nobody finds out we've been here.[40]

1067. *Fourteenth floor interior:* MS *of John, silhouetted in the frosted window of the men's room. He seals an envelope. Tilt down to his feet as he exits; track right as he walks to a mail chute and deposits the envelope; track right as he moves toward the door to the roof.*[41]

1068. MLS *of the men on the roof, panning right with them as they start back to the door. D.B., hearing something, signals the others to stop.*

1069. *Frontal* MLS *of the group. D.B. leads them off to the right.*

1070. *High angle* MLS *from the other side, as the men hide in the shadows behind the open door.*[42]

1071. *High angle* LS *of the roof. John's elongated shadow precedes him as he slowly passes through the door. He pauses, looks around, then moves toward the parapet, his shadow shrinking with each step.*

1072. LS *behind John as he reaches the parapet.*

1073. MS *of D.B. and the others, looking on. In the darkness their eyes gleam.*

1074. MLS *from a three-quarters angle of John looking over the low wall. He removes a second envelope from his pocket.*

1075. CU *of the envelope, marked: "To All John Does Everywhere."*

1076. *High angle, frontal* MLS *of John, with D.B.'s group visible in the background. John returns the letter to his pocket and takes a drag on his cigarette.*

1077. MCU *of John. He looks upward, then briefly closes his eyes.*

1078. MS *of D.B.'s group, as 1073.*

1079. MLS *profile of John from the left. He tosses his cigarette aside and places his hands on the wall.*

1080. MCU *of John's back. He begins to lift himself up on the wall.*

D.B. *(off):* I wouldn't do that if I were you, John.

John spins around, startled to hear D.B.'s voice.

1081. MS *of D.B.'s group.*

1082. MLS *of John, staring blankly.*

1083. MS *of D.B.'s group as they take a step forward.*

D.B.: It'll do you no good. The Mayor has policemen downstairs . . .

1084. MLS *of John, listening.*

D.B. *(off)*: . . . with instructions to remove all marks of identification you may have on your person.

1085. MS *of D.B.'s group.*

D.B.: You'll be buried in Potter's Field and you will have accomplished nothing.

1086. MCU *of John. He stares at them, thinking.*

1087. MS *of D.B.'s group. D.B. looks away nervously.*

1088. MCU *of John.*

JOHN *(softly)*: I've taken care of that. I've already mailed a copy of this letter to Mr. Connell.

1089. *D.B. steps into* CU.

D.B.: John, why don't you forget this foolishness?

1090. MCU *of John.*

JOHN: Stop right where you are, Mr. Norton, if you don't want to go overboard with me.

1091. MCU *of D.B., with the others behind him, as they recoil.*

1092. MCU *of John. A slight smile forms on his lips.*

JOHN: I'm glad you gentlemen are here. You killed the John Doe movement, all right, but you're going to see it born all over again.

1093. MCU *of D.B., watching John intently.*

1094. MCU *of John. He turns toward the wall.*

JOHN *(his eyes shining)*: Now, take a good look, Mr. Norton.

1095. MCU *of D.B. Alarmed, he starts to step forward again, but is interrupted by the sound of Ann's voice.*

ANN *(off)*: John!

1096. CU *of Ann, now on the roof, racing toward John.*

1097. MCU *of John, turning back around.*

ANN *(off)*: John!

1098. MLS *of John as Ann comes forward and collapses against him.*

ANN: Oh, John. Don't do it! I won't let you! I . . .

1099. CU *of John, the top of Ann's head visible against his chest.*

ANN: . . . love you, darling. Oh, please.

1100. MCU *of John and Ann. Grabbing onto the lapels of his coat, she supports herself and faces him.*

ANN: Please don't give up. We'll start all over again, just you and I. It isn't too late. The John Doe movement isn't dead yet.

Turning her head, Ann notices for the first time the presence of D.B. and his entourage.

1101. MS *of D.B. and the others.*
ANN *(off)*: You see, John, it isn't dead, or they wouldn't be here.

1102. *Low angle* CU *of John from behind Ann. He glances toward D.B.'s group.*
ANN: It's alive in them. They kept it alive, by being afraid of it! *(John looks back down at her.)* That's why they came up here!

1103. *High angle* CU *of Ann, over John's shoulder.*
ANN: Oh, darling! Sure, it should have been killed. It was dishonest! But we can start clean now! Just you and I!

1104. *Low angle* CU *of John, as 1102.*
ANN: It'll grow, John, and it'll grow big, because it'll be honest this time!
John looks off into the distance.

1105. *High angle* CU *of Ann, as 1103.*
ANN: Oh, John, if it's worth dying for, it's worth living for!

1106. *Low angle* CU *of John, as 1102. He turns away.*
ANN: Oh, please, John!

1107. MLS *of Connell and the Colonel as they lead the Millville club members through the door onto the roof. They are stopped in their tracks by what they see.*
ANN *(off)*: Oh. Oh, please, please God, help me.

1108. *High angle* CU *of Ann, as 1103.*
ANN: John. *(She takes his face in her hands.)* John, look at me.

1109. MCU *of John and Ann, as 1100.*
ANN: You want to be honest, don't you? Well, you don't have to die to keep the John Doe idea alive! Someone already died for that once! The first John Doe!

1110. *Low angle* CU *of John, as 1102.*
ANN: And He's kept that idea alive for nearly two thousand years!

1111. *Pan left over the faces of the Millville club members.*
ANN *(off)*: It was He who kept it alive in them, and He'll go on keeping it alive forever and always!

1112. MS *of D.B.'s group.*
ANN *(off)*: For every John Doe movement these men kill, . . .

1113. *High angle* CU *of Ann, as 1103.*
   ANN: . . . a new one will be born! *(She looks out over the city.)* That's
   why those bells are ringing, John!
1114. *Low angle* CU *of John, as 1102. He is watching her closely now.*
   ANN: They're calling to us, not to give up, but to keep on fighting! To
   keep on pitching! Oh, don't you see, darling?
1115. MCU *of Bert and his friends.*
   ANN *(off)*: This is no time to give up!
1116. *Low angle* CU *of John, as 1102.*
   ANN: You and I, John, we c—
1117. *High angle* CU *of Ann, as 1103. Tiring, she wraps her arms around*
   John's shoulders.
   ANN: Oh, no. No, John, if you die, I want to die, too!
1118. MS *of Ann and John, as she weakens.*
   ANN *(her voice waning)*: Oh. Oh, I love you so—
   Ann collapses against John's legs.

1119. MS *of D.B.'s group, watching.*
1120. MCU *of Bert's group, watching.*
1121. MS *of John. He reaches down to lift Ann up.*
1122. MCU *as John lifts up Ann in his arms and gazes at her.*
      BERT *(off)*: Mr. Doe, you don't have to—
      His voice breaks off as John looks up.
1123. MCU *of Bert, with his wife to the right and the Colonel to the left.*
      BERT: We're with you, Mr. Doe. We just lost our heads and acted like a
      mob. We—
1124. CU *of Mrs. Hansen, stepping forward.*
      MRS. HANSEN *(interrupting)*: What Bert's trying to say is that we need
      you, Mr. Doe.
1125. CU *of John, as he stands before them with Ann in his arms.*
      MRS. HANSEN *(off)*: There were a lot of us that didn't believe what that
      man said.
1126. CU *of Mrs. Hansen.*
      MRS. HANSEN: We were going to start up our John Doe Club again,
      whether we saw you or not. *(She glances over to the left.)* Weren't
      we, Bert? And there were a lot of others that were going to do the
      same thing. Why, Mr. Sourpuss even got a letter from his cousin in
      Toledo, and—
      SOURPUSS *(off)*: I got it right here, Mr. Doe.
      MRS. HANSEN: Only, only . . .
1127. CU of John.
      MRS. HANSEN *(off)*: . . . it'd be a lot easier with you. Please.
1128. MS *of the group from Millville.*
      MRS. HANSEN *(softly)*: Please come with us, Mr. Doe.
1129. CU *of John, thinking. He glances over at D.B.'s group.*
1130. CU *of D.B., then panning left over the faces of Hammett and Mayor
      Lovett.*
1131. CU *of John. He looks down at Ann, then takes a step in the direction of
      the door. (The music to "The Ode to Joy" softly rises on the soundtrack,
      and is heard, along with the church bells, throughout the remainder of
      the scene.)*
1132. MLS *of John, carrying Ann in his arms as he walks toward the door.
      D.B.'s group watches in the background.*

1133. MCU *of Mrs. Hansen, between her husband and Sourpuss.*
    COLONEL *(off)*: Long John!
    MRS. HANSEN: Mr. Doe! *(Entering the shot, John walks between the Hansens on his way toward the door.)* Here, we'll help you with her. She'll be all right.
    SOURPUSS *(following John as he exits)*: Mr. Doe, take her right to my car. That's it, right out front.
    The other club members join in escorting John and Ann out. The Colonel exits with them. Connell steps into the foreground.
1134. CU *of D.B., staring at the departing group.*
1135. MCU *of Connell at the doorway. He points with his thumb over his shoulder to the departing group.*
    CONNELL: There you are, Norton! The people! Try and lick that!
    As Connell follows the others out, the music to "The Ode to Joy" swells on the soundtrack.

1136. *Dissolve to bells swinging and ringing in a belfry. Over this the end title appears. Fade out of both image and soundtrack.*

Fade in to ELS *of the snowswept city at night, with the clock tower to the right, as credits for the principal characters are scrolled. Scored under this is a medley composed of "Roll Out the Barrel," "Take Me Out to the Ballgame," and "Oh, Susanah."*

Notes on the Continuity Script

As independent producers at Warners for *Meet John Joe,* Frank Capra and Robert Riskin did not follow standard studio procedures for filing scripts; as a result, only fragments of their early drafts survive. However, lawsuits filed against Warners and Frank Capra Productions by novelist Henry W. Clune and playwrights Robert Shurr and Pat A. Leonard gave rise to a detailed study of the development of the script, the results of which are retained in the studio's legal files at Princeton University. A complete copy of the script that Capra submitted to the Production Code Administration, dated 13 June and delivered to the PCA on 24 June, is held in the Dimitri Tiomkin Collection at the University of Southern California. The Capra Collection at Wesleyan University has a bound copy of the director's estimating script, which includes a shooting script dated 27 June, amended by numerous revisions made just prior to and during shooting, and accompanied by extensive handwritten comments by Capra; Slavko Vorkapich's scripts for the three montage passages he produced for the film; and a shooting schedule and related materials concerning the logistics of production. From the studio's Daily Production and Progress Report for *Meet John Doe,* which is held in the Warners Archives at USC, one can discern which scenes from the shooting were actually shot, when they were shot, and the dates and locations of postproduction filming. My notes here are drawn from these varied sources. For purposes of convenience, I have abbreviated the 13 June script submitted to the Production Code Administration as the *PCA script,* and the 27 June shooting script as *SS.* All dates are from 1940, unless another year is specified.

1. These three songs return (along with other folk songs) at various points in the film, and are woven together as a medley under the end credits. When Dimitri Tiomkin was commissioned to compose the score, trade papers made much of the fact that the music was to be based entirely upon American sources, but somewhere along the line Germanic music such as "Oh, Tannenbaum," "Silent Night," and "Ode to Joy" also found its way into the score (*Daily Variety, The Hollywood Reporter,* 10 Oct. 1940).

2. In the PCA script, there is brief vignette placed between the removal of the old sign and the elevation of the new: an older man, "Grandpa," opens a newsboard poster heralding oil magnate D. B. Norton's acquisition of the paper. This character returns four more times in the script, responding on each occasion to recent news reports concerning John and the John Doe movement. He last appears after the third montage, when the clubs have disbanded. To the news of this he responds, "Well, that's the end of that," and walks away from a Santa's helper who is soliciting donations with an outstretched tambourine.

   It is also interesting to note that an alternative opening was scripted on 22 July and shot on 25 July, in which the *Bulletin's* elderly ex-owner (played by Harry Davenport) storms Norton's estate. Intending to kill Norton, he discovers he can't do it, but he angrily accuses Norton of destroying the "only free voice" in the area, a newspaper that had been in the ex-owner's family for eighty years, and which he hoped to pass on to his son. He warns Norton that he'll live to regret his action. Police drag the assailant off. (The scene appears to have combined aspects of a farmer's attack on Deeds in *Mr. Deeds Goes to Town* and an ex-business associate's challenge to tycoon Kirby in *You Can't Take It with You.*) Capra notes in the margins of the script that D.B. should be found reading Hitler's *Mein Kampf,* and possessing medals and Legion of Honor ribbons. It is unclear whether this alternative opening was ever tried out on preview audiences.

3. In an early version of this scene, dated 25 March, it is indicated that Pop is

the former editor of the *Bulletin*. D.B. agrees to retain him as long as Connell assumes responsibility for boosting circulation.

4. In the PCA script, Christmas Eve is first mentioned when Ann changes the suicide date in the letter she is writing from Labor Day to the less secular holiday. The film, however, follows the SS; no date is mentioned in the letter.

5. In the SS, the phrase is "typical John Doe." Capra penciled in the change to "typical American" on his copy.

6. Prior to 13 May, the character's name was simply (and perhaps implausibly) John Doe, as in the treatment by Connell and Presnell. The use of the name Willoughby after that date was considered key evidence in the lawsuit filed by Clune, since Chester Willoughby is the name of the protagonist in Clune's novel, published in April 1940. In the novel, Willoughby achieves national celebrity, and is touted for the presidency, because of the message of Christian brotherhood he delivers over the radio. See Henry W. Clune, *Monkey on a Stick* (New York: William Morrow, 1940).

7. The Colonel first appeared as a character in the 22 April script.

8. The SS version of Ann's direction of the photography section was revised extensively by Capra, with his handwritten suggestions incorporated into a new draft on 2 July.

9. The SS, calling for the use of newspaper inserts, a few quick images of newspapers being sold and read, and a rising circulation graph, outlines the information that is conveyed in this scene. (Capra notes in the margins to the passage, "Who is John Doe?") Vorkapich's script, dated 8 August, adds to this outline detailed suggestions for vignettes and graphic effects. Not included in the film version of the passage, however, is a series of superimpositions planned by Vorkapich to make the point that money directly buys votes at the ballot box.

10. In the SS, after Ann and Ted depart, D.B. is distressed to discover in his foyer two men whom he has ordered never to visit or phone. "We had to," one man replies, "Hinkler is in a jam with the FBI. We need money to get him out of the country!" D.B. tells them to "get hold of Carl," and orders the men out. The name "Hinkler" perhaps was designed to evoke the specter of Adolph Hitler, or Charlie Chaplin's satiric version of Hitler, Adenoid Hynkle, in *The Great Dictator* (1940).

11. In the PCA script, Ann's first scene at home with her mother is located

prior to her meeting with Norton, and emphasis is placed on her elation over the bonus money she had exacted from Connell. Her house, moreover, is described as a "worn-down wooden structure somewhere in the suburbs." In the SS, as in the film, she is first seen at home when she writes the speech, but the scene was revised several times during production. In the SS, the scene opens with a photograph of her father, inscribed, "To Ann: whose head and heart are always having an argument. I bet on her heart, Dad." Looking at it, Ann murmurs, "You bet wrong, Dad," and returns to her typewriter. Her mother enters and advises Ann to forget politics and write something simple and hopeful, as would her late father. She also notes that she has met John and sees something of Ann's father in him. "Guess I'm just blind," Ann replies. The children (with a younger brother added to the two sisters) interrupt, and the girls mockingly read aloud extracts from Ann's speech. The diary is brought out after the children have retreated to bed, and Ann recalls how her father died: struck by a truck after dragging himself out of his own sickbed to help someone else who was ailing. (In addition to underscoring the martyrdom plot, the cause of death may have been intended to parallel Ann's illness and departure from her sickbed at the end of the film.) Revised in July, and again a few days before it was shot in mid-August, the scene was condensed. Moreover, its ending was modified so as to make Ann appear more receptive to her mother's advice. On 23 January 1941, several months after principal photography was completed, the scene between Ann and her mother was reshot one more time, reportedly in an effort to further condense it. This seems to be part of a general pattern at the editing stage to cut back on Ann's scenes with her mother.

12. Ann is referring here to a remark by her mother that was cut from the film (see note 11). In the SS, Ann describes to Long John in greater detail the romantic ideal John Doe represents. "A man like that wouldn't exist," she tells John, "but if he ever did I'd follow him to the ends of the earth."

13. In early drafts of the script, John tears up the speech by Ann (or "Dot Brush" in some versions), declaring he wants to speak without anybody's help, and his invocation of the principles of the Sermon on the Mount at once strikes a chord in the audience. Although this allowed Capra and Riskin to sidestep some of the difficult questions of the hero's authenticity inherited from the treatment, by 22 April Ann was reinstated as ghost writer for John and her role in the film expanded. In the PCA script, the

radio speech makes more direct reference to contemporary political problems and Christian solutions. Although originally scheduled to be shot in July, Capra waited until the end of principal photography in September to record the scene, and kept the set closed.

14. In the PCA script, this was a much longer scene in which the competing claims of the Colonel and Ann on John were explicitly drawn. The Colonel suggests that John's baseball career may be over, sparking off a brief quarrel. Then, as he massages John's sore arm to calm him down, the Colonel explains why he has come to abhor money; once the owner of a grocery store, he was so overwhelmed by bills that one day he walked out of the store and never came back. "Let's get away where there are trees—and rocks—and mountains—and sky," he urges. "You can trust them." Meanwhile, John observes that he has never known a girl who possessed sentiments like those Ann expressed in the speech. A guy would be lucky to win her, he muses, but he would have to be more than a bush-league pitcher to do so.

15. The PCA script called for a hitchhiking scene with John and Colonel following their ride in the boxcar. In the passage, allusion is made to the famous hitchhiking scene in Capra's 1934 comedy, *It Happened One Night,* where Claudette Colbert's legs attract a ride after Clark Gable's thumb has failed. Parodying Colbert's gesture, John and the Colonel pull up their pants legs, but the only car that stops is that of a policeman. The scene was deleted from the SS, but on the back pages of his script Capra jotted down lyrics for it, to be sung to the tune "Hi-Diddle-Dee-Dee." They include a comic reference to Colbert, as well as couplets such as: "The Heelots come and the Heelots go / But they go alone without John Doe," and "The pavement's hot—and my feet are sore / But I'm free as air—and I want no more." (In his script, Capra also jotted down ideas for another song or jingle: "He's come from many a shore / But he's American to the core / He's the man who lives next door / Meet John Doe," etc.) The hitchhiking scene apparently was shot; in the early months of 1941, the press reported that Cooper was to make his singing debut in the film, and a production still from the scene is included in *Life's* photo essay on *Meet John Doe* ("Movie of the Week," 10 March 1941, p. 44).

16. In early drafts of the script, the John Doe clubs are a grass-roots phenomenon and establish contact with John by writing to him and inviting him to speak at local meetings. In the 22 April script, the idea of using the radio

to build a third party on the back of the movement appears, and Norton (originally D. B. Wells, then D. B. Hatch) begins to assume a larger role in developing the movement by way of the media. Capra's handwritten notes on his script, furthermore, frequently suggest ways that the power of radio, the press, and communications technology can be elaborated visually or through dialogue in the film.

17. The second montage sequence follows the SS fairly closely. Slavko Vorkapich's script, dated 8 August, eliminates a shot from the SS in which a priest, rabbi, and Protestant minister announce that they are pleased by the movement, and substitutes plaques for John Doe dolls in a scene in which these items are shown to be big sellers. Neither scene appears in the film. Another passage in both scripts was shot but eventually cut from the film in which a foreign dignitary warns the State Department that John Doe clubs are spreading in his country. The Wall Street sequence was originally more pointed in both scripts, with a tycoon demanding that the movement be stopped. This seems a vestige of earlier versions of the script in which Wall Street big shots attempt to crush the movement.

18. The idea for a John Doe convention first emerged in the 3 June script; prior to this, the announcement of a third party was to be made over the radio.

19. This scene, and the one to follow in the airport lounge, was scripted on 17 July, and replaced a single, longer scene that, in the SS, takes place in airplane. Flying home after a long trip, John holds a skein of wool while Ann winds it into a ball, and they talk. She is anxious to see her mother and sisters; he wonders if the Colonel will be waiting for him, and describes his changing attitude toward the people he has met, in a fashion similar to the airport lounge scene in the film. John then relates a dream from the night before, as in the hotel scene. In effect, the 17 July revision divides and reverses the two halves of this passage. It also eliminates the humor that is derived from their cooperative venture with the yarn (woolgathering?), the only playful moment between the couple in the entire SS.

20. In the SS, two scenes appear between the airplane flight (see note 19) and Ann's receipt of the fur coat and jewelry from D.B. In the first, Ann returns home to a new apartment, furnished by D.B., and, while dressing for the appointment that evening with her boss, talks with her mother. Admitting for the first time to her mother that John resembles her father, she worries that he takes the John Doe movement too seriously. As for herself, she figures that although people currently get a "big kick" out of

the clubs, it will soon be supplanted by another fad. Ann's comments
perturb her mother. (The tension planted here is developed in a subsequent
scene; see note 24.) This was followed by a parallel passage in which
John, dropped off by Beany at the bridge, rejoins the Colonel where they
first camped out. The companions play some music together. In the PCA
script, the scene in which Ann receives the coat and jewelry also was extended. D.B. expands on the idea of a third-party movement and tempts
Ann further with the prospect of being the first woman to write a platform
for a major political party.

21. In the first draft of the script, dated 26 January, D.B. intends to use the
movement to gain support for a candidate from an existing party, but is
threatened with economic destruction by Wall Street if he does so. (The
draft ended, unfinished, at this point.) By the 1 March draft, D.B. plots to
form a third party, with nephew Ted (then Tim) Sheldon as the presidential
candidate; financial and corporate kingpins are still opposed. In the 13 May
script, John exposes D.B. to Hammett's group (who at this stage are D.B.'s
opponents), and Norton has to leave the country. When John is exposed as
a fake himself, he attempts to rekindle the movement by addressing individual clubs. It is not until the 3 June script that D.B. emerges as the
presidential candidate and there are no antagonists from Wall Street.

22. The SS describes a sequence here in which people attending the convention approach the city by car, bus, and train, and are steered toward motel
rooms paid for by Norton. The passage, however, was never shot. The
introduction to the convention by the radio announcers was originally part
of the scene in which John arrives following his confrontation with Norton.
In the SS, Norton's associates also appear outside the stadium prior to Norton's appearance.

23. Knox Manning and John B. Hughes regularly broadcast for the CBS and
Mutual networks. The NBC announcer is played by actor Selmer Jackson.

24. In the SS, John's visit to the Mitchell apartment was preceded by a lengthy
scene between Ann and her mother, as Ann readied herself for Norton's
convention eve dinner. The scene helps to explain Mrs. Mitchell's sober
mood in the film when John arrives at the door, and perhaps also Ann's
reaction when John appears at Norton's dinner party. Shot on 21 August,
the scene was eventually cut, perhaps to shorten the film. It includes the
following conversation between mother and daughter:

MOTHER *(complainingly)*: The only times I've seen you since your return is when you come home to change. You haven't spent five minutes with the children.

ANN: This convention tonight's a big thing, Ma. What time is it? *(She glances at her watch.)* Oh, my goodness! Tim [Ted] will be here any minute. D.B. asked me specially to come over early.

MOTHER: It's a wonder you haven't moved inside D.B's house.

ANN *(unperturbed)*: Oh-oh! Ma's mad!

Her mother steps in front of her.

MOTHER: I wish you'd give this whole thing up, Ann. Let's go back to the little house. I called them up today. We can move right in.

ANN *(horrified)*: Back there! And live like beggars again!

MOTHER: We never lived like beggars.

ANN *(sharply)*: Yes, beggars! Frightened little beggars! Not me!

Her mother looks at her a moment, then with a helpless gesture turns and starts to leave the room. CU of Ann—she turns, her face softens.

ANN: Aw, Ma! *(The camera pans with her as she goes toward her mother, whom she catches at the door. She takes her in her arms.)* Don't pick on me, Ma. Big exciting things are happening—and I've got to keep a clear head.

MOTHER *(quietly)*: You've changed. You don't seem like my daughter any more.

ANN: Aw, don't be silly. *(She shakes her playfully.)* You know I love you.

MOTHER: Something's wrong, Ann. *(She releases herself and walks away.)* I don't like it. I don't like living here. I don't like what you're doing. *(Ann's face clouds. A look of irritation and impatience comes over it. Her mother has sat down on the bed. Ann stands rooted, watching her.)* I don't trust this man Norton. What's he after? While you were gone he sent me flowers every day. Why? And that pompous Tim Sheldon! A hand-kisser! I don't trust a man who kisses hands—particularly mine!

ANN *(explaining tolerantly)*: Oh now, Mother! Of course they're catering to you. I'm important to them.

MOTHER *(vehemently)*: They pay you a salary, don't they? What's the ermine wrap for? And the diamond bracelet?

Ann grabs her comb and starts running it nervously over her hair.

ANN *(irritably)*: You certainly are suspicious! D.B. has political ambitions like hundreds of other men in this country. What's wrong with that? I dropped the John Doe clubs in his lap and he's paying me for it.

Her mother shrugs resignedly and rises.

MOTHER *(bitter sigh)*: All right, Ann. If it's as simple as all that. *(She is on her way out and stops.)* And what about you? Doesn't it bother you that millions of decent people are taking this seriously—while you laugh at them? *(Contemptuously:)* How can you do it?

ANN: Oh, so that's what's bothering you.

Ann writhes under her mother's attack.

MOTHER: You've gone so money-mad you haven't any conscience left!

ANN *(irascibly)*: I don't see that any harm's being done! It's just a fad! In six months, it'll be forgotten like the "Handies" and "Confucius Say!" If the saps go for it, that's perfect! It's keeping us off the breadline.

Her mother grimaces bitterly.

MOTHER *(quietly)*: I'm one of those saps. I'm a member of a John Doe Club myself.

Ann turns, unable for a moment to believe her ears.

ANN *(ironically)*: That's a funny one!

MOTHER: Yes. Funny, isn't it? Funny that I believe in everything your father held sacred. That *you* went and sold for a mink coat. *(Ann winces. This accusation is devastating to her. Her mother glares at her, contemptuously.)* You can be proud of yourself, Ann Mitchell!

Ann suddenly jumps up, flings the brush down with a clatter.

ANN *(overwrought, her voice shaky)*: I wish you'd let me alone! *(She strides around, irritatedly, for a second. Trying to justify herself:)* I put over one of the biggest things in the country—people think I'm brilliant—I get credit everywhere—everywhere but here! Here, I'm something small and loathsome! *(She suddenly stops.)* Well, I'm not giving it up! *(She grabs the ermine wrap.)* It's given us security for the first time! *(A wave around the room.)* It's given us this! *(She throws the wrap over her shoulders.)* And I like it!

Something collapses inside of Mother. She struggles to control herself.

MOTHER *(quiet, but grim)*: You can have it, Ann. *(Strained voice.)* The children and I won't be here when you come home tonight.

She turns and leaves. Ann stares, shocked.

Sheldon then arrives, and Ann departs with him in state of bewilderment. Capra and Riskin's willingness to cut this scene, and to preserve instead John's visit with Mrs. Mitchell, is indicative once again of Ann's diminished role in the final cut of the film.

25. Capra penciled into his script the phrase: "Lighthouses, John, lighthouses in a foggy world." The metaphor is used again in *Prelude to War* (1943), the first of seven orientation films Capra produced as part of the *Why We Fight* series for the Army during World War II.

26. In the SS, after John leaves the bar, he is seen reading Ann's speech by the light of a streetlamp.

27. In the SS, D.B. takes John to his study, and Ann follows. John tests D.B. by pretending he wants a piece of the action. Relieved, Norton offers to put him on the payroll as head of the John Doe clubs at $25,000, with more money in store if he will "play ball." Ann is confused. Norton then takes John to the dining room to meet his associates, introducing him fulsomely as a "man of destiny" whose speech that night will be "a warning to all outmoded political institutions that their day is ended." At this point John interrupts to announce that he has other plans instead. The confrontation with D.B. then unfolds in a fashion similar to the film, although in the earlier version, D.B. reveals that in his vault he has the agreement that John signed with the *Bulletin,* John's receipt for cash advances, and a written confession by Ann, and John hints that he might resort to suicide to preserve his reputation, a suggestion that terrifies Ann. John's plea to the cabal, which evokes the memory of the men's ancestors who fought in the Revolutionary War and the future of their children, is also less biting. Commencing work on the scripted version of the scene on Friday, 2 August Capra spent Saturday on the set without filming a shot. He resumed work on Monday with an overhauled script, and over the next three days shot the scene that appears in the film.

28. In the version of *Meet John Doe* released on 12 March 1941, John at this point observes: "I'm beginning to understand why decent people have had to take up guns and give up their lives to protect themselves from vultures like you. Yeah, vultures who are responsible for most of the bitterness in the world!" A justification for violence, the lines were deleted when Capra altered the ending of the film a few weeks later.

29. In the SS, this is one of ten blurbs from the newspaper that are read aloud by people in the audience. Most remarks simply anticipate Norton's accusation at the podium, but three provide supplemental information: that the police have been given Ann's signed confession, that she and Connell have been arrested, and that the mayor is convinced of John's guilt.

30. In the version released to theaters on 12 March 1941, John's remark was

preceded by a catcall from one man ("You dirty double-crosser!") and
followed by a series from another ("You five-and-ten phoney! You cheap
chiseler! Cheap racketeer!") These were excised after the film release,
perhaps to tone down the ugliness of the crowd's behavior at the convention.

31. In his handwritten notes, Capra added the reference to a crucifixion to
the SS.

32. This scene was not in the SS. From existing documents, it is unclear when
it was scripted and shot.

33. In the SS the scene is rather different. It opens with John weeping because
he was unable to get people to listen to him at the convention. Soaking a
handkerchief in hot water, the Colonel applies it to a bump on John's forehead. "*She* wasn't there, Colonel," John says, "Maybe, if she'd been
there—." Sympathetic, the Colonel remains silent throughout the scene.

34. The third montage deviates greatly from the SS, which only describes a
series of headlines announcing Norton's exposure of John, and two brief
vignettes: the discarding of John Doe dolls, and the tearing of John Doe
signs from buildings. However, the structure of the sequence as filmed—
including its subjective, expressionistic quality—closely conforms to
Slavko Vorkapich's script, dated 8 August.

35. In the version of the film released on 12 March 1941, the carolers sing
"Good King Wenceslaus" upon finishing "Silent Night." The second carol
was deleted before the revised version went into distribution in April.

36. In the SS, the scene of D.B. at home is followed by one in which Hammett, in his hotel room, is informed by his valet that he has a phone call
(presumably from Norton), and another in which Weston and Bennett are
staked out in a hotel room across from City Hall, waiting to see if John is
going to jump. The latter scene was never shot; the former was shot but cut
from the film.

37. This scene was shot on 23 March 1941, two weeks after *Meet John Doe*
had been released, as part of Capra's decision to bring the club members
from Millville to the City Hall roof for a revised ending of the film.

38. In the SS, the men have the following conversation as they walk:
D.B.: This is ridiculous! Whose idea was this? *(To Weston:)* Yours?
WESTON: If we don't stop him, he'll become a martyr.
D.B.: Absurd!

39. In the SS, a much more vocal, defensive D.B. breaks the silence.
NORTON: The poor fool! He had a vision of purifying the world. *(There*

is again silence. After a few minutes, he continues although no one is willing to refute him.) How'd he think he could do it? By a miracle? Change the nature of people? Expect them to embrace their neighbors with love and kindness in their hearts? Bah!

Capra penciled in the remarks by Weston and Bennett that follow.

40. In the SS, D.B. adds, "We'd certainly be made a laughing stock," and Weston's line is spoken by Hammett. Moreover, the exchange is placed after John's exit of the fourteenth-floor men's room, rather than before.

41. In the SS, the letter John deposits in the mail chute drops past Ann as she leans against the corner of a landing to catch her breath, and then lands at the bottom of the chute next to the Colonel on the first floor.

42. The complete SS for the remainder of the film is included in the variant endings reprinted in the next section.

Variant Endings

Existing records suggest that the alternative endings to *Meet John Doe* previewed by Capra and Riskin in the fall and winter of 1940–1941 were not widely divergent: all involved a decision by John to retreat from the ledge of the roof. But extant script material also suggests that the endings varied greatly in tone and projected a different future for subordinate characters. The following excerpts from the shooting script, and the revised ending scripted for reshooting on 3 January 1941, help to clarify Capra and Riskin's conception of, and perhaps confusion about, the ending during the course of the production of the film.

Shooting Script: The City Hall Roof

The following excerpt is from the City Hall roof scene in the 27 June shooting script, beginning with John's exit onto the roof where Norton and his associates are waiting. According to the daily production log, this passage was filmed at a Los Angeles icehouse on 12–14 August. The footage shot that day appears to have given Capra and Riskin a base to work from when crafting variations on the ending.

INT. TOWER

604. FULL SHOT: *The place is silent except for occasional scraping of feet as several of them move around. They continually refer to their watches. Finally, D.B. gives up impatiently.*

    D.B.: I give up. Whatever gave us an idea he'd attempt anything like this!

    HAMMETT: Guess you're right. I'm afraid the joke's on us. Let's go.

    D.B.: Hope nobody finds out we were here. We'd certainly be made a laughing stock.

    They all start to exit, when suddenly D.B. stops.

    D.B. *(whispering)*: Wait a minute.

    He puts his hand out and they all stop to listen. They hear footsteps, and back into the shadows.

605. MED. SHOT: *Shooting toward stairs. John appears around the bend and mounts the last few steps.*

606. MED. SHOT: *Of the huddled group. They watch breathlessly. In the darkness, their eyes dominate the scene.*

607. MED. SHOT: *Over their shoulders. As John, expressionless, his cigarette in his hand, crosses to the parapet, and looks out. He takes a puff of his ciagarette and exhales the smoke.*

608. MED. SHOT: *Of the huddled group. The Mayor is for stepping forward, but D.B. with an extended hand stops him, indicating for them to wait and see what happens.*

609. CLOSE UP: *Of John. He takes the envelope out of his pocket and withdraws a paper from it.*

610. CLOSE SHOT: *Of the group. Their eyes glued on him, tensely.*

611. CLOSE SHOT: *Of John. He reads the paper.*

612. CLOSE UP: *Over his shoulder. We read the beginning:*
    "To All John Does everywhere—"
    It is as far as we get, for the paper is folded over.

613. CLOSE UP: *Of John. As he continues to fold the paper, inserts it in the envelope—and slips it into his pocket again.*

INT. STAIRS

614. MED. SHOT: *Of Ann. Dragging herself effortfully up the stairs. She glances up and a hopeful light appears in her eyes, as she sees the top landing.*

INT. TOWER

615. CLOSE SHOT: *The group. Their eyes riveted on John. They feel the moment has come. Several of them glance toward D.B.*

616. WIDER SHOT: *To include them all, and John. He drops his cigarette on the ground, and, bending over, crushes it with his foot. Just as he straightens out again, D.B. speaks.*

D.B. *(restrained voice)*: I wouldn't do that if I were you, John.

617. CLOSE UP: *Of John. As he turns sharply, startled. He stares blankly at the five people.*

618. MED. SHOT: *Of the group. They move slightly forward and stop.*

D.B.: It'll do you no good.

619. CLOSE UP: *Of John. He continues to stare at them, strangely.*

620. WIDER SHOT: *To include them all.*

D.B.: The Mayor has policemen downstairs with instructions to remove any identification you might have on your person. You'll be buried in Potter's Field and accomplish nothing.

621. CLOSE SHOT: *Of John. After a moment, he speaks.*

JOHN *(in a sepulchral voice)*: I'm afraid you're wrong. I just mailed a copy of this letter to Mr. Connell.

622. MED. SHOT: *Of the group. Amazed that he thought of this, they feel themselves helpless.*

623. CLOSE UP: *Of John. His mouth screws up bitterly.*

JOHN: You stopped me once, Mr. Norton—but you're not going to do it again.

624. WIDER SHOT: *To include all. He holds them spellbound.*

JOHN *(wild look in his eyes)*: I'm glad you rats are here! You killed the John Doe movement but you're going to see it born all over again.

D.B. tries taking an authoritative tone.

D.B. *(his throat is dry)*: You better forget this foolishness, young man.

He steps forward as he speaks.

JOHN *(quickly—threateningly)*: I'd stay right there if I were you, Mr. Norton—unless you want to go overboard with me!

625. CLOSE UP: *Of John's face. His eyes have a wild, maniacal look in them.*

626. CLOSE UP: *Of D.B. He stares into John's eyes and a terrified expression covers his face.*

627. WIDER SHOT: *As D.B. instinctively backs up.*

JOHN: I may be a fake to the John Does today—*(grimly)* but tomorrow I won't be.

INT. LANDING TO TOWER

628. MED. SHOT: *As Ann practically has to pull herself up to the last step. Her face is wet from fever and exhaustion.*

ANN *(an outcry)*: John!

INT. TOWER

629. FULL SHOT: *As everyone, startled by the outcry, turns. Ann staggers into scene.*

ANN *(crying)*: John!

She rushes in and throws her arms around him.

ANN *(muffled sobs)*: Oh, John, darling. No! No!

630. CLOSE SHOT: *John and Ann. He stares down at her, blankly. Ann clutches him, her head buried in his shoulder.*

ANN *(muffled sobs)*: I won't let you. I love you, darling.

631. MED. SHOT: *Of the group. They remain motionless, watching.*

632. CLOSE SHOT: *John and Ann. She emits wracking sobs, then lifts her eyes up to his.*

ANN *(in a desperate plea)*: John. Please, John, listen to me. We'll start all over again, just you and I. It isn't too late. The John Doe movement isn't dead yet.

Suddenly, she becomes conscious of the others present, and she turns her head. CAMERA PANS *over to what she sees. The group of men watching, silently.*

CAMERA PANS *back to Ann. Her eyes widen slowly. She looks from them to John and back again, and her face takes on an excited, breathless look, as the reason for their being here becomes comprehensible to her.*

ANN *(excitedly)*: See, John, it isn't dead, or they wouldn't be here! They thought they killed it, but they didn't. It's still alive, darling! It's alive in *them*. They *kept* it alive. By being afraid of it. By coming here. Don't you see?

633. MED. SHOT: *Of the group, featuring D.B. He is awestricken by the scene he is witnessing.*

ANN'S VOICE: Don't you see what a great idea it is—if it can frighten big men like that.

634. CLOSE SHOT: *Ann and John. He continues to stand with his hands at his sides, looking at her, while she clings to him desperately. While she*

speaks, he turns his face from her and stares at the men.

ANN: They thought they killed it, but they didn't. They killed it in everybody but themselves! Sure, it should have been killed before. It was dishonest.

635. CLOSE UP: *Of John. He is staring strangely at the group of men—as slowly, gradually, the curtain is being lifted from his clouded brain.*

ANN'S VOICE: But we can start clean now. Just as you and I. It'll grow again, John. It'll grow big. And it'll be strong, because it'll be honest.

636. CLOSE UP: *Of Ann. Her strength is fast ebbing away. She clings to John more tenaciously.*

ANN *(last bit of effort)*: Oh, darling, if it's worth dying for, it's worth living for.

Then suddenly, as if the thought terrifies her.

ANN *(a frantic whisper)*: No, no. If you die, I want to die, too. *(her lips form the words—scarcely audible)* I love you, John.

Her eyes, slowly close. Her body goes limp. Unconsciously she clutches at him. John's arm goes out, bracing her.

CAMERA PAN *up to John's face. He is looking down at her, his eyes softening.*

637. CLOSE UP: *Of D.B. Obviously touched. The hardness has vanished from his face entirely. There is a suspicion of moisture in his eyes.*

638. WIDER SHOT: *Quietly, John bends down and lifts Ann in his arms. Without a further glance at the men, he walks out of the scene. All heads turn to follow him.*

639. MED. SHOT: *The group stands, transfixed. They have gone through an emotional experience which leaves them speechless.*

Shooting Script: Epilogue

Appended to the 27 June shooting script was a "tag" scene, set on a street in an unidentified neighborhood. There is no record that the scene was ever shot.

EXT. A NEIGHBORHOOD STREET. DAY.

640. MED. SHOT: *Of sidewalk. Organ grinder is at the curb. Children play on the sidewalks. Housewives carry market baskets.*

CAMERA PANS *over to a small store. In front of it John stands smearing paste on the window with a brush. He lays the brush down, and picks up a rolled sheet of paper. Just as he is about to unroll it, Ann enters, eyes sparkling, her arms laden down with bundles.*

ANN *(excited)*: I got two people in the neighborhood to say they'll come.

JOHN: Swell.

ANN *(holding up packages)*: And look! The makings of a stew—all donated.

JOHN: Wonderful.

While they speak, John has been unfolding the sheet—and it is a hand-painted sign, reading "JOHN DOE CLUB." Ann keeps the packages and starts to help him.

641. WIDER SHOT: *As pedestrians go by. Upon seeing the sign, they roar with laughter.*

AD LIBS: Hey, get a load of this!

A John Doe Club!

You must be screwy, buddy!

The crowd grows bigger and the laughter becomes louder.

642. MED. SHOT: *Ann and John turn to the crowd and smile at them. John waves his hand in the most friendly fashion.*

From inside the store the Colonel comes. He wears an apron and has a pot in one hand and a ladle in the other. He stares belligerently at the laughing crowd.

CAMERA *moves down to him and he looks right into the camera as he speaks.*

COLONEL: Listen, you Heelots. I'm giving you just one more chance.

FADE OUT

Revised Ending: 2 January 1941

Having suspended production of *Meet John Doe* uncertain how to end the film, Capra reassembled key cast members at the Los Angeles icehouse for additional filming on 3 January 1941. Added to the original City Hall roof scene now are the figures of Connell and the Colonel, new dialogue for John and Norton, and an extended argument by Ann. The script fragment reprinted below was dated 2 January. Capra appears to have experimented with different permutations on this ending over the next two and one-half months. The final ending, however, was to require additional filming.

ANN: John!

She rushes in and throws her arms around him.

ANN: Oh, John darling. No! No! I won't let you! I love you darling! *(desperately)* John, please, please don't give up! We'll start all over again—just you and I. It isn't too late! The John Doe movement isn't dead yet! *(she sees the men)* See, John, it isn't dead—or they wouldn't be here! It's alive in *them!* That's why they came up here! They're keeping it alive by being afraid of it!

She clings to John, pleading desperately.

ANN: Sure, it should have been killed—it was dishonest. But we can start clean now. And it'll grow, John. It'll grow big because it'll be honest this time. It'll be clean. *(desperately)* Oh, darling, if it's worth dying for, it's worth living for.

Throughout her plea John has intermittently stared at her—and at the men, his befuddled mind struggling to comprehend her torrent of words.

ANN: Please, John.

She looks up at his face, seeking some sign of his relenting—but she finds none.

CLOSE UP: *Of Ann, who still clinging to him, lays her cheek on his chest— and lifts her eyes heavenward.*

ANN *(a murmured prayer)*: Oh, please, God—help me.

FLASH

Of the men—as they stare transfixed, waiting breathlessly.

CLOSE UP: *Of Ann. Suddenly she stares before her—as a divine inspiration comes to her. Her eyes light up with a wide, ecstatic fire.*

TWO SHOT: *Ann and John. Ann turns and glances up at John's face.*

ANN *(tensely)*: John!

She takes his face in her two hands and turns it to her.

ANN: John darling, look at me! You want to be honest, don't you? Well, you don't have to die to keep the John Doe idea alive! Some one already died for that once! The first John Doe. And He's kept that idea alive for nearly two thousand years. *(with sincere conviction)* It was He who kept it alive in *them*—and He'll go on keeping it alive forever and always! For every John

Doe movement these men kill, a new one will be borne [sic]! *(ecstatically)* That's why those bells are ringing, John. They're calling to *us*—*not* to give up—but to keep on fighting! To keep on pitching! Don't you see, darling? This is not time to quit!

CLOSE UP: *Of John. (To inter-cut with above.) While she speaks, his eyes are glued on her in profound absorption. Finally, when she has finished, his face slowly lifts upwards—into his eyes comes the light of understanding, and his whole face brightens up in a warm, beatific glow. (With the raising of his head, the music also rises—suggesting the emergence from darkness and confusion— to light and understanding.)*

CLOSE UP: *Of Ann. Her eyes riveted to his face. She sees his expression—and knows her prayer has been answered. She throws her arms about him—and holds on.*

ANN *(reverently)*: Oh, dear God—thank you.

Then having let go, her strength leaves her—and as her eyelids slowly shut, she collapses limply at his feet.

MED. SHOT: *As John lifts her into his arms, draws her closely to him, and kisses her cheek. He then glances toward the men—and a faint smile appears on his face.*

JOHN *(warmly)*: Merry Christmas!

As he starts out with Ann in his arms, the men remain transfixed, watching.

MED. SHOT: *At door. (To inter-cut with Ann's speech). The Colonel and Connell come running in, breathlessly. They hear her voice—and stop to listen in respectful awe.*

WIDER SHOT: *At door. As John carrying Ann reaches Connell and the Colo- nel. Their faces are lit up in expressions of exultation. All they can do is murmur "John," and "Gosh, Long John." A smile appears on John's face as he exits.*

CLOSER SHOT: *Of Connell and the Colonel. They watch, exultantly, as John exits. Suddenly they hear D.B.'s voice.*

D.B.'S VOICE: Connell!

They turn—as D.B. enters to them. Connell glares belligerently at him.

D.B. *(quietly—sincerely)*: He mailed a copy of a letter to you, telling the whole story. Will you come to see me soon as you get it. I want to publish it. I want all the John Does to know the truth.

Connell's belligerent expression slowly vanishes and his face lights up happily.

CONNELL *(emotionally)*: Gosh. That's swell, D.B. *(holds out his hand)* Merry
   Christmas!

D.B. smiles and murmurs: "Merry Christmas."

CLOSE UP: *Of the Colonel. He grins joyously.*

COLONEL *(gaily)*: Well, looks like I gotta give the Heelots one more chance.

Revised ending: 12 March 1941

Dialogue transcripts taken from the version of *Meet John Doe* released on 12 March 1941 indicate that the ending composed on 2 January had been scaled back considerably. Nevertheless, Norton's statement of conversion remained in the film. After Ann's plea to John, the soundtrack concluded as follows:

COLONEL *(laughing)*: Long John!

D.B.: Connell! He sent you a copy of a letter. As soon as you get it, I wish you'd come and see me. I want to publish it on the front page of the *Bulletin,* because I want all the John Does to know the truth.

CHORUS *(humming and singing, off)*:
Sing, oh, sing the joyous song,
Hope is our eternal guide,
Brothers all we fear no wrong,
Marching onward side by side,
Let us sing our joyful song.
My country tis of thee,
Of thee I sing!

Contexts, Reviews, and Commentaries

Reports and Recollections

Frank Capra's celebrity status as a director ensured that the production of *Meet John Doe* would be widely covered in the press. Interest was compounded within the film industry, moreover, by Capra and Riskin's attempt to embark on an independent production. The importance of that attempt was the subject of an April 1940 editorial in *Film Bulletin,* the trade journal of independent exhibitors in America.

Lewis Jacobs's report on Capra's working methods first appeared in *Theatre Arts* in January 1941, three months prior to the release of the film. It offers a detailed account of the shooting of the police station sequence in *Meet John Doe* and presents a portrait of Capra (meticulous and immersed in details, yet a rule-breaker and risk-taker) that is very much in keeping with the director's reputation during this period.

As co-owner of Frank Capra Productions, Robert Riskin was active in the financial side of the company's first project as well as writing its screenplay. Riskin is profiled and interviewed in an article by *New York Times* reporter Theodore Strauss on the occasion of Riskin's arrival in New York to handle the distribution arrangements for *Meet John Doe.*

Less public a document is a letter Capra wrote in response to a viewer who had attended the Los Angeles premiere of *Meet John Doe* and had felt personally betrayed by its depiction of the John Doe club members as mindless sheep. Capra received a good deal of mail from moviegoers about *Meet John Doe,* much of it highly appreciative, but a substantial portion registered dismay at the ending, and a few provided detailed critiques. Written with great passion the day after the premiere, the letter

Capra responds to here was of the last kind. Capra waited to reply until he had a revised ending, and his letter describes what he hoped to accomplish in *Meet John Doe*. He calls attention to a religious impulse behind the ending, but confesses that he may not have gotten his ideas across in the film.

Capra's retrospective account of the production, excerpted from his 1971 autobiography, however, points to another ambition beyond that detailed in his letter: the desire to win critical approval for his work. Capra colorfully recalls his experience on the project, from his decision to embark on an independent production in November 1939 through his final re-editing of the film eighteen months later. Occasionally inaccurate with respect to minor details (in the book's introduction, Capra disavows responsibility for historical precision), the passage nevertheless provides a candid account of Capra's professional, financial, and psychological investment in the project, and the insecurities the production generated.

An Inspiring Experiment

Considerable Hollywood interest is centered on the experiment going on at Warner Bros. Burbank studio, where Frank Capra and Robert Riskin have set up offices and are preparing for their forthcoming production, "The Life and Death of John Doe."

No ordinary independent unit, this. It has been formed solely with Capra-Riskin money—drawn from their own investments and in the form of personal loans from banks. The stages, props and production crew will be furnished by Warners, but Capra and Riskin will pay all the other bills, including cast salaries. Neither will draw a red cent of salary until the picture is completed, released and the returns start rolling in.

For years now this pair of artists have been turning out pictures that were both artistic and commercial successes. They have every reason to anticipate another hit. Yet, they are gambling with that intangible "if"—"If the public will like it."

The spectacle of two men of the calibre of Capra and Riskin, who could write their own tickets—in four figures—with any major studio, deliberately setting out to stand or fall on their own individual merits and with their own money, is not a familiar one in Hollywood.

There aren't many like them around Hollywood, but there are plenty of capable production people whose talents are being literally crushed by the mass methods that have taken hold of film making during the past decade or so. "Speed up production" is the cry today—and four out of five pictures show it. The accepted attitude is turn them out in a hurry and pray that one will click. It takes courage to resist that system and very few in Hollywood have enough fortitude to fight back.

The Capra-Riskin experiment is inspiring. There is always that possibility that their "John Doe" will not click, but we're betting on them. Their's is the sort of spirit and courage that could carry motion pictures to greater heights. If only there were more Capras and Riskins!

From *Film Bulletin*, 6 April 1940.

Film Directors at Work: Frank Capra

Lewis Jacobs

rank Capra is one of the rare directors in Hollywood whose name appears above those of his stars. Sober, judicious, he has definite and logical ideas about his work. "There must be a reason behind a picture—and that reason must be the kernel of the story. To me that is axiomatic." He is particularly distrustful of the Hollywood formula and "factory method" of turning out pictures and likes to break all the rules.

To prove the success of his credo, Capra lists the productions which convinced him that breaking the rules was responsible not only for his making better pictures but for their paying greater dividends. "*Lady for a Day* was one of the first productions in my new order of things. They told me that the story was impossible, that actresses past middle age could not hold the interest of an audience. The box-office proved they were wrong." When he made *It Happened One Night*, "they told us we were crazy." But when the picture was released, the Academy of Motion Picture Arts and Science awarded it a flock of gold statuettes. He was told that race-horse pictures never made money. He made *Broadway Bill*. It, too, was a smash at the box-office. Both *Mr. Deeds Goes to Town* and *Mr. Smith Goes to Washington* met with the same objections as *It Happened One Night*, and again they were disproved.

Now once more Capra stakes his reputation in order to "make what I like and then hope and pray that other people will like it too." His latest undertaking, *Meet John Doe*, is an independent venture, financed by himself and his scenarist. Capra has mortgaged his house and farm. Robert Riskin, who has worked with him for many years, "has put all his stocks and bonds into the kitty in order to make the kind of movie we believe in."

When you face Mr. Capra on the set of Warner Brothers Studio where he is shooting *Meet John Doe*, you see a short, stocky man with a square face and olive complexion topped by thinning black hair. The most striking thing about him whle he is directing is his complete immersion in the film problem. He is

From *Theatre Arts* (January 1941): 43–48.

seldom to be found in the chair marked "Director." Instead, he is continually roving about, seeking ways and means to heighten the scene. Every set-up absorbs his attention.

His effort is endless to make every detail significant and to maintain a continuous pace, even in short and relatively minor scenes, such as that in a police station toward the end of *Meet John Doe*. While the crew sets up, Capra is busy placing the actors. The police captain is in the foreground, sitting with his back to the camera, playing solitaire. Opposite him is Jimmy Gleason, a drunk in a battered derby, drinking milk. Against the wall Capra groups Barbara Stanwyck, crying, in the arms of her mother, Spring Byington. It is raining outside and a reflection of the drops is made to fall across their faces. Capra signals an assistant that the effect is too hard—"Soften it."

A moment later he is seated in Jimmy Gleason's chair meditating on a piece of business. He experiments with the policeman's hat to have it throw a significant shadow on the wall beside Miss Stanwyck. Then he whispers to her to get her into the mood for tears. He goes to the camera, and while he watches through the lens, the players rehearse their action. What he sees dissatisfies him; he is off the camera and, with viewfinder in hand, roams the set for a better angle. Finally he has the camera re-set on a track for a dolly shot, and again the actors go through the scene. This time he studies it through the moving camera. 'This is it!' he says, pleased.

While the crew prepares for the take, Capra is off again, surveying, suggesting, making last-minute changes, equally concerned with technicians and players. Throughout he speaks calmly, in low tones, and gives his instructions directly rather than relaying them through an assistant, the usual procedure.

Finally the scene is set. "Ready, boys?" asks Capra. His assistant blows the 'all quiet' whistle. Capra whispers, "turn 'em over." Then, alert, on tiptoe, he cues the cameraman to begin his dolly forward. The policeman, who has already started his solitaire, interrupts his game to turn on the radio. Capra signals his dialogue director, who speaks the announcement supposed to come from the radio. At its close, it is Capra who again cues the policeman as to the exact moment to turn off the broadcast.

Almost simultaneously—so timed is the action—the camera pans to the drunk. Capra cues him and Gleason lifts a half-filled bottle of milk and says, "well, you can chalk up another for the Pontius Pilates." Before that speech is finished, Capra has cued Barbara Stanwyck so that when the camera and microphone pan and dolly in to her, her sobs can be heard before we see that she is crying. She speaks through her tears, and the camera continues to hold her after her speech is finished, while the microphone picks up only the sound of the rain as it beats against the window.

Suddenly Capra calls, "cut! Try it again. Much faster." The scene is repeated. Again Capra is dissatisfied. "Still too slow," he says.

The camera moves back to first position, Capra confers with Miss Stanwyck. The "all quiet" whistle blows. The shot is retaken—swiftly, smoothly. At its end, Capra says, "that's about how it should run, boys. O.K."

The script girl indicates the third take as the one to be printed; the crew prepare the next set-up. Capra kisses Barbara for her good performance; she can't stop crying, having gone overboard on her tears.

All this has been done with a minimum of noise and motion. Although there seems to be a tremendous store of energy in Capra's lithe movements, it is never unleashed in the form of harangues, temperament or jitters. He transmits his instructions with so much reserve and regard for others that crew and cast act similarly. By his own example, he seems to draw the best out of everyone. He is a director who displays absolutely no exhibitionism.

"The pictures I direct," Capra says, "are practically finished before I go on the set. I work right along with Robert Riskin, the writer. It takes three times as long to complete a workable script as it takes to shoot the picture. Even then I don't consider it iron-clad. I'm apt to change any sequence or incident, if it doesn't feel right to me when it gets before the cameras."

What concerns Capra most in a movie is the story. "I have some general rules that I abide by religiously in selecting a story. My first rule is that it must have charm. This is pretty hard to define, but if a tale leaves you with a glow of satisfaction, it has the quality I seek. Second, it must have interesting characters that do the things human beings do—or would like to do if they had the courage and opportunity. My third and last requisite is that the members of the cast must in real life be the nearest thing possible to the characters they are to portray, so that their performance will require the least acting. Give me these three things and a lot of story formulas that I can violate, and I am completely happy."

Mr. Riskin Hits the Road

Theodore Strauss

Despite a private conviction that no one, with the exception of a few fanciful folk who always see idealized portraits in mirrors, continued to believe that the "artistic temperament" is directly opposed to everyday common sense, the notion is still expressed with distressing frequency. Atavisms of this sort, we suppose, are hard to stamp out and the fond belief that the artistic temperament is a state of exalted lunacy probably will remain current as long as cats can look at queens and schoolmarms read Swinburne. But whenever any one repeats it to us hereafter we shall retort: "Oh yeah? Well, look at Mr. Riskin. . . ."

Robert Riskin is the full name. As practically everyone knows, he is by achievement and personal preference, a writing man. With Frank Capra, the director, he has in the past nine years turned through his typewriter the yarns for "American Madness," "Lady for a Day," "It Happened One Night," "Broadway Bill," "Mr. Deeds Goes to Town," "Lost Horizon," "You Can't Take It With You" and the unreleased "Meet John Doe," of which no one, and especially Mr. Riskin, will give you a hint but of which the rumor daily grows larger. These are Mr. Riskin's credentials and good ones, too. By any standards they have been tiptop entertainment.

But if Mr. Riskin falls into the category of mad artists there is daylight in his madness. Although he is able to set a group of characters moving believably across the pages of a scenario, he is also, when need be, as hardheaded a drummer as ever hit the road to peddle his wares. When Mr. Riskin blew into town a week ago it was not merely to read scripts and look over the current crop of plays. He had come on a business trip to drive a bargain on the distribution and promotion of "Meet John Doe," on which Frank Capra is presently putting the finishing touches on the West Coast.

A crisp fellow, Mr. Riskin. Sitting in the luxuriously appointed Radio City quarters of David O. Selznick, which he is using for the nonce, he seemed as dapper and assured as any promotion expert. Now and then, for a moment of indecision, his eyes would search the ceiling as he swiveled back and forth in his

From *The New York Times*, 26 January 1941.

chair. But usually his mind worked at trigger speed and without pause. It will take a shrewd tradesman to outwit Mr. Riskin.

As it happens, Mr. Riskin knew a little about the "strange and mysterious" world of business long before he ever began writing scripts in Hollywood. Beginning at 17 he produced some fifty-one short subjects for a venturesome shirt manufacturer and later, during the middle Twenties, he produced plays as well as wrote them on Broadway. Thus, when a year ago he and Capra finally decided to become an independent producing unit, most of the furniture for the "front office" was installed in Mr. Riskin's hat.

It was a little dizzying at first, Mr. Riskin admitted. Simultaneously with the writing of the script, Mr. Riskin was also concerned—as was Mr. Capra—with arrangements for the financing of the film; there were the rental arrangements for the use of the Warner Brothers studio and other facilities; there were budgets and shooting schedules, players to be dickered for—and finally, the picture to be made. Despite the fact that both of the co-producers are inclined to putter interminably with a film, it was begun and completed on schedule and expenses were kept within the budget. Mr. Riskin, the businessman, is very proud of that.

The reasons are several. First of all, if the Capra-Riskin outfit succeeds in its lone venture it may encourage other writers and directors to cut their studio moorings likewise. Secondly, the efficiency with which "Meet John Doe" was completed is another refutation to an old adage among Hollywood impresarios that writers are an essentially crack-brained and totally un-reliable breed.

Asked why he and Capra decided on their independent venture, Mr. Riskin hesitated. He didn't know precisely, he said, because he and Capra had always been allowed the most complete freedom of action on the Columbia lot and elsewhere and sometimes during the filming of "Meet John Doe," with all its contingent headaches, he was at a loss to justify their rash procedure.

"But it was the sense of freedom, rather than actual freedom itself," he reasoned, "which led us to do it. Also there was the adventurous side to it, which one doesn't feel when working on a stated salary. We were just a pair of dice-shooters at heart."

At this point Mr. Riskin began to muse softly on his own authorial idiosyncrasies and on the writing animal in general. Ordinarily, after he and Capra have seized upon an idea, the two retreat to some nearby watering-place or tug at trout while they discuss pivotal points of action. After that Mr. Riskin retires to his own corner and hammers out a tentative first draft which usually emerges as a veritable tome, "long as hell." Then begin the arguments between the two over the script, but so closely are their artistic points of view allied that the debates usually concern comparatively minor detail. After all these years away from Broadway, however, Mr. Riskin says that in construction of the scenario he still finds himself thinking in terms of first and second act curtains.

For the moment, however, neither Mr. Riskin nor Mr. Capra is concentrating on further efforts.

"We've got to get 'Meet John Doe' out of our hair first," said Mr. Riskin.

Letter from Frank Capra
to Viewer

April 8, 1941

My dear Mr. Gluck:

I am extremely grateful to you for writing me that interesting letter about your reactions to "MEET JOHN DOE."

The end of the picture is my own—that is, I'm responsible for it. You evidently missed the point I was trying to make, and it's not your fault, it's mine.

Briefly, my point was this. The Golden Rule is the only law or commandment that can make for happiness. Up to the convention the John Does were following it and their lives were happier. By contrast I wanted to show them what happened when they listened and followed human leadership, the greedy men after power whom people are wont to listen to. Also I wanted to show them an example of what was happening in the world when people listened and believed in this type. They were turned into a howling mob, their peace and happiness shot to pieces. And then I wanted to hold out hope for them at the end, if they understood and were willing to follow spiritual leadership.

Your point is that the John Does wouldn't have turned on John Doe. You say you wouldn't do it, and neither would any other John Does. I say the world today is a pretty good example that they do do it.

People have urged me to let John Doe jump off the roof. My argument against that is that his blood would be on the souls of the John Does.

But evidently my point is missed, or at least I missed it, and perhaps I was wrong to start with. Anyway, I have put a new ending on the picture in which some John Does who had faith in the man are the ones who keep him from jumping. I think it will suit you better, although perhaps you still won't like it.

The picture has caused a great deal of healthy discussion. Please know that I am grateful for your excellent comments.

Sincerely yours,
Frank Capra

From *Meet John Doe* correspondence files, Frank Capra Collection, Wesleyan University Cinema Archives.

Five Endings in Search of an Audience

Frank Capra

Mr. *Smith* ended my contract with Cohn and Columbia. It was time to leave. David O. Selznick offered me office space at his Selznick-International studios in Culver City. I accepted and moved out.

Thirteen years before I had entered Columbia's Poverty Row doors as a bitter, discouraged run-of-the-mill Sennett gag man. Now I was leaving Columbia's major studio doors as Hollywood's acclaimed number one filmmaker. My first year's salary at Columbia—for producing, writing, and directing five feature-length films—was under ten thousand dollars. My last year's salary (plus percentage profits) was over three hundred thousand dollars for making *one* film. Time to strike out on my own. But I needed a partner—a gambling, sympatico, creative spirit—to join me in my independent film company. Robert Riskin was a natural. But he was off making a name for himself with Sam Goldwyn.

Before making a move I don't consult astrologers, fortune tellers, or Ouija boards. And yet, as I have noted before, whatever happens to me seems to happen for the best. The rose-tinted glasses of a super-optimist could be one explanation—"Ill wind" . . . "Silver lining" . . . "Bright side" . . . ad nauseum. Another, the rationalizing of a super-ego; unwilling to admit defeat. When you're a combination of both, you say, "It always happens for the best"—implying you are the pet protégé of some benign mystic power.

Whatever it is, I recommend it highly; for when I approached Bob Riskin about a partnership, I expected a turn down. But no. He agreed, joyfully. Even though, as the major stockholder, my word would be final. Creatively, as well as socially, there was a psychological affinity between Riskin and me, an afflatus that quickened creative impulses, stirred up wavelets of sympatico ideas that reinforced each other's crests rather than canceled them out.

And so, in August, 1939, the State of California issued incorporation papers to Frank Capra Productions, Inc. (F.C.P.). Riskin owned one-third of the stock, I

From *The Name Above the Title* (New York: Macmillan, 1971), pp. 294–297, 302–305.

owned two-thirds. Expenses and initial investments were shared proportionately. My long cherished dream—in business for myself—was a legal reality. "Good luck!" messages poured in; some sent rabbit feet. Harry Cohn was a hold-out. His telegram: "You'll be back."

The team of Capra-Riskin was a one-two punch with negotiating power. Offers from major studios came fast—financing, profit-splitting, three-picture deals; six-, ten-picture propositions. The most tantalizing proposals came from the prominent independents. Samuel Goldwyn wanted the Capra and Goldwyn companies to join up with Howard Hughes in a new production-distribution set-up. David O. Selznick proposed a simlar combine: Selznick-Hughes-Capra. But neither Riskin nor I wanted any part of long-term contracts again. What we demanded were one-picture-at-a-time arrangements, first come first served, with any major distributing outlet, and no profit-splitting or outside approvals of subject, cast, or budget. These were hard terms. The offers cooled off.

But there was one nonconforming, irrepressible spirit among the studio heads—Jack Warner. Jack was a jokester, a self-confessed wit who was loved and laughed at more for his garrulous non-wit. But beneath his "jokes" Jack Warner ran a taut, well-disciplined major studio. The first to introduce sound, the frère Warners were among the first to develop a stable of great stars, including Bette Davis, Humphrey Bogart, Edward G. Robinson, James Cagney, Olivia de Havilland, Errol Flynn, Paul Muni, Ronald Reagan, Kay Francis, Ann Sheridan, Jane Wyman, and Rudy Vallee.

By reputation, Jack Warner was a martinet, not noted for giving aid and succor to independent mavericks. Hence, eyebrows raised all over town when Jack offered us a one-picture proposition on terms far better than any previously imagined. In essence, this was the deal: Warner Brothers would advance all costs for production, prints, and advertising and—providing Capra and Riskin donated their time and invested one hundred thousand dollars in cash—Frank Capra Productions would own the film—and *all the profits!* Only Seward made a better deal when he bought Alaska. It had to be one of Jack Warner's unpredictable whims. Perhaps he wanted to find out if there really was a Frank Capra, and if there was, he wanted to see how he made pictures. Oh, I forgot his most important concession: He asked for no approval of story, budget, or east. Riskin and I swallowed, blinked, and asked Jack Warner, "Where's the pen?"

And what film story would we choose for our first independent production? We toyed with Rostand's *Cyrano de Bergerac* and with the *Life of Shakespeare*. I say toyed, because I had raced my motor many times before about filming some costumed, historical classic, but when time came to put it in gear my instinct said: "Whoa! Charlie. Contemporary Americana is your blue-plate special."

Well, up popped a story as American as baseball. One day in November, 1939, while sitting in my office in David Selznick's Culver City studio (two months before our deal with Warners), a writer friend, Robert Presnell, walked in with a long treatment he had written with Richard Connell. They called it *The Life and Death of John Doe*. I read it. A bell rang. Riskin read it. A carillon chimed. We bought it before Presenell left the office.

In a matter of days, Riskin and I headed for the desert and lucky La Quinta where the muses were kind and mockingbirds and linnets darted in and out of smoke trees and flowering bougainvillea. Lu came along with little Lulu; Frankie remained in school at the Urban Military Academy. But Riskin was alone—still the most eligible bachelor in Hollywood; his recent romance with wonder-gal Carole Lombard had phffft! as W. W. would say.

Outside our red-tiled adobe bungalow, sitting in shorts, at card tables strewn with yellow pads, Bob and I hammered out scene after scene. Enthusiasm bubbled; ideas outraced pencils. Each new film was a new Arabian Nights adventure. Each evoked its own moments of hot excitement.

In one of those moments I said to Riskin: "For all the tea in China, Bob— this'll be the greatest film we ever made."

"Down, boy, down!" he laughed. "We haven't got a finish yet."

"We'll find a finish. And when we do, a few highbrow critics are going to eat under-done crow."

"Oh, oh. Now I'm worried," said Riskin. He hummed Cole Porter's "I've Got You Under My Skin."

Were critics getting under my skin? Well, let us say that because I had not come into films via the footlights I had no preconditioned reverence for the elegant cognoscenti. In fact, I thought they were getting by with murder.

In the United States a newspaper is a private enterprise in a free country. So is a restaurant, department store, Ford agency, or theater. Each sells a specific commodity to the public. Now let's take New York City. What metropolitan daily dares run a daily column which tells its readers: "Stay away from the Twenty-One Club, the food is lousy," or "Macy's dresses shrink in the rain," or "the new Ford is a pile of junk?" None.

But just seven drama critics can close a theater on opening night if a majority of them publicly print thumbs-down ukases which state, in effect: "The new show at the Winter Garden stinks. Save your money."

Later in life I became a fishing pal of Harold Ross, publisher of *The New Yorker* Magazine. "Harold," I asked him, sitting around a fire, "why do you hate Hollywood?"

"I don't hate Hollywood. But who reads our magazine? Mostly the horsy set of the East. It tickles their vanity to read that your Hollywood heroes are really spavined bums."

"Harold, how would you like it if I had an actor, on the screen, pick up your magazine in a dentist's office then throw it in the waste basket, saying: "That's the crummiest magazine I ever read?"

He laughed merrily. "I'd probably sue the hell out of you. But go ahead and do it, and I'll print why you did it."

Did I ever shoot the scene? No. I realized that if there were no critics, show business would have to create them. For the manic outbursts of squealing joy or tearful despondency with which we "read our notices," are the very heart of the mystique of the theater. We caress the notices, save them, press them in clipping files, to read them later to our children in pathetic attempts to impress them that we, too, were once somebody.

No, it wasn't the existence of critics that really riled me. It was their super-cilious attitude that got under my skin. I had made seven smash hits in a row. Had I performed that feat on Broadway I would have been canonized. Shubert Alley would have been renamed Via Capra. As it was, not one of my last three films—*Lost Horizon, You Can't Take It with You,* and *Mr. Smith Goes to Washington*—had made the New York Critics Annual Poll of their selected "ten best" films.

So I can truthfully say that it was the box-office customers who made Frank Capra whatever he was or is. I was not invited into motion pictures, nor did I enjoy special favor of finance, nepotism, or critical influence. I simply did my thing with films and the people responded.

And yet, and yet—an ego like mine needed—nay, required—the plaudits of sophisticated criticism. Childlike, creativity thirsts for the heady wine of the connoisseur's acclaim. The "Capra-corn" barbs had pierced the outer blubber.

And so, *Meet John Doe,* my first completely independent film venture, was *aimed* at winning critical praises.

Hitler's strong-arm success against democracy was catching. Little "führers" were springing up in America, to proclaim that freedom was weak, sterile, passé. The "new wave" was Blood Power! Destroy the weak, the Jews, the blacks; destroy Christianity and its old-hat commandment "Love thy neighbor." Arriba the Herrenvolk!

Riskin and I would astonish the critics with contemporary realities: the ugly face of hate; the power of uniformed bigots in red, white, and blue shirts; the agony of disillusionment, and the wild dark passions of mobs. We would give them a brutal story that would make Ben Hecht sound like Edgar Guest. [. . .]

[. . .] Making a film out of *Meet John Doe* proved to be as full of surprises as breaking a half-rogue wild stallion to the saddle. Precisely when I thought it would make one of the world's great show horses, it would leap and buck and throw me over the fence. It was still untamed when, with blinkers on it, we shoved the maverick into a theater for its opening night.

However, in the beginning it had been docile and full of promise. For instance, seldom does a filmmaker ever assemble his dream cast—his druthers for every role from the world-wide firmament of stars. That rarity happened in *Meet John Doe*. For the part of "John Doe"—a lanky hobo, an ex-bush league pitcher with a glass arm—I had but one choice: Gary Cooper. I wouldn't have made the picture without him. But I had no script for him to read when I asked him to play the part. Surprisingly, he said: "It's okay, Frank. I don't need a script." His wife, Rocky, put it this way: "John Ford sent Gary a script of *Stagecoach*. Gary was on the fence about it. I read it, and advised him to turn it down. *Stagecoach!* It made a star out of John Wayne, but we turned it down."

Moreover, all the other star names in my first-choice dream cast—Barbara Stanwyck, Edward Arnold, Walter Brennan, James Gleason, and Spring Byington—were available and signed for the film. And, as with Cooper, they all accepted their roles before reading the script—which is about the highest compliment a director can be paid.

Long before we began principal photography, *Meet John Doe* had stirred up world-wide press speculation; primarily for two reasons: First, it was news when a writer and director put their own money into a film; most of the film scriveners called it "brash," "reckless." And second, we made news because we wouldn't tell the press what the story of John Doe was all about.

As for being reckless, all Riskin and I could lose was our shirts, but that was small disaster when film company presidents stood in line holding fur coats to cover our backs. But making the press privy to our story was another matter. Not that we played hard-to-get as a publicity gimmick, or stole a nook from Garbo's seclusion ("I vant to be alone") bit. *John Doe* was a secret to the press because it was still a secret to *us*. To admit it publicly might give Jack Warner and the Bank of America second thoughts.

Our story problem was self-inflicted. To convince important critics that not every Capra film was written by Pollyanna, and that I could handle hard-nosed brutality with the best of the groin-kickers, Riskin and I had written ourselves into a corner. We knew we were loaded with entertainment; we had a startling opening and a powerful development that rose inexorably to a spectacular climactic wow. But—we had no acceptable SOLUTION to our story. The first two acts were solid; the third act was a wet sock.

We had abandoned our usual formula—a sane, honest "man of the people," thrust into a confrontation with the forces of evil, wins out with his innate goodness. This time our hero was a bindle staff, a drifting piece of human flotsam as devoid of ideals as he was of change in his pocket. When the forces of evil tempt him—fine; no skin off his nose if they call him John Doe, the "Messiah of goodness," in exchange for steaks and fancy clothes. But—discovering he is being used to delude and defraud thousands of innocent people, he rebels. When he tries to tell the deluded people that he had been a fraud, but now believes as they do, the people turn on him, try to tear him limb from limb. So far so good. But now, what happens to John Doe? to the thousands that believed? to the forces of evil? We didn't know. Up to there the story wrote itself; beyond that point, it balked.

We called in Myles Connolly, my friend and severest critic—but also my ace-in-the-hole story constructionist. Connolly suggested several possible endings but admittedly, he, too, was stumped. We called in Jules Furthman, Hollywood's most sought after story "doctor." Furthman—a noted rarebook collector, he inoculated me with the bug—was in demand not for us inventive originality, but for his encyclopedic memory of past authors and their story plots. Filmmakers would tell him their story hang-ups; nine times out of ten, without recourse to research, Furthman would say: "Oh, that plot was used by Shakespeare—or Chekhov, De Maupassant, Sheridan, Goethe, Kipling, Stevenson, Conrad, Cooper, or one of a host of other authors—"and this is the way *he* solved it." Plagiarism? We like to call it borrowing.

Anyway, "Doctor" Furthman listened; then hemmed, hawed, dredged the fathomless depths of his recall for a plot like ours—novels, plays, poems; legends, myths, sagas; the New Testament, the Old, the Apocryphy; Egyptian writers, Sumerian, Sanscrit; hieroglyphics, cuneiform, the Rosetta Stone. Nothing. Annoyed, "Doc" Furthman fell back on quackery. "Hell, it's simple," he declared. "You guys can't find an ending to your story because you got no story in the *first* place."

Riskin, Connolly, and I threw him out on his ear. His diagnosis was enough to put us all in the hospital. The picture was cast, we had a starting date, our own money was on the line—and he tells us we've got no story in the first place.

Meet John Doe's inside joke was on the bizarre side—"The Mystery of the Unsolved Ending," we called it. It is astonishing, but true; *Meet John Doe* missed becoming a lasting film classic because *we couldn't end it!* For seven-eighths of the film, Riskin and I felt we had made The Great American Motion Picture; but in the last eighth, it fizzled into The Great American Letdown.

It was mea culpa, of course. From the first day of script-writing, Riskin fretted about the ending. I didn't. "Stop worrying, Bob. The picture will dictate its own ending."

"But Frank, it's murder to start shooting a picture without knowing how it's going to end."

"Haven't you heard? Everything happens for the best. Wait and see."

Bob waited, but didn't see much. In desperation—setting some kind of a pointless record—I was to photograph five different endings, and then try them out on theater audiences; all collapsed like punctured balloons. Why? Why did the hundreds of scenes integrate into a jigsaw puzzle that had greatness written all over it except for one gaping hole no last scene would plug up? I never found out why.

Of course, the press had a field day with the new phenomenon of playing musical chairs with film endings. Jay Carmody (Washington *Star*) wrote: "Mr. Capra, whose 'rightness' in disposing of his magnificent little people . . . has been one of the miracles of the screen, finally has landed in the middle of a hornet's nest . . . When his *Meet John Doe* opens at the Earle . . . it may have any one of four endings . . . a new world's record in indecision . . ."

And Beau Broadway quipped in his New York *Telegraph* column: "The new giggle around town is this:

"Do you know why today is so refreshing?"
"Why, because the sun is out?"
"No. This is the day Capra isn't shooting a new ending for Doe . . ."

How did *Meet John Doe* finally fare? With some reservations, it finally won me what I long had coveted: acclaim from the intellectual critics.

Kate Cameron (New York *Daily News*) gave it her rare top rating—"Four Stars." William Boehnel (*World-Telegram*) called it: "The finest film Frank Capra ever made, bar none . . ." Howard Barnes (*Herald-Tribune*): "The full power of the screen is unleashed in Frank Capra's *Meet John Doe* . . . With an artist's fine perception he has gone to the heart of the issues which are troubling us so profoundly these days . . . It is a testament of faith as well as brilliant craftsmanship . . .''

Those words, "an artist's fine perception," had seldom been applied to my work before. And Bosley Crowther (*The New York Times*) upped my rating: ". . . eloquent with love for gentle people . . . it marks a distinct progression in Mr. Capra's—and the screen's—political thinking . . .''

The hard-nosed *Variety* seldom used unpragmatic phrases of this sort: "A showman's pride . . . Much comedy, much humor, much sly wit and broad fun . . . Pictorially and technically, the picture is a masterpiece . . . the dramatic narrative is one of the literary milestones of the screen."

Archer Winston (New York *Post*) felt as I did: ". . . [They] have made seven-eighths of a great and timely film . . ." Leo Mishkin (*Telegraph*) echoed the appraisal: "At least one may say that the first half of *Meet John Doe* is undeniably . . . one of the great pictures of any year . . . You'll never see anything better . . ."

But the audiences, my John Does, about whom and for whom I made my films, they left the theater somewhat disappointed—no matter which ending they saw. This was shrewdly predicted by movie critic Edwin Schallert (Los Angeles *Times*) when he first saw the film: "Frank Capra's *Meet John Doe* . . . an admirable challenge to the spirit of life today, is a picture that should make history and give a new turn to the thoughts of the nation, if—and the IF is very large, indeed—it does not die abornin' . . . [because] it lacks the inspiration of a great ending."

And then—after the film had been playing a couple of weeks in six major cities—I received a letter signed "John Doe." It read: ". . . I have seen your film with many different endings . . . all bad, I thought . . . The only thing that can keep John Doe from jumping to his death is the John Does themselves . . . if they ask him . . ."

A large bell rang. I called back all the east and shot *Ending Number* FIVE!

I called back all the outstanding prints of the film and spliced on ending number FIVE. And that finished our crazy game of "Five Endings in Search of an Audience."

That last ending was the best of a sorry lot, but *still* it was a letdown. Was an acceptable ending *ever* possible for *John Doe?* I still don't know. Perhaps readers will. I do know that at the time, I was much harsher on the film than the critics. I *knew* Riskin and I had written ourselves into a corner. We had shown the rise of two powerful, opposing movements—one good, one evil. They clashed head on—and *destroyed each other!* St. George fought with the dragon, slew it, and was slain. What our film said to bewildered people hungry for solutions was this, "No answers this time, ladies and gentlemen. It's back to the drawing board." And the people said, "Oh, nuts!"

But whether Cooper jumped or not, we were not prophets without honor in our own filmland. A sample telegram: David O. Selznick—"ONCE IN A BLUE MOON A PICTURE COMES ALONG THAT MAKES ONE PROUD TO BE IN THE PICTURE BUSINESS . . ."

Reviews

When *Meet John Doe* was finally released on 12 March 1941, critical reaction was by and large enthusiastic, but praise was rarely unqualified, and perspectives on the film varied considerably. The sample of reviews selected here indicate something of the range of these responses.

Bosley Crowther and Edwin Shallert—movie reviewers for *The New York Times* and *Los Angeles Times,* respectively—offer immediate impressions of the film the day after its premiere on opposite coasts. In keeping with most press coverage, they treat the release of the film as an important cultural event; the seriousness of the film's subject matter and pertinence to the contemporary political scene is respected, and they have high praise for Capra's direction and the performances of his cast. But having seen the version of the film in which D. B. Norton converts to the John Doe cause at the close, they also express reservations about the way the film ends. Crowther, in passing, describes the ending as a "sop," a criticism he was to pursue in greater detail in a (still celebratory) Sunday "think" piece, "How to Be a Good American," published by *The New York Times* three days later. More elaborately, and somewhat vertiginously, Shallert punctuates his lavish praise for the film with recurring expressions of doubt about the success of the final scene. Signs of ambivalence can also be found in Shallert's laudatory survey of the acting; Cooper's character in the early stages is "not too well defined," Stanwyck's is equivocal, and Arnold's insufficiently motivated at the close.

James Shelley Hamilton, writing for *New Movies,* the monthly publication of the National Board of Review, expands on certain ideas found in the remarks of the daily reviewers such as Crowther and Shallert. Situating *Meet John Doe* in relation to Capra's earlier work, especially the development of a social thematic and narrative formula in *Mr. Deeds Goes to Town* and *Mr. Smith Goes to Washington,* Hamilton seeks to identify the possible sources of the weakness of the ending. That the closing scene has been revised since the film's release, Hamilton argues, suggests either an inherent flaw in the plot or an unfortunate timidity on Capra's part. But having posed the problem in this way, Hamilton backs away from any further analysis along these lines. Regardless of how much Capra's reputation has made it incumbent upon critics to scrutinize his work closely, Hamilton questions whether a coherent social message should be required of a film that, despite its thematic confusions, is effective as drama.

Jay Leyda and Herbert Biberman, writing from the Left, both keep a fix on political questions, but come to somewhat different conclusions about the value of the film. A still photographer and documentary filmmaker who studied under Sergei Eisenstein at the Moscow Film School and served as Russian correspondent for *Theatre Arts* in the 1930s, Leyda compares *Meet John Doe* with Fritz Lang's *The Testament of Dr. Mabuse,* proposing that both films use the medium of motion pictures to expose native fascism. This represents for Capra, Leyda claims, a bolder, more courageous step than the struggle against "straw bosses" in *Mr. Smith,* and, with films such as *Citizen Kane* and *Native Land* waiting in the wings, raises the possibility of new political maturity in American cinema. In contrast, Biberman, a Hollywood screenwriter who was active in the Communist Party, sees the protagonist of *Meet John Doe* as lacking the honesty, dynamism, and depth of Capra's early heroes. Adopting an epistolary form to "speak" to Capra as a fellow craftsman, and working from a realist model of fiction, Biberman argues that a failure of character development betrays an inadequate grasp of contemporary social events, and worries about the depiction of the common people as politically immobilized. Leyda registers similar reservations about this last point, despite his general enthusiasm for the film.

Otis Ferguson, film reviewer for *The New Republic,* shares few of the assumptions of the other critics and writes against the current of their comments. A champion of Capra's unassuming comedies of the mid-thirties, Ferguson had gotten off the bandwagon when Capra's films had taken a socially ambitious turn five years before. In *Meet John Doe,* he finds sufficient evidence that Capra is still distracted by the "business of promoting a thesis," and with a skeptic's wit critiques the general phenomenon of the commercial packaging of patriotic sentiments, no matter how fervently held. But

he also finds signs of the director's former unobtrusive style, sense of timing, and eye for behavioral eccentricities, for which he is grateful, and proposes that Cooper's sheer physical presence evokes human dignity in a more compelling fashion than the "two hours of talk." Ferguson thus assumes the possibility of the co-existence of different registers of formal expression in the film, not all of which are exhausted by a thematic reading of the plot.

The New York Times

Bosley Crowther

Call him Joe Doakes or George Spelvin or just the great American yap—he is still the backbone of this country and as sturdy a citizen as there is. You've seen him at the ball parks, on buses, at country fairs and political rallies from coast to coast. You've even caught glimpses of him—and seen him squarely, too—in films once and again. But now you will see him about as clearly as Hollywood has ever made him out in Frank Capra's and Robert Riskin's superlative "Meet John Doe," which had its local premiere last evening at the Rivoli and Hollywood Theatres—you and countless other John Does. For, in spite of a certain prolixity and an ending which is obviously a sop, this is by far the hardest-hitting and most trenchant picture on the theme of democracy that the Messrs. Capra and Riskin have yet made—and a glowing tribute to the anonymous citizen, too.

Actually, this is not our first introduction to John Doe. Mr. Capra has already presented him under the names of Longfellow Deeds and Jefferson Smith, the fellows, you remember, who went to town and to Washington, respectively. He is the honest and forthright fellow—confused, inconsistent but always sincere—who believes in the basic goodness of people and has the courage to fight hard for principles. When he went to town, he was fighting for a vague but comprehensible social idea; in Washington, his adversaries were those who would use the United States Senate for corrupt and venal purposes.

But now, under the pseudonym of John Doe—John Willoughy is his real name—he finds himself confronted with a much more sinister and pertinent foe: the man—or, rather, the class—that would obtain dictatorial control by preying upon the democratic impulses and good-will of people of the land. In substance, the Messrs. Capra and Riskin are hinting broadly at the way this country might conceivably fall into the hands of a ruthless tyrant. It could happen here, they say—if it were not for the American John Doe.

For their story is that of a young fellow, a genial and aimless tramp, who is hoaxed into playing the role of a cynical social firebrand for the sake of a news-

From *The New York Times,* 13 March 1941, p. 25.

paper stunt. At first he lolls in luxury while articles ag'in this and that are ghost-written for him and printed in the aggressive, unscrupulous sheet. Then, under the pleasantly romantic influence of his beautiful "ghost," he goes on the radio with a stirring and encouraging appeal to the "little man" for brotherly love and democratic good-will.

Immediately, and by virtue of his simple, sincere address, he becomes a national hero, the messiahs for little people all around. John Doe Clubs are formed, a spontaneous "movement" gets under way. But then the guiding hand behind the whole set-up appears: the owner of the paper, a Napleonic industrialist, indicates his intention of using the voting strength of the clubs to bludgeon his way into power. And, at this point, John Doe takes the bit in his teeth and gives courageous battle. The outcome is not resolved; in the end, John Doe is almost licked. But so, too, is his opponent, and an ideal has been preserved.

With an excellent script by Mr. Riskin—overwritten in many spots, it is true—Mr. Capra has produced a film which is eloquent with affection for gentle people, for the plain, unimpressive little people who want reassurance and faith. Many of his camera devices are magnificent in the scope of their suggestion, and always he tells his story well, with his customary expert spacing of comedy and serious drama. Only space prevents us from enthusing loudly about individual "touches."

And his cast is uniformly excellent. Gary Cooper, of course, is "John Doe" to the life and in the whole—shy, bewildered, non-aggressive, but a veritable tiger when aroused. Barbara Stanwyck plays the "ghost" and, incidentally, the dea ex machina with a proper brittleness, and Edward Arnold is, as usual, the diabolically disarming tycoon. In supporting roles James Gleason makes a forbiddingly hard-boiled managing editor whose finer instincts are revealed in a superb drunk scene; and Walter Brennan, Harry Holman and Regis Toomey are distinguished among a host of character bits.

John Doe may not be the most profound or incisive fellow in this cross-purposed world of ours today. But he has an inspiring message for all good Americans. And he is charming company. We most heartily suggest you make his acquaintance at once.

Los Angeles Times

Edwin Schallert

F rank Capra's "Meet John Doe," an admirable challenge to the spirit of life today, is a picture that should make history and give a new turn to the thoughts of a nation, if—and the IF is very large indeed—it does not die abornin'.

This is by far his most significant film in all respects except one: it lacks the inspiration of a great ending.

He has seized the dilemmas that are to be found in modern life, wrestled with them like a Sandow, but one feels that in the long run, he has compromised with sentimentality.

"Meet John Doe" had its premiere last night at Warners-Hollywood Theater, with showings to continue at that house today and the Downtown. It is a valiant work of the cinema, revealing that its director, and his writer, Robert Riskin, have their fingers on the pulse of existence today in America. It is a rich picture that they offer in its realism, bigness of an idea, and—to use a now almost trite phase—social significance.

The director is, as always, a marvel in bringing to life hidden talents of people whom he chooses to appear in his scenes. He transforms James Gleason into a new man of destiny in the studios, and Gleason goes with him all the way in a dazzling performance. He awards Regis Toomey one scene which is so pregnant with humanness and feeling that this actor is certain to enjoy a new zenith.

The entire philosophy expressed in the picture is magnificent. It presents the theme of good will toward men revived all over again—the spirit of Christmas not limited to a brief period, but spread through the entire year.

So fine are the thoughts projected that they could well start a new Moral Rearmament movement. There is the practical thought put forward that each human being should endeavor to achieve understanding of his fellows, break down the fences which stand between individual lives, come to a more definite appreciation of problems that are mutual. It is a grand idea that is projected.

All that lacks in the picture is the spell of a great sacrifice to make the whole impression convincing. Instead we witness John Doe, willing to give his life for a

" 'Meet John Doe' Hailed as Capra Victory," from the *Los Angeles Times*, 31 March 1941, p. 16.

cause, won over to living by the persuasions of a woman who has double-crossed him. We also behold the man who had exploited him, and who never showed any previous signs of relenting in his crafty ways, suddenly developing the milk of human kindness.

If you can accept the situation that ends the picture you will be able to consume all of it with a gratefulness that is surpassing. But I fear that many will feel that John Doe should have paid a fatal price—something apart from the suicide he contemplated—for the sake of a theory of brotherly love.

The finish, as it stands, makes it difficult to believe that the fine principles of the philosophy he espouses, purely as a stooge at the outset, and later as a devout believer, would or could be revived anew. He has been dubbed a fake and the John Doe idea has been shattered.

However, this need deter no one from visiting "Meet John Doe." It offers enough—in fact so much more than ordinary pictures—that it will be chronicled as an event of the current year and be well remembered. There are other endings that might possibly be devised to give it more potent meaning, but the one that it has will probably be popularly received, notwithstanding it may not be wholly appealing to more discriminating followers of the screen.

At all events, director and scenarist have made exceptional use of their theme. It is the old "Miracle Man" idea—something conceived to deceive the public which turns out to be so worth while that it becomes greater than those who participated in the birth of the enterprise.

Barbara Stanwyck, as a newspaper columnist, is the one who accidentally brings it all about, when she prints a letter from a supposed John Doe as her final contribution to a newspaper from which she has been fired.

This purely fictitious Doe stands as a symbol of revolt against modern conditions. It becomes necessary to produce him by some hook or crook.

With the assistance of a new editor of the paper, played by Gleason, Miss Stanwyck essays to do that, and they pick Gary Cooper as their pawn. He's a former baseball player who has lost the use of his pitching arm. He accepts the assignment which they hand him, despite the protestations of his buddy played by Walter Brennan, who doesn't believe in such a fallacy or even the advisability of acquiring wealth and comfort.

By degrees John Doe becomes a national figure, with clubs formed right and left in his name. He is exploited to the nth degree, all for the good until the man who is pulling the wires through it all (the newspaper owner, played by Edward Arnold) decides to capitalize on the popularity of his protege.

Here the hero's native honesty comes forward and he refuses to fall in with the plans which would aim to make Arnold President of the United States for his own advantags and uses—practically a dictator.

The house of cards topples, Doe loses all his followers overnight through Arnold's machinations.

But as Doe in the first faked letter had been made to assert that he would commit suicide at midnight of Christmas Eve as a protest against the ways of present civilization, it seemingly becomes incumbent on him to do this in order to save the ideal of life for which he has been the apostle. He himself is willing to, but is prevented in the manner already indicated.

One feels that it is a pity that some more compelling solution was not reached in this picture which is clearly ennobling in its spirit, and which is so deeply moving in many of its scenes, as well as being told with all the Capra vigor, power and cleverness.

For many reasons, though, "Meet John Doe" will deserve high appreciation and commendation, and a Capra picture, particularly after a long lapse of time, is something indeed to be welcomed.

Plenty could be written about all those who undertake leading parts in "Meet John Doe." Gary Cooper in such scenes as his radio address, his recital of his dream to Miss Stanwyck, the one with her mother, provides a portrayal which he has never excelled. In the earlier stages the character itself is not too well defined, but Cooper seems to develop it admirably under the Capra direction.

The role that Miss Stanwyck plays is somewhat equivocal, in that she is drawn into a veritable net of intrigue, and only belatedly manages a regeneration. She gives the interpretation everything of which she is capable and that is much.

In the case of Arnold the transition to the better life is all too quick, but he supplies throughout the earlier part of the picture a splendid impression of a scheming businessman.

The work of Gleason in a part that is genuine throughout is, as already suggested, noteworthy. Brennan, too, stays to his course most competently, and has the chance to do this. Spring Byington endows the heroine's mother with charm. Rod La Rocque is a striking personality in a heavy role, and should do more of these.

Gene Lockhart, Irving Bacon, J. Farrell MacDonald, Warren Hymer, are among the excellent performers seen in the large company. The Riskin screenplay was taken from a story by Richard Connell and Robert Presnell.

New Movies

James Shelley Hamilton

t is Frank Capra's own doing that he has become the object of the most careful kind of critical scrutiny when he brings out a new picture. He has made himself one of the most enjoyable of directors by putting a lot of American life on the screen with affectionate warmth and sympathy, and with a remarkable gift for discerning and expressing the humors and sentiments and crochets of American character. His highly individual style as a director is full of that not too common quality that we call good natured, and his expertness as a craftsman has put him in the top rank as a maker of American films. His success has been enormous, with both critics and audiences.

For some years now he has been concerning himself with something more than being merely entertaining. His social conscience has been more and more evident, leading him more and more to consideration of the lot of the ordinary, the "little," man, and questions of wealth and poverty and the workings of democracy. *The Lost Horizon* was his first approach to such matters, but laid in a far-off setting with more fantasy than fact in its set-up. Beginning with Mr. Deeds he took up a character that has remained practically unchanged ever since, involved in problems that have become a pattern—a pattern so little varied that it is getting almost too apparent. Mr. Deeds and Mr. Smith, and now Mr. Doe, are easily interchangeable, and whether they appear in the person of Gary Cooper or James Stewart they are always the same—a simple, honest young man, naive and innocent in worldly matters, suddenly forced by circumstances to confront some immense social-political problem, always coached by a wise-cracking disillusioned girl to whom he gives back her lost ideals and faith, and always, in the end, confounding the powers of darkness by his simplicity and honesty.

Meet John Doe follows this formula faithfully. The ingenious story that Richard Connell wrote called "The Life and Death of John Doe" provided a parable most pertinent to Frank Capra's feelings and philosophy—save for its ending. Starting with a faked letter to a newspaper column, announcing that a certain John Doe is going to kill himself on a certain date as a protest against the

From *New Movies: The National Board of Review Magazine*, April 1941, pp. 13–15.

injustices of living, public interest is so aroused that the paper's editor has to admit he has been bamboozled or find a real John Doe to satisfy it. Mr. Deeds-Smith-Stewart-Cooper, a broken-down ballplayer temporarily being a tramp, gets the job of being John Doe. The gag becomes a circulation builder for the paper—John Doe becomes a public personage, preaching goodwill and neighborliness over the radio as the cure for all the world's ills. Backed by the tremendous publicity that money can get with modern methods, John Doe becomes a national figure—John Doe Clubs spring up everywhere. And the owner of the newspaper, who is a man with fascist ideas and ambitions to be an American dictator, has been behind it all, ready to use the immense John Doe following to put himself in power when the time is ripe. It is when John Doe discovers this plot that he becomes the Deeds-Smith fighter for the common people.

That's where Mr. Capra ran up against his great problem. How could John Doe win out, and defeat the evil personified in the would-be dictator? He is branded—justly enough on technical grounds, with all the proofs—as a fake: he had never intended to jump off any roof as a protest. His followers desert him because he was a fake. But he has been won to the ideals he has been preaching—all supplied by the girl, who provided them in the cynical pursuit of her own job. The only way he can win back the trust of his followers is actually to kill himself as threatened in the fake letter. But every provision has been made to keep his suicide from getting into the news, or from ever being known except by those whose interest is in keeping it hushed up. How could that be an effective ending, being merely one man's tragedy and completely futile as a blow or even a gesture against the enemies of righteousness? It would solve nothing—and nobody would like seeing Gary Cooper killed.

A plot-problem that is the hugest kind of a headache for any writer or director. The first solution to reach the public was John Doe kept from suicide by a plea by the girl—herself now converted and in love—to start all over again, and the wicked newspaper man and his henchmen announcing they were completely reformed. Since then the startling reformation of the villians has been simply lopped off from the picture. Another ending is reported to have been made with John Doe Clubbers repenting of their distrust and—instead of the girl—being the agents to save their hero. Which sounds as if it might be the best way out. But the need to experiment with so many different solutions is a measure either of weakness in the plot itself or of an unfortunate timidity in resolving the plot, gambling on audience reaction rather than tackling the situation firmly one way or another. Which isn't satisfying in a picture that means to treat serious problems seriously.

Since Mr. Capra has got people into the habit of seeing meanings and lessons in his pictures they are sometimes apt to examine what he does with more probing an eye than may be called for. *Meet John Doe* can easily be taken for just a dramatic story, with a powerful and unscrupulous man plotting to use the sentimentality and gullibility of ordinary people for his own ends. Is it necessary to take this as Mr. Capra's solemn conviction that sentimentality and gullibility are the chief American characteristics, and that if they are used in the right way all would be well with us and with the world?

Anyway, Capra is as skilled as ever in keeping things moving along briskly and dramatically—though here and there are some pretty long speeches which for all his artful manipulation have something of the effect of a set aria in an opera. He is still gifted in making characters, particularly background characters, vivid and alive—though there is a reporter in this picture who appears to perform on the principle that tripping over a spitoon is always funny. Sentimentalities are neatly balanced with sharp commentaries on sentimentality. Folkways are brilliantly pictured again and again, particularly in the small-town mayor's befuddled antics, and in the broadcast of the John Doe convention. Such a characterization as James Gleason's is deep and revealing.

But it's a pity Mr. Capra, with so much good stuff to work with, had to fumble the point of it.

Direction

Jay Leyda

Courage is the best and the rarest quality of the American film—the courage of artistic convictions, the courage of a determined philosophy. When a philosophy that fights *for* the American people finds a forceful expression in an industrial medium that is lending its almost unanimous support to a fight *against* this people—that is a film to be seen. That is the courage of *Meet John Doe,* produced in an era when the "discretion" of *Back Street* and *Mr. and Mrs. Smith* is much the better part of a valor that even in normal times is none too firm.

The other week I witnessed another, perhaps more sensational display of courage, which in a way prepared me to see the best in *John Doe.* At an unsuspecting German movie house in New York's Yorkville—sandwiched between a Nazi newsreel and a military farce, Fritz Lang's last German film, finished in 1933, was given its American premiere. On its surface *The Testament of Dr. Mabuse* was a police thriller. Underneath it was an intricately detailed exposé of the true character of the Nazi ideology, as understood in 1932. The means of the attack was extraordinary, necessarily taking on the disguise of an allegory; it was begun when the Nazi party had already been financed for power (*by the same money that was behind the German film industry*) and completed *after* power had been taken. The production history of *The Testament* is in itself an exciting story of ingenuity and risk, of outwitted studio heads and smuggled rolls of film, etc., but that is not the outstanding importance of Lang's film. What is important is that the motion picture medium was used by a grave group of film-makers to fight against a crisis in the way they knew best.

Maybe I'm reading too much into the efforts of Frank Capra and Robert Riskin, but their *Meet John Doe,* with its realistic, motivated portrait of a native American fascist, with its genuine sympathy for ordinary people, seems an instinctive fighting gesture, using the best means at hand, an American analogy to Lang's more conscious work.

In *Mr. Smith Goes to Washington* Capra played safe, played demagogue, and fought straw bosses. The issues were tiny and the technique was enormous. *Meet*

From "Courage in Films," *Direction,* April-May 1941, p. 27.

John Doe might have pursued this dangerous path further, but instead the Capra-Riskin team (now independent producers) returned to pick up the decency of *Mr. Deed*'s where they dropped it for the temptations of *Lost Horizons* and the stuff you can't take with you.

In the film's fight against native fascist tendencies, the parallel theme—of brotherhood-of-man—becomes secondary, and if a weakness must be found in *John Doe* this is it. The greatest weakness as well as one of the greatest braveries of the film is its exposure of the technique of manipulating the American people, but surely the American people know how to do more than be manipulated. It is not enough for Capra and Riskin to demonstrate how fiercely they are fighting fascism. Their fight is incomplete so long as it ignores the fight of the American people itself.

But the release of *Meet John Doe* is the first great film event of 1941. And 1941 is no ordinary year. I think we can hope that *Citizen Kane* will make more than an artistic contribution, too. And then—*Native Land*—which Paul Strand, Leo Hurwitz, David Wolff, Marc Blitzstein and Paul Robeson are now completing. This is the courageous film we all have been hoping would be made—not by a miracle, but by a brave group of filmmakers expressing their belief in American ideals, in the way they know best.

New Masses

Herbert Biberman

Dear Frank Capra,

No one can have watched and studied your work or known you in the Screen Directors Guild without recognizing the purposefulness of your character. You are the only director I have known who regularly called his fellow craftsmen together to discuss scripts in advance of shooting. Your pictures have, in the main, revealed the search for content. Your probing of chosen material has marked you as no flighty purveyor of "pure" entertainment. On the contrary, you have emerged through your work as an artist who believes that what is most pertinent to men's lives is most relevant to their culture and entertainment.

If, therefore, you last work, *Meet John Doe,* presents much that needs challenging, respect for you demands that your friends wrestle with a tabulation of shortcomings and inaccuracies, and also attack the reasons for them. Let us base our examination, Frank, upon the uncontroversial question: are the characters and their relationships truthfully presented? If we also examine certain political generalizations emanating from the picture, this will be done not to engage in a political discussion, but to study your characters in relation to those generalizations. For it is, finally, by character and situation that your work must be judged. In attempting to measure this work, I shall use your two pictures which preceded *Meet John Doe, Mr. Deeds Goes to Town* and *Mr. Smith Goes to Washington.*

What characterizes those pictures? The resourcefulness, the creative humanity, and the utter honesty of your protagonists and of many around them. They were not isolated from material cultural traditions. They acted in accordance with and were deeply conscious of the militance and independence of traditional earthy Americanism. Your protagonists led the action. They assailed the forces of evil. They were positive and dynamic, quietly in the case of Deeds, pugnaciously in the case of Smith. For all the superficial difference in their personalities, they were brothers at heart in the union sense of the word. Suddenly, into this gallery of young Americans steps John Doe and with him, as a great shadow, comes a new theory. This theory had its inception in *You Can't Take It With You,*

"Frank Capra's Characters," from *New Masses,* 8 July 1941, pp. 26–27.

but in *Meet John Doe* it is no longer a tenatative but a full-fledged philosophy. It is now so strongly felt by you that, for the first time in any of your pictures, the theory overwhelms the characters and takes the play away from them.

This theory is that politics are of no use; that "unpolitical organized neighborliness" should take over. Now, Frank, is this observed from life and people, or is it a special plea from you? Has it not forced you to distort the American character in order to make that character speak this special plea? And whose plea is it, and where does it lead? Are you counseling that politics be wiped completely out of American life, *or only out of the life of the common people?* For this assault on politics is not necessarily unpolitical. Nothing, indeed, is so political as the suggestion that politics be forgotten. You would apparently counsel the people to give up politics even though the fascist newspaper owner does not. You ask that people give their neighbors odd jobs to eliminate relief. You suggest that 10,000,000 unemployed accept permanent status as handymen, supported by airplane workers who, even after winning the Vultee strike (for example), make the munificent wage of twenty-five dollars a week. This private charity, you tell us, holds a more creative future for millions of Americans than does the WPA.

Where is there a factual basis for such a theory in the whole of American history? Was the Revolutionary War a manifestation of organized neighborliness of an unpolitical character? Were the Democratic Party under Jefferson, the Civil War, the right to free public education, the Wagner Labor Relations Act, women's suffrage, the Bill of Rights, or the Screen Directors Guild unpolitical events? Will "unpolitical neighborliness" prevent the eight-hour day from becoming the twelve-hour day? Our American political history is of prime importance to the creative artist because it underlies American character. An artist who ignores historical facts and the experiences behind the American way cannot make his story or characters work or play. No man can think or create for the people in opposition to the people.

Can you, after Deeds and Smith, accept the notion that "politics is a mug's game"? Do you believe politics should be left to the mugs? The mugs, from Hamilton to Hitler, have tried to spread such a belief. They invented the phrase, hoping to engender surly disrespect for politics in the common people in order to abscond with the profit and power that sole control of politics would give them. Let us examine *Meet John Doe* to determine whether by accident or design it fits "politics is a mug's game." Who is the initiator of the John Doe clubs? John Doe? No; the fascist newspaper owner, who wished to use the discontent of the people to gain his own ends. This was not the way the Abolitionist Clubs grew.

Who leads the John Doe Clubs: a Thomas Jefferson, a William Garrison, an honest member of the Progressive movement? No. The leader of the John Doe Clubs is a declassed derelict, heading a movement he does not understand, believe in, or love. For him it is a job which will pay him enough money to recondition his pitching arm. Although such an objective is perfectly intelligible from his point of view, to present such a man as a typical leader of the American people is a travesty upon our history and our fellow citizens. American history has not been and will not be made by declassed derelicts.

John Doe constantly runs away, hides in hotel rooms, does the devious bidding of a conglomeration of culprits; and his final acts of "decency" for love of his girl make no sense at all, since they spring from nothing but animal impulse. *Meet John Doe* has no such scene as that in *Mr. Smith* in which the young senator strengthens himself with the memory of Lincoln before the Lincoln statue. Mr. Smith is a defender of America's present because he understands and defends America's past. There is no defeatism in him, nor is he an advocate of "unpolitical neighborliness." He was a fighting, "No For An Answer" American. So was Deeds.

In the two earlier films you began with the people; in *Meet John Doe* you began with the fascist. In the former the people act, in the latter they are acted upon. In the former they were observed from life, in the latter concocted out of theoretical confectionery. Deeds and Smith had faces. You could photograph their alertness, their wit, their humanity. In John Doe you presented an expressionless mask; not John Doe, the average American, but John Doe, the legal abstraction, first created to suit the needs of corporate law and then used by you to suit the needs of a story of corporate treachery. And here, Frank, is the crux of the matter. *Meet John Doe* is not a story of John Doe or the people but a story of corporate treachery out of which you try to twist a moral for the people without consulting them.

The proof of this is in your character development. There is only one rich, positive, resourceful, and convincing character in *Meet John Doe*. That is the fascist, the real protagonist of your picture. The world is his state, and all the men and women on it his players. It is no surprise that the philosophy which emerges from the film is *his* philosophy: politics is a mug's game. And that philosophy is not only a negation of the best in the American tradition; it is also a negation of the tradition of Frank Capra as represented by Mr. Deeds and Mr. Smith.

Let us examine the passivity of your people. They are drawn like filings to a magnet when the fascist sends out a call through his newspapers. They play no part in developing, qualifying, or creating the movement. They just join. There is no more democracy in the John Doe Clubs than in the storm troopers. And since the people have no part in the movement's struggle, the whole thing falls apart when the leader rats. Contrast this with the history of the United Automobile Workers and their erstwhile leader Homer Martin; when he ratted, they threw him out and went on to organize and grow. It was their movement, not Martin's. They have a saying of Jefferson's—there should be an upsurge of the people every twenty years, but in auto it's every two years.

You may ask whether your exposure of the fascist does not make the film true and valuable for the people. But when you merely say that the fascists are mugs and the people should have nothing to do with them, you speak the mug's language. If the people do not struggle against the mugs the people are canceled out. For as long as you present no program of opposition to the powers of decadence and destruction, your rescue of the people from the "messy political struggle" leaves the people completely unprepared and helpless against attack. To ask the people to make the best of the present is to subscribe to pessimism, to counsel against growth, to negate and proscribe a better future. Nothing could be more opposed to the historical necessity which makes of the people the force of progress.

You yourself recognize this in part; for when your people are faced with destruction, you do contrive to set them in motion again. But when you warn them against the full implications of their actions, you lead them in two opposite directions at once; one historical and effective, the other abstract and immobilizing. Those in power always attempt first to cajole into immobility those whose common needs are drawing them together. Moral Rearmament, which swept the front pages of all the newspapers a few years ago, asked us all to forswear selfishness, but it asked us to do so in the relative positions of the *status quo*. It hopes thus to perpetuate existing inequalities and to end the struggle of the dispossessed for their rights. Moral Rearmament failed because it was not of the people and invited them to frustration and self-destruction.

Workable theory cannot be spun entirely out of the head of one individual; neither can workable character. Politics can be brushed aside neither in life nor in the movies. There is no escape from the struggle of reality. The people make history, they do not concoct it. They make it under tremendous pressures, on the basis of vast common interests and needs, under tested leadership, and independently of ruling classes and their false leaders and phony slogans. The genuine slogans come out of the mouths of Deeds and Smith, but never out of the mouth of John Doe.

We in Hollywood have a tremendous responsibility to American history; a responsibility not to distort, to malign, to misrepresent motives. There is no better way to understand what our people are than to understand what made them that way. Study of our history and character will lead us to tap the boundless resourcefulness, the independence, and the creative energy of the average American, the real John Doe.

The New Republic

Otis Ferguson

T hough Frank Capra is still right in the formula he has been holding to for five years now, *Meet John Doe* is at least a promise that he may be coming back to pictures. It is almost a point-for-point replica of *Mr. Smith Goes to Washington,* but some of the old felicity is there again and there are actually comedy sequences in it. I am not holding out too much hope, for today there is nothing Americans so like to be told from the screen as that they are Americans. So why should anybody with a formula and a credit line like skywriting bother with making a swell simple movie as his "production for 1941"?

The John Doe of the story is Capra's familiar and favorite American type, the easy shambling young man, shrewd and confused, rugged, a lovable innocent but don't tread on him—the uncommon common man, in short, with a heart of gold and a limestone fist, and integrity in long fibers. Eyewash, of course, but there is something in it, for a national hero is some sort of national index after all, and it is not so much how miserably short we fall of being an ideal as what ideal we choose to dream of. Anyhow, this young man, a bush-league baseball player with a glass arm, is caught up in a freak stunt for tabloid circulation-building which turns out to be dynamite both ways. As J. Doe, he is supposed to be a social reformer with a deadline for a suicide of protest; as a national news personality, he becomes so arresting and eloquent in his plea for love and understanding—the Sermon on the Mount with a drawl—that miracles are passed and John Doe clubs are formed, and it is presently worth someone's while to own him as political property. It started as fraud but eventually led to the young man's believing his own spiel and wrecking the sinister plans when he found out their anti-democratic aim. Love was a part of it, of course, and there are various clever wrinkles; but the outline is enough.

The fascination of gossip and the awe of prestige make it impossible that the question of what makes a picture should ever have a chance against the question of who. But while the names of Robert Riskin and Frank Capra are behind the production and writing and direction of *John Doe,* I think we can see even behind

"Democracy at the Box Office," from *The New Republic,* 24 March 1941, pp. 405–406 the names to what is under our noses. The message is that since it is all the little men who truly make the big world, they should live together and hang together, doing away with hate and suspicion and bad-neighborliness. Fine. Ringing. Of course there are present among us oppression and injustice and scorn for all unsung heroes whose names are Moe Million. Too bad; an outrage; something should be done. So the lift of the story comes in the doing, in the rallying to a new simple faith, as people and as Americans, through homely things but as a mighty army under the flag. In this story the powers of darkness are able to check the advance, but the victory in defeat is that there will be advance again.

I have no doubt the authors of such theses believe in them, just as it is easy for a song-writer to believe that God should bless America after he has glanced over the recent sheet-music sales. But sifted in with any such half-thought-out hoorah must be the true motivating conviction that the box office is out there and will be terrific. And that is where the thing begins to crack like Parson Weems's Liberty Bell, for in art there is a certain terrible exaction upon those who would carry their show by arousing people to believe, and it is that any such show must be made out of belief, in good faith and pure earnest, in the whole of belief itself. This rhetoric and mortising of sure-fire device of a success today is its sure betrayal by tomorrow—the flag in a game of charades, the mock prayer at a picnic.

As a picture, it does well the things which have proved highlights before: the tender concern over the little fellers with great faith; the underdog finally getting on his hind legs to tell them off; the regeneration of even a hard-boiled newspaper gal; the final blow-off scene with the nation as audience. But it talks too much to no purpose and in the same spot. The musical score is both arch and heavy (the most undeveloped department in all Hollywood anyway). And one of the saddest things is to find Capra so preoccupied with getting over a message of holy-hokum that he lets in half a dozen of the worst montage transitions—mumming faces, headlines, wheels and whorls—that have been seen in a major effort since the trick first turned stale.

Whether this much of hollowness and prefabrication will spoil the picture for you, I wouldn't know. There are things in it to see. The business of promoting a thesis has distracted Frank Capra's attention from much that he was superb at doing, and he still skips over many of the little fitted pieces which make a story inevitable. But now and then he lingers and you can see the hand of the loving workman bringing out the fine grain—as in the direction of the little crowd around the local mayor when Joe Doe is apprehended, with its naturalness and light spontaneous humor: as in the edge of satire in the management of the radio broadcast; as in the bringing out of homely humorous quirks in John Doe himself; and as always in the timing of a line, its cause and effect, so that it comes out with just force and clarity among the shifting images. But Capra and Riskin now seem content to let good actors fill out a stock part and stop at that, so Edward Arnold, Walter Brennan, Gene Lockhart, J. Farrell MaDonald, and several others have nothing more incisive to do than they would in any B picture. Barbara Stanwyck has always needed managing, and apparently got it here, though her idea of a passion is still that it is something to tear to firecrackers. But one man the director did give a chance to and smooth the way for, and that is James Gleason, who made more of this chance than there was in the lines and their meaning. The one scene which came through all these streamlined Fourth of July exercises with true sincerity and eloquence was Gleason's drunken talk in the bar, the one that starts, "I like you, you're gentle. Take me, I've always been hard. Hard. Don't like hard people, you hear?" It was just talk, with business, but he made it his, and it will remain one of the magnificent scenes in pictures.

That leaves only the star, who is so much an American John Doe type you could never say whether he was cast in a part or vice versa—Gary Cooper. It is he who has the human dignity which this two hours of talk is talking about, and talking about; and it seems impossible for him to be quite foolish even in the midst of foolishness. His is the kind of stage presence which needs no special lighting or camera magic; he makes an entrance by opening a door, and immediately you know that someone is in the room. *Meet John Doe* has its humor, inspiration, and interest in uneven degrees; but whether you find it good, fair, or merely endurable depends more on Cooper than on what we know as sound movie making.

Commentaries

Many of the motifs found in the reviews of *Meet John Doe* in 1941 reappear in the three critical commentaries selected here, but the perspective of these recent writers is very different. This is in part a function of a certain historical distance; writing long after the immediate impact of the film has faded, critics have much less a stake in measuring or predicting its direct use or social effect, and greater interest in placing a given work within a broader social, cultural, or aesthetic context. With time, as well, comes different kinds of material to work with; Capra's autobiography, in particular, has emerged as a seminal sourcebook in contemporary exegeses of *Meet John Doe,* and the increased availability of other kinds of archival materials makes historical scholarship possible for the first time. It is also important to keep in mind that sustained critical work of the kind included here is supported by and circulates within an academic environment. These critics thus assume a different audience, and draw on critical methods imported or developed for systematic, analytic study of cultural forms. In the cases of the last two essays, they also explore methodological issues that their own criticism raises. All three testify to the sustained fertility of *Meet John Doe* for the elaboration and reformulation of new critical work.

Richard Glatzer's commentary crossbreeds an auteurist analysis of a director's personality as evidenced in his or her films with a method of cultural criticism common to American

Studies. Social mythmaking, a cultural activity traceable in America to William Bradford and the Puritans, is understood by Glatzer to find contemporary form in the work of a Hollywood director like Capra in the 1930s. But in *Meet John Doe,* Glatzer argues, Capra's role as social mythmaker is undermined by his personal doubts about the use of mass media for social persuasion. Thus Glatzer reads the film's plot and disconcerting tone autobiographically, with a view toward explaining the trajectory of Capra's career during these years. *Meet John Doe* emerges as a project Capra must work through on his way to the more personal, postwar film, *It's a Wonderful Life.*

Dudley Andrew is similarly interested in the ways in which *Meet John Doe* illuminates Capra's role as a Hollywood director, but from a perspective that calls into question the very possibility of "personal" filmmaking within the economic and textual constraints of the Hollywood studio system. Inflected by contemporary notions of discourse as a force that is at once hetereogenous and constrained, Andrews's argument turns on not only the possibility of reading the plot of *Meet John Doe* autobiographically, but also locating at the level of filmic narration symptoms of a struggle between the film's implied author (Capra) and various subvoices

(Slavko Vorkapich's montages; actors Cooper, Stanwyck, and especially Brennan) that the author seeks to control. However distressing to the filmmaker (see Capra), or disconcerting to a viewer in search of a clear message (see the reviewers), discords of this kind are productive, Andrew contends, for they expose tensions in a style of filmmaking that critics have "prematurely labeled 'classic.'" Under the terms of this argument, the value of the film resides neither in its consequence for the career of its director not in its impact on the original audience but rather in the lessons it provides analysts of film texts.

For Nick Browne, the larger issue at stake is the relationship of the film to its social ground. Prefacing his analysis of *Meet John Doe* with a brief survey of models for examining this relationship, Browne situates the Hollywood studio system, and the "textual systems" of Hollywood films, within an institutional history of American film, and that history, in turn, within a large-scale history of social, political, and economic relations. *Meet John Doe* invites study from this perspective, Browne suggests, because the story it tells, and the rhetoric it adopts, figures the media, the economy, and the state in a particularly intricate fashion. Drawing on the legal documents drawn up for the production of the film, Browne furthermore is able to present specific evidence of Capra's contradictory pursuit of "independence" within a matrix of interlocking, but historically variable, institutions. The autobiographical subtext glossed by Glatzer and the textual disturbances scrutinized by Andrew are thus read by Browne as symptoms of ideological contradictions at a particular historical moment.

Meet John Doe:
An End To Social
Mythmaking

Richard Glatzer

As of 1935, *It Happened One Night* had enlisted an enthusiastic following of millions, almost put the undershirt industry out of business, and gathered a bushel of Oscars for its deserving director. Frank Capra's immediate response to his success was a feeling of elation, but elation soon gave way to anxiety and self-doubt: would his future film-making career merely prove to be an anticlimax? "Then it came to me," Capra writes in *The Name Above the Title,* "—a brilliant out! Burnish my halo with martyrdom—get sick!" Capra's illness, at first purely imaginary, soon became a brutal physical reality: he was wishing himself to death. Then an anonymous stranger visited him, and chastized him for wasting his God-given talents. Capra tells us that he listened to the man, was overcome with shame, and abruptly began to recover. It was at this point in his career, he insists, that he became a socially dedicated film-maker: "I knew then that down to my dying day, down to my last feeble talent, I would be committed [to the service of man]. . . . Beginning with *Mr. Deeds,* my films had to *say* something."

Clearly, Capra's earlier films often "said" something; *American Madness* in particular ambitiously and successfully dealt with timely social questions in a manner somewhat similar to his post-1935 works. Yet *American Madness* is severely, pragmatically focused in a way the important later films are not. *Madness* straightforwardly confronts particular problems and suggests particular solutions while minimally dealing with classic American types and broad national preconceptions. In *Mr. Deeds Goes to Town,* for the first time, Capra meticulously and self-consciously attempted nothing less than to create an American mythology that might reinforce the nation in its time of financial and social crisis.

In assuming this responsibility, Capra linked himself irrevocably with an American tradition of conscious mythmaking that harkens back to William Brad-

From *Frank Capra: The Man and His Films,* ed. Richard Glatzer and John Raeburn (Ann Arbor: University of Michigan Press, 1975), pp. 139–148.

ford and the Puritans. Bradford wrote his history of the Plymouth Colony to awaken a spirit within third generation Puritans that was apparently dying—that pioneer spirit that had underlain their ancestors' bold decision to travel to a new world. Similarly, Capra, in *Mr. Deeds Goes to Town,* attempted to remedy, not merely the concrete financial, political, and social problems that the Depression presented, but the more profound and difficult problem of national morale. Army veterans were marching against their government; radical political ideologies were growing in popularity; the power of charismatic celebrities seemed unlimited: Americans' belief in their country was crumbling under diverse pressures unlike any they had felt previously. Frank Capra—in 1936, a man very sure of his control over a mass audience—wanted to revitalize their faith by renovating dusty national archetypes and dreams.

In *Mr. Deeds Goes to Town,* and later (to a somewhat lesser extent) in *Mr. Smith Goes to Washington,* Capra accomplished this revitalization in part by creating his heroes and their small town communities as incarnations of the composite ideals and philosophies of historical figures whose enthusiasm for the possibilities this country presented had been deeply felt—figures like Jefferson, Lincoln, Thoreau, and Washington. The rural village comes to symbolize such values as a stress on personal relationships, the celebration of unselfconscious individualism, a healthy lack of interest in irrational progress and excessive materialism, and an acute sense of the worth of strong spiritual ties to one's friends.

Yet Capra was very much aware of the idealized nature of the small towns he envisioned. *Deeds* and *Smith* gain their mythic power and drive when Capra's rural protagonists make archetypal journeys to the city, and there encounter Capra's notion of the chaotic, very unidealized "present"—a world where political and moral corruption abound, where moneylove is the prime motivating factor, and where interpersonal relationships, even within families, prove to be pragmatic, selfish, and loveless. Atomization and mass conformity result.

Clearly, the values of the cities are inimical to those of the small towns. Deeds and Smith (the emissaries from the past) must inevitably confront the urban present; and in their ultimate victories over their foes lies Capra's prognosis for the future—a future in which the spiritual will triumph over mindless progress. Yet, when Deeds and Smith finally conquer the city, enabling us to glimpse the happy future, only the most irretrievably villainous—the political bosses and the shyster lawyers—are truly defeated: the majority of the urbanites are converted to a belief in traditional values. Longfellow Deeds and Jefferson Smith merely awaken a moral sense that the city has lulled to sleep. As such, they are symbols of the basic decency of every American, a decency so strong that, once tapped, it is capable of overcoming any evils and of carrying this country through to a glorious future. In *Deeds* and *Smith,* Capra used national types and placed them in the urban present so as to ultimately update the mythical notion of the American national character. Capra gave his countrymen a positive self-image.

In 1940, the dangers which Americans faced were perhaps greater than any they had encountered previously. In addition to the still unresolved economic problems at home, totalitarian Fascism ranged virtually unchecked over the European continent and threatened to engulf liberal democracies everywhere. For the United States, war was on the horizon. All the values Capra had celebrated in *Mr. Deeds* and *Mr. Smith* were in danger of being eclipsed. A restatement and reaffirmation of those values—a vote of confidence—was sorely needed.

When Capra began working on *The Life and Death of John Doe,* he had every intention of casting that vote. "The people are right," he told an interviewer at the time, "people's instincts are good, never bad." In *Meet John Doe* (as the film was finally titled), Capra would attempt to dramatize once more his faith in America and its people by creating another variation on the *Deeds* formula of the guileless rustic reawaking the finer instincts of the misguided urbanites. Ironically, however, the film proved to be the bleakest work of the director's career. With insight gained after the fact, Capra would write thirty years later that *Meet John Doe* was made, not so much to show faith, but rather to prove that he could "handle hard-nosed brutality with the best of [them]." A dark vision of the dangers implicit in American democracy, rarely permitted to surface in *Deeds* or *Smith,* erupts in *Doe,* and instead of reaffirming those values he had advertised so successfully in the previous films, Capra here discovers that they are inadequate to a new set of problems posed by the rise of Fascism. *Meet John Doe* marks the end of Capra's career as social mythmaker: after it he would turn to the more personal cinema of *It's a Wonderful Life.*

The seed of *Doe*'s problems is apparent in its enormous physical scale. *Deeds* had taken place in a limited arena—New York City—but *Doe* encompasses the entire nation in its scope, indicative of Capra's desire to give the film a comprehensiveness which would underline its mythic intent. The mythological resonance of *Mr. Deeds,* however, was a result not of sheer numbers, but of Capra's inspired manipulation of meaningful, well-defined symbols which were a part of a shared American experience. Deeds's victory over his adversaries clearly implied the triumph of individualism over conformity, of the personal over the mass, of the spiritual over the material. There was no need to render explicit the importance of this victory by painting on an exceedingly large canvas.

Mr. Smith Goes to Washington represents Capra's first increase in the scale of his national mythology over that of *Deeds:* in it one can see the germ of the problems *Doe* would later present. The courtroom of *Deeds* in *Smith* becomes the Senate of the United States. Deeds's activities are the talk of New York; Smith's are the talk of the entire nation. And the public media that, in *Mr. Deeds,* is apparently contained by the big city, branches out to reach Smith's home state. Rather than heighten our sense of the traditional, the increased scale of *Smith* brings with it an increased sense of modern corruption. We find evil in the person of Boss James Taylor in a rural (and presumably traditional) western state. And since Smith's foes are not entirely urban, Capra could not easily tie up all the strings in one neat, decisive victory. Consequently, the film's original ending, depicting the dismantling of Taylor's political machine following Smith's Senate victory, proved to be anticlimactic. Capra chose to cut it, leaving us somewhat in doubt as to Taylor's fate. Still, the present ending is hardly open-ended; in *Mr. Smith Goes to Washington,* the mythological *Deeds* structure remains basically intact.

With the further increase in scale of *Meet John Doe,* this structure breaks down completely. The distinction between small town and city, so important to *Mr. Deeds,* virtually disappears. Although *Doe*'s backdrop is the entire map of the United States, the moral geography of the film is urban; no longer is there any contrast between citified and rustic views of social reality. Correspondingly, the idealized past of *Deeds* and *Smith* is dissolved. There is in the first half of *Meet John Doe* no traditional moral sense similar to those that energized Longfellow Deeds and Jefferson Smith.

The film opens with the changing of the *Daily Bulletin*'s motto from "A Free Press for a Free People" to "A Streamlined Newspaper for a Streamlined Era," and we immediately find ourselves in the center of a modern moral chaos. Ann Mitchell (Barbara Stanwyck), a reporter for the *Bulletin,* is fired along with many of her colleagues for being out of step with the times. In retaliation, she composes a letter under the name of "John Doe" protesting the injustice of the modern world and threatening to commit suicide by jumping off City Hall on Christmas Eve if social conditions do not improve. This letter becomes her final column for the *Bulletin.* When a political, social, and journalistic controversy ensues, Ann is rehired—provided she reveals the identity of John Doe. Ann admits to having penned the letter herself, then convinces the *Bulletin*'s editor (James Gleason) to hire a John Doe rather than publicly acknowledge the letter as a hoax. (If no sincere moral figure exists in the modern world, then fake one—especially if it will boost your circulation.) Long John Willoughby (Gary Cooper), a freight train hopping ex-bush-league pitcher, is chosen from a long line of eager derelicts. In return for posing as John Doe, he will receive an operation that will mend his bad arm and a one-way ticket out of town on Christmas Eve.

Doe's premise is as unrelentingly cynical as any Capra has ever treated. Yet a traditional, ethical figure does emerge out of this world of self-serving fast-talkers, improbably enough: Long John's tenuous link with the past (the speeches Ann writes for him, containing the wisdom of her dead father), and his growing sense of responsibility that comes of being a public figure finally transform him into a moral force in this chaotic present. The John Doe letters attract public attention—including the attention of D. B. Norton (Edward Arnold), the *Bulletin*'s Fascistic owner, a powerful monopolist, and a man with extreme political ambition. Norton puts Long John on the radio to increase Doe's following, and it is at this point that Willoughby finally awakens both to the extent of his control over his audience and to the moral dubiousness of the Doe affair. He runs from the studio at the end of his speech; he and his friend the Colonel (Walter Brennan) hop the first freight train out of town. However, Long John's anonymity is short-lived: when he and the Colonel stop over in Millville, a nearby small town, he is recognized as John Doe, cornered by the townspeople, and told how positively he has affected community relations. Willoughby is deeply moved by these testimonials. His moral transformation is now complete, and he decides to pose once again as John Doe, this time hoping to promote brotherhood among his followers.

It seems, for a while, that the newly transformed Willoughby might conquer the corrupt present and lead us to an ideal future. The John Doe movement gains momentum. Willoughby is sent on hectic speaking tours; John Doe Clubs—encouraging a sense of community and personal relationships among average Americans—spring up across the continent; a national John Doe Convention is planned. But D. B. Norton has had personal reasons for promoting the movement. The night of the convention, Norton privately demands that Willoughby choose him as the John Doe's third party candidate for the Presidency of the United States. Willoughby refuses, and leaves for the convention stadium, planning to tell the John Does the truth about the movement. Before he can speak, however, Norton rushes upon the stage, reveals Willoughby as an impostor, and has his private police force cut the microphone wires. Hearing no explanation from Willoughby, the violently disillusioned mob turns on him. He is lucky to escape with his life.

Long John decides that he can only prove his sincerity and thereby resurrect the John Doe movement by committing suicide on Christmas Eve as the original John Doe letter said he would. In the film's present ending (Capra shot five different endings, all of which he found unsatisfactory), a group of John Does— the very Millville citizens who first persuaded John to become a public crusader— now convince him that he is more valuable to the movement alive than dead. But is he? The film's finale, with the small group exiting from the City Hall roof to the strains of Beethoven's Ninth, is utterly unresolved. Lacking a clear notion of an idealized past, Capra is unable to provide us with a convincing realization of an ideal future. The struggle of these few to revive the John Doe movement just begins as the film ends, and we are left anchorless in an ugly, tempestuous present.

Clearly, this breakdown of the *Deeds* structure results in a drastic departure in meaning from Capra's earlier films. What forces within the film make it much darker and more troubled than either of its predecessors? *Doe*'s magnification of the evils of *Deeds* and *Smith* is in large part responsible. The relatively limited danger of the city shysters in *Deeds* has grown cancerlike, paralleling the film's increase in scale, giving us the Hitlerian national menace that D. B. Norton poses. Norton's villainy surpasses Cedar's and Taylor's financial greed: Norton lusts after cold power. Capra introduces him brilliantly, immediately impressing upon us the enormity of his ambition. We see a long shot of a motorcycle troop preparing to drill on a large field, then a medium shot of Norton on horseback, watching the drill through binoculars. We then return to the field, where a dazzling, dangerous pattern involving dozens of speeding, intersecting motorcycles is being performed. All this is for one man's benefit. It comes as no surprise, then, to learn that Norton believes "What the American people need is an iron hand" or that he controls almost every important communications medium in the country.

Indeed, it is the mass media that serve as Norton's prime means of controlling America. Capra's ambivalence toward this impersonal means of communication, a tangential issue in earlier films, here becomes a focal point. Radio and the newspapers, in *Meet John Doe,* exert an almost supernatural influence over Americans. The media become arbitrary fates: if Doe's climb to fame is achieved through them, his decline—the result of the simple clipping of a microphone wire—is likewise, in a sense, their work.

Yet, after all, D. B. Norton and his villainous use of the media do not entirely account for the darkness of the film: to isolate the aspect of *Doe* that makes it so much more pessimistic than either of its predecessors, one must look beyond the obvious dangers of Norton to the more subtle ones Long John Willoughby suggests. Unlike Longfellow Deeds and Jefferson Smith, Willoughby, when he is anonymous, is absolutely amoral. He accepts the *Bulletin*'s offer so that his bad arm may be mended—thinking nothing of the moral consequences of his action. Only when he becomes a celebrity does he grow into the moral decency that Smith and Deeds possess from the start. If taken symbolically, Willoughby's conversion implies, not that most Americans are traditionally ethical, but rather that the anonymous "little man," so long as he remains anonymous, is little more than a moral blank slate.

This is obviously an atypical notion for Capra, and one would be tempted to disregard it if the bulk of *Meet John Doe* did not bear it out. When Ann Mitchell selects Cooper as her choice for John Doe, she tells her editor, "That face is wonderful. . . . They'll believe him." As a veteran newspaperwoman, she believes that the American public can be manipulated by mere appearances. And her belief is shared by her colleagues. In an almost surrealistic sequence, reminiscent of Nathanael West, we see newspapermen create perverse symbols for an undiscriminating public: just prior to his first radio broadcast, Long John is being photographed for the newspapers when a young woman in a bathing suit is ushered in, a banner draped across her breast. "I'm getting a Jane Doe ready," a newspaperman explains. She is photographed with Willoughby, then leaves, and two midgets are brought into the room. The midgets, "symbols of the little people," we are told, perch on John's shoulders, and again a picture is taken.

Soon after this sequence, we are given a direct indication of the eagerness with which ordinary Americans accept symbols produced by the mass media, when John and the Colonel visit Millville. One can easily see how far Capra has travelled from the solid community of Deeds's Mandrake Falls: Millville residents illogically worship John Doe, a man whom they at this point have only heard once, on the radio. The owner of a small diner (Sterling Holloway) becomes inordinately excited when he recognizes Doe eating in his restaurant, then telephones an operator: "Tell everybody in town! John Doe was just in my place!" The situation of John Doe—the symbol of the average man—receiving this perverse celebrity worship is extraordinarily ironic. Similarly, Millville's Mayor Hawkins (Harry Holman) lures John to the town hall, then patrols the main entrance. "Don't do anything to disgrace a little town," he tells some townsfolk as they push their way in to see their god. He denies entrance to others because they did not vote for him. "Haven't had so much excitement since the city hall burnt down," he remarks; "people were so excited they nearly tore his clothes off." The small town, once the locus of traditional values, is fast becoming a center of selfishness and ugly credulity.

There is a huge potential for disillusionment among these Millville residents, a potential that is realized in the film's climactic convention sequence. The crowd, gathered together from many states, is at first a model of harmony, a sea of umbrellas, singing together in the rain. The people are, as Long John tells us, "hungry for something. . . . Maybe they're just lonely and [want] . . . somebody to say hello." They are at their most open, their most vulnerable, yet this vulnerability renders them more volatile. They need only vaguely sense that they have been duped, and they will emotionally snap shut like clams. D. B. Norton gives them that sense, and in the ensuing bitter turmoil ("We've been taken so long, we're getting used to it," one man snarls), the latent dangers of unthinking innocence are brilliantly realized. What began as Capra's denouncement of Nazi tactics finds the seeds of Fascism lying dormant in American Democracy. *Meet John Doe* presents America, not with the good self-image that *Deeds* and *Smith* provided, but with the underside of that image—with all of Capra's doubts about democracy and the American people.

Yet Capra's consciousness of his role of social mythmaker, coupled with his fundamentally comic world vision, did not permit him to be comfortable with *Doe*'s pessimism. The more the film shows us his disillusionment with the American people, the more it tells us of his love for them. His sentimental scenes, normally so poignantly effective, are unconvincing in *Meet John Doe*. The sequence in which Long John is convinced by the Millville residents to resume his posture as John Doe is typical of the film's unsure treatment of sentiment. One townsperson after another bears witness to his faith in Doe. The first speeches are somewhat affecting, but by the time old Mrs. Delaney (Emma Tansey) tells Long John (in close-up), "God bless you, my boy," the sequence has become excessive.

Similarly, the decision on the part of the three Millville "John Does" (Regis Toomey, Ann Doran, J. Farrell MacDonald) to journey to the City Hall roof to prevent Doe from committing suicide is unbelievable. We have just witnessed their profound disillusionment in the convention sequence, then suddenly they are racing to the roof, insisting that they trust Willoughby.

Indeed, Capra himself seems to be often acutely aware of the implausibility of such sequences. His characteristic comic undercutting of the potentially maudlin (Cooper, in *Deeds,* trips over a trash can after a romantic scene with Jean Arthur) here becomes extreme, rendering the film's tone uncertain and disconcerting. The character of the Colonel seems to have been created solely to serve as a constantly cynical (yet sympathetic) reference point throughout the film. When Stanwyck first explains the John Doe letter to him, the Colonel replies, "You couldn't improve the world if the buildings jumped on you." Long John, in his first radio speech, suggests that people tear down the fences separating them from their neighbors: later, the Colonel insists that, "If you tore one picket off of your neighbor's fence, he'd sue you." The Colonel summarizes his world view in one phrase: "The world's been shaved by a drunken barber." And in the afore-mentioned sequence in which Millville residents tell John of how his speech has helped them to understand each other, the Colonel's skeptical scowl, repeatedly shown in reaction shots, constantly punctures the scene's mawkishness. Yet the Colonel is never proven wrong: unlike other likable cynics in *Deeds, Smith,* or even *Doe,* the Colonel is never converted to optimism.

At times, the corrosively skeptical aspect of the film, embodied primarily in the Colonel, seems to take on a perverse sense of self-parody. The midget se-quence preceding Long John's radio debut in particular seems to have a self-directed irony to it. When the two midgets are placed on Long John's shoulders, and Willoughby is told that he is supporting twin symbols of "the little people," Capra seems to come dangerously close to commenting caustically on his own conception of himself as social mythmaker.

And therein lies a possible key to one of the most perplexing questions *Meet John Doe* poses: why did Capra, so aware of his influence over the American public, so socially dedicated, allow himself to create as disturbing a film as this? The answer lies in the autobiographical nature of *Doe;* for the film, obsessed as it is with the importance of mass media, proves to be Capra's only work to deal directly with the issue of American mythmaking. Long John's accidental trans-formation from drifter to national figure parallels Capra's own early drifting ex-perience and subsequent involvement in moviemaking. Willoughby's awakening to his power over the studio audience during the key scene of his first radio speech, his initial fear of that power and his subsequent responsible acceptance of it parallels Capra's emotional and physical illness which followed the success of *It Happened One Night,* and his ultimate decision to create social myth in *Mr.*

Deeds Goes to Town. Yet Willoughby eventually learns the fruitlessness of attempting to create community by the impersonal means of mass preaching: the movie's finale ultimately accepts only the personal as a valid manner of dealing with others. Perhaps Frank Capra allowed himself to make as troubled a film as this because the rise of Fascism had caused him to doubt the value of his previous social mythmaking, and he now desired to express himself in a more personal, less strictly symbolic manner than the *Deeds* structure would allow.

Meet John Doe, then, was an attempt to work out his own fears and questions; unfortunately, they were not quite fitted to the structure of the film. It was, however, a fruitful effort: five years and a world war would intervene before Capra would again direct an ambitious feature film, but *It's a Wonderful Life*—a much less mythological work than *Doe,* on a smaller, more personal scale—would prove to be the crowning masterpiece of a long and stunning career.

Productive Discord in the System: Hollywood *Meets John Doe*

Dudley Andrew

Millions watch each year when Hollywood bestows its Academy awards, genuflecting before the ideals of art. This moment confirms its ordained episcopal role: worthy or unworthy, Hollywood, like the Church, claims to be the mediator through which its members may attain the sanctity of art and, in doing so, guarantee the rightness of a universal hierarchy headed on this earth by the leaders of studios and distribution companies. No recitation of its alleged misdeeds, of its spreading secular dominion, of the crass behavior of its potentates, can contaminate the grace that flows through it to its devotees. Hollywood has never pretended to be virtuous, except in this: that its cruelty and bad faith, its greed and its groveling, have created a versatile culture industry in which genius may achieve the pure and spiritual goals of art.

The film artist in Hollywood has always been treated as the favored son of a ruthless industrialist. Off at the best finishing schools, he knows little of the murky origins of the family fortune. The sins committed in the quest for power are to be expiated by this innocent Siegfried. When a conflict does arise, when the hegemony of power is at stake, it is always the son who must capitulate or, in the usual gesture of defiance, leave. Murnau must have felt this as he set sail with Robert Flaherty for pristine Polynesia, and Welles when in disgust he fled to Europe in search of patrons who knew something about the care and fostering of genius.

But how can we say that Hollywood has ever been uninterested in art? How can we forget Welles' glorious invitation to RKO, where he was given "the most expensive electric train" any adult had ever toyed with, sheerly on the promise of genius he had displayed? Murnau, too, came to Hollywood under a million-dollar contract because William Fox was so eager to upgrade and sanctify his enterprise. In that era Hollywood plundered European film talent without thought of cost. This is hardly the neglect of art.

From *Film in the Aura of Art* (Princeton: Princeton University Press, 1984), pp. 79–97. Published, in a slightly different form, in *Enclitic* 10 and 11 (Fall 1981 and Spring 1982).

But the cinematic art celebrated each spring in Southern California is popular art, not the pure marginal discourse of aliens like Murnau and Welles. For the cinema that has been touted as the art of our century is precisely the cinema of genres and mass taste, not the cinema that contorts itself into the postures of painting or poetry.

From this point of view, the men and women whom Hollywood beatifies are not at all those pampered children, referred to above, who have been kept far from the filth of the factory, but instead those children brought up to move into the firm, eventually to run it. The difference they make, the energy they bring, is not the excess of rebellion, obtuseness, or effete obsession. It is the productive difference that all capitalism feeds on, especially in this industry, where novelty is a chief value of the product sold.

Such novelty has most often been attributed to the "craft" of studio personnel or at best to their "artistry." But the tension between the institutional norm and each ambitious film emerging from the system is precisely the tension we recognize in the case of the lone genius who struggles against the system. And so it should hardly surprise us when, from time to time, Hollywood personnel, the sons of the industry, adopt the inflated vocabulary of art in parrying the stifling rules of their powerful parents.

In all events, by now few retain the image of the classic Hollywood cinema as a vast undifferentiated mass of mindless filmmaking. Tension and experiment are part of this era as they are in every period of every cultural institution. Naturally the Hollywood machine systematizes individuality and today forthrightly markets it. But even in the heyday of the system when Hollywood was proud of its image as "dream factory," the counterdreams of the great *auteurs* must not be seen as altogether separate from Hollywood but as bound up with Hollywood in a single, though variable network of links and causes.

In this context Frank Capra must energe as a figure worthy of continued study. The system's most consistently successful practitioner, he was immensely proud of the general popularity of his films, not to mention the incredible salary that popularity permitted him to accept without qualms. He was Mr. Hollywood, the man who directed its greatest stars: Jimmy Stewart, Gary Cooper, Jean Arthur, Barbara Stanwyck, Clark Gable. Yet Capra never tried to disappear behind the system as, say, Mervyn Leroy or Michael Curtiz seem to have done. He was "the name above the title" who knew, better than any of his peers, how to use the system.

There is reason to entertain his claim to a kind of moral distinctiveness, for after his fame had given him a sense of personal strength, he immediately hoped to separate himself somewhat from the system that had reared him in order to speak with a still more personal voice. In 1939 Capra began his adventures as an independent producer. Admittedly his primary goal was financial. He hated to see Columbia Pictures picking off the best fruits of his effort and his talent. Yet he was also genuinely anxious to get away from the prying paternal eyes of executive producers. Why should he have to bargain for script ideas or for personnel? Why couldn't he now choose his own projects and his collaborators in the French manner, since he had earned this independence by rising to the top of the system? Why couldn't he begin speaking directly his own ideas with his own voice? The mere fact of financial independence gave him a sense of moral rectitude.

It is, I think, crucial that Capra saw his first independent production *Meet John Doe* as a chance to prove to both the system and to the critics and intellectuals on the edge of the system that he was a man of conscience, insight, and intelligence. He himself said:

No it wasn't the existence of critics that really riled me. It was their supercilious attitude that got under my skin. I had made seven smash hits in a row. Had I performed that feat on Broadway I would have been canonized. . . . As it was, not one of my last three films—*Lost Horizons, You Can't Take It With You,* and *Mr. Smith Goes to Washington*—had made the New York Critics Annual Poll of their selected "ten best" films.

So I can truthfully say that it was the box office customers who made Frank Capra whatever he was or is. I was not invited into motion pictures, nor did I enjoy special favor of finance, nepotism or critical influence. I simply did my thing with films and the people responded. And yet, an ego like mine needed—nay required—the plaudits of sophisticated criticism. The Capra-Corn bards had pierced the outer bubble.

And so *Meet John Doe,* my first completely independent venture, was aimed at winning critical praises. Riskin and I would astonish the critics with contemporary realities. We would give them a brutal story that would make Ben Hecht sound like Edgar Guest.[1]

1. This and later citations concerning the film's production history come from Frank Capra, *The Name Above the Title* (New York: Macmillan, 1971), p. 297.

The film did indeed make the critics sit up. It was lavishly praised. More important to Capra, his peers in the industry applauded his daring. David Selznick said that this film made him "proud to be in pictures."[2]

What Selznick and the critics seemed to like was the direct presentation of a conflict between good and evil in which the outcome wasn't clear. The age was ugly: Hitler in Europe, fascists in America made hatred and evil representable concepts. In *Meet John Doe* these bitter representations "hit a standoff" with Capra's good folk, discoloring the limpid moral solutions his populist films had advanced. "My spirit and those of the audience would now have to seek a solution."

Meet John Doe was self-consciously ambitious in its aspirations. Capra conceived it as a personal film, a film that would address Hollywood from a position of independence, a film that would address the crisis of the depression and the lure of fascism. He wanted to speak with an authentic voice. If the film is less pleasurable than *Mr. Smith* or *Lost Horizon,* it was due, he felt, to the truth of what he had to say.

This was the "other side of the Pollyanna Capra." Instead of the small town virtues flowing like mountain streams through the corrupt city to purify it (as in *Mr. Deeds,* for instance, or *Mr. Smith*), now we find the big city mentality pushing across the country. Indeed, the politics in the villages is already seen as corrupt. Even the heroic little man has lost his innocence. Gary Cooper as John Doe is very nearly a moral cipher, a tabula rasa waiting to be used for good or evil. More disturbing, the John Does of the world can achieve morality only in nonpolitical social union, yet in 1940 it was clear that such moral power as the people may attain on their own could be quickly corralled and, in a single stroke, used by political forces. Because of Germany, it was not a matter of more or less politics. Politics was inevitable and in Capra's world inevitably bad.

The contradiction here was insurmountable. People alone are amoral, together they achieve morality, but as soon as that togetherness is organized politically they become immoral. This was something Capra believed: it was systematization that killed the best impulses in human beings.

At the very moment of *Meet John Doe* Capra was organizing his huge Hobby Shop in Los Angeles according to these precepts. It was to be a building full of work areas and supplies. His hope was that, by allowing craftsmen who were out of work to tinker free and at their leisure, new inventions would bubble up. All patents would be held by the Hobby Shop and one-half the proceeds from them

2. Ibid., p. 305.

would be plowed back into the operations of an ever expanding, Santa's work-shop. Capra's partner in this naive scheme was Howard Hughes who was to supply most of the money, Capra contributing the spirit. Like all naive schemes it went under at the first collision with reality. Ironically, in this case it was *Meet John Doe,* a film about the little people, that killed Capra's real-life hope for aiding those people. Capra claims it was Hitler and Hirohito who subverted his venture. He blamed them as well for siphoning warmth and optimism from his film. He even suggested that the *era* was responsible for his failure to come up with a natural ending to his film.

Capra saw the relation of film to history as direct and immediate. If his films were dark and murky, it was because this was the tone of politics throughout the world in 1940; this was also the tone of Hollywood, or so Capra felt as he struggled to gain his independence. Not only would *Meet John Doe* carry the tone of the times, it would explicitly dramatize the problems facing the average John Doe in the world and the individualist in Hollywood.

While not an allegory in the strict sense, *Meet John Doe* nevertheless turns on the opposition between power structures and the little man, mediated by the technocrats of the press whose job has much in common with Capra's own. When Barbara Stanwyck loses her position in the opening sequence, it is because of a command from the top which is insensitive to her talents and needs. Her ability not only to survive in this milieu, but to thrive and, in some respects, master that milieu expresses Capra's sense of his own accomplishments in the cutthroat Hollywood system.

Typically, Capra poses the opposition between power and the everyday citizen as dramatically as possible; most interesting for us is the fact that it is posed directly in relation to questions of media and of persuasion. On the one hand we have D. B. Norton's vast telecommunications network, with its broadcast station and its newspaper. The man of politics speaks via the voice of technology, ampli-fied beyond all reasonable proportion, drowning out counterstatement. On the other side, the ideas of the ordinary citizen express themselves through intimacy and personal contact: Barbara Stanwyck in the silence of the night draws inspira-tion from her father's diary, at once the most homespun and most trustworthy of media; the soda jerk calls over the hedge to old "sourpuss," leading to the house-to-house personal organization of the John Doe Clubs; finally, the power of an embrace and even of the threat of suicide is the ultimate authentic means of persuasion in which the body itself becomes the means of communication.

While Capra evidently fights so that intimacy might conquer technology, presence conquer absence, what kind of medium does his own discourse represent? What form of communication and persuasion is *Meet John Doe?* In serving as his own executive producer and personally taking charge of nearly every aspect of the film, Capra surely felt he could sustain in his film the aura of personal presence symbolized by the father's diary. Naively, Capra could only believe that if the individual is pure, then his ventures or statements can be trusted if the organization by which he states them is independent; thus anything confused or disorienting in such statements must be the product of some outside force, usually politics.

But this is nonsense. First of all, Capra's so-called independent company was not only linked to Hollywood through every element and member of its production, it was indeed the apotheosis of Hollywood. From 1937 on big producers and directors were finding it lucrative to break with the studio contract system in setting up independent companies, *Gone With the Wind* being the most famous example. In other words, Capra was at the forefront of the economic history of a changing but very healthy Hollywood system. Secondly and most importantly, the movies are not a means of expression so much as an apparatus expressing itself. Capra could say only what this apparatus permitted him to say. No one believed in this apparatus more than Capra. All his films speak the language of Hollywood and necessarily represent its values.

Meet John Doe is no exception to Hollywood. After all, it is an explicit reworking of Capra's earlier films. Its complication develops as a mixture of genres, particularly the newspaper film and the Warner's hobo film. The system, rather than Capra's spirit, dictated the direction and look of the picture. His inability to end the film in a satisfying way testifies to this. Showing it to numerous preview audiences, he tried no less than five endings hoping to find one that worked. Obviously it was convention, not Capra, that would dictate what worked and thus what would be said. Even his vocabulary betrays this homage to the filmic apparatus. "Why did hundreds of scenes integrate into a jigsaw puzzle that had greatness written all over it except for one gaping hole no last scene could plug up?"[3]

Meet John Doe, like all Capra's films, is indeed a jigsaw puzzle: hundreds of pieces fitting cleverly and nearly seamlessly together to present a single clear picture. This is the method of the classic Hollywood film, a method employing a rigorous and restricted set of techniques all aimed at suppressing interest in the fragment (in the sound or image) to further interest in the story. Not only are the

---

3. Ibid., p. 304.

stories drawn from conventional genres and subjects with a rhythm of exposition, conflict, complication, and resolution; but the story is presented in the clearest possible light. The entire apparatus of the cinema is brought to bear simply to clarify character relations and plot progression. This means framing characters and lighting them to bring out their importance, miking them to allow human dialogue to overcome natural sounds, using background music to key audience sympathies, maintaining consistent light and noise levels even when this means tampering with profilmic situations, using camera movement to focus interest, match-cutting on action to hide shot changes, setting up internal visual relations through glance-glance or glance-object cutting and through close-up inserts which organize the world around the characters, and employing visible transitions such as dissolves, fades, and wipes for clear punctuation.

These techniques are so common it is hard to accuse Capra of using them insidiously. What is ironic, however, is that he did employ them without question while figuring they would deliver his personal message of freedom and spontaneity. In fact his filmic system is as totalitarian and powerful as the political machinations of the film's villain, D. B. Norton. Both employ nice sentiments and the labor of the little guy to produce something unstoppable, something that can't be argued with, and, most important, something that is so monolithic that it dwarfs the pieces that gave it existence. We have learned how to analyze the monolith of the classic Hollywood system; nothing would be easier than to demonstrate the working of that discourse in *Meet John Doe*. But what gave life to this system is of the same order as that which gives life to *Meet John Doe*, a tension between the nearly military regularity and precision of the dominant discourse and the engaging lilt of the smaller voices it dares to include. The system is challenged by these small moments of counterstatement even if it ultimately harmonizes them. In *Meet John Doe* alternatives to the classic register are found first in the montage sequences prepared by Slavko Vorkapich, and second in the individual voices of its three principal actors, speaking as they do with the trailing echo of their careers, bringing to the spectator an intimacy won in other films, in radio interviews, in magazine stories, and other organs of publicity. As Capra wanted to speak his own mind even within the world of Hollywood, so Vorkapich, Cooper, Stanwyck, and Brennan seem to want to speak their own way within the prison of the film's logic.

The montage sequence is one of the few clear legacies of the silent film carried over into the 1930s. It remains almost indigestible in the belly of the classic Hollywood system, for although functioning to benefit that system, it disobeys the rules we have constructed to describe that system, rules concerning invisibility of technique, clarity of development, primacy of character, and most crucially, homogeneity of narration.

By the time of *Meet John Doe,* of course, the etiquette of such sequences had been firmly conventionalized: montage sequences might appear for short sections (seldom over ninety seconds) to provide narrative transitions. They had to be dispersed through the film, never threatening to take over the discourse. They were particularly appropriate as prefaces to the main body of the narrative. The conventions of their construction were just as rigorous, permitting strong juxtapositions, but no shock-cutting. Dissolves and inventive wipes must ease the viewer through the disparate visual elements. Superimpositions fading in and out sometimes result from this strategy, frequently putting a complicated graphic image atop a more stable and recognizable one, such as a word, a calendar page, the face of a key character. The sound accompaniments of montage sequences are often loosed from their narrow tracks and allowed to roam freely amongst the images. This freedom asserts itself either with a rhythmic nondiegetic score or with a concatenation of sound pieces overlayed on one another in imitation of visual dissolves.

Such wild, experimental intrafilms are justified by the syntagmatic logic of the full text so that they serve a single function, act as one syntagmatic unit. Originally they replaced titles denoting temporal, spatial, or causal change. Indeed, they might be thought of as distended dissolves between locales, the projector mysteriously winding down to show the atomic subevents and the liquid chemistry animating them which permits the movement from one scene to the next. In this way the energy of the montage segment is held in by the function it serves in the narration, a single unambiguous function; so that for all its pyrotechnics, for its seeming challenge to discursive clarity and method, the montage sequence submits to the standard logic of the Hollywood narrative voice.

All of this is precisely the case in *Meet John Doe.* The three montage sequences are equally distributed (one in the middle of each reel on the 16mm print). Their lengths are fifty-four, fifty-seven, and thirty-two feet, that is, between a minute and ninety seconds. They feature an average of one new image every three seconds, but this is complicated by the use of superimpositions, which are sometimes multiple.

The principle of contiguity behind these sequences varies from graphic similarity, to mini-narrative, to screen direction, to rhythmic alteration. The first such sequence is exemplary in this regard. Gary Cooper is caught with an irate expression on his face by the press camera. That expression graces the front page of the paper which is seen in several locales and as an object of exchange (money and a doorbell are inserted to thematize the issue of exchange already signified by the successive shots of the paper). Two mini-narratives find Barbara Stanwyck madly typing (framed in a cocked low-angle shot), putting out stories that expose graft and the scandal of medical aid to the poor. We see dirty money being passed; we see a poor family. These little motifs are anchored by a headline which once again asserts the priority of the textual as the commodity of exchange. In a series of three varied shots, papers are shown being purchased at an accelerating pace, leading to the standby of all montage sequences, the animated graph. Here the soaring fame of John Doe as well as the increased circulation of the paper is explicitly displayed on a grid, superimposed over mounting piles of papers. When those papers reach a crescendo, the sequence's most daring transformation occurs: they begin to move not upward but foward in a march that becomes a literal march on city hall. A caricature of the mayor fainting gives way, as it must, to a shot of the governor trying to defend himself. The governor is given a sync-sound speech to bring us out of the sequence, but not before a telling track in on his face match-dissolves to the face of D. B. Norton holding binoculars and looking back at the camera. This is the introduction of the film's last key character, and it is quite an introduction at that.

The modes of contiguity in this sequence are many, as is the iconography (printed words, caricatured scenes, pixillated objects, long shots of crowds, close-ups of money, graphics). Throughout, the metaphor of circulation is explicit and with this metaphor the suggestion that every element in the sequence, and by extension in the narrative, attains its significance only in the system that moves it and that it helps move. As money passes from hand to hand, hardly mistakable is the implication that the newspaper itself is part of the system of graft it pretends to expose. We can find a similar analogy when we look to the source of the sequence's power. D. B. Norton looking back on us with his binoculars, owner of the newspaper, is the man who dictates its policies and personnel, and this includes the benign ignoramus Gary Cooper. In terms of the allegory of narration, Frank Capra finally wrests power away from Slavko Vorkapich, the creator of the sequence, assembling the peculiar gains of the sequence into a precise and calculated summing up. Recall that the entire sequence is triggered by a trick of photography: Gary Cooper, feigning anger over a miscalled pitch, becomes a social rabble-rouser. Even the social issues he purportedly raises are only the necessary preconditions for the march of the papers and the rise of economic and political power which the sequence chronicles. It is a peculiar chronicle, suggesting in its very form the revolutionary disruption of the life of the press and the life of politics that D. B. Norton's entry into public life has caused.

The montage aesthetic, purportedly Hollywood's daring concession to experimental cinema,[4] is given full play first of all in order to make an efficient narrative gain, taking us in this instance up a chain of command from lowly Gary Cooper to the seat of political power. At the same time it thematizes the issue of free expression and spontaneous experimentation. The montage sequences are like the sudden joyous outbursts that Walter Brennan and Gary Cooper spit out on their "doo-hickeys." This analogy permits us to theorize the aesthetics of spontaneity, or rather, extend the theorization already attempted by Adorno in the case of jazz to the aesthetics of standard cinema. The montage sequence seems exemplary in this respect, for, like the cadenza or jazz solo, it addresses us with its freedom, its authenticity, and its bravura. Yet it always is authorized by the dominant rhythm and by the rules established in the introduction of the piece, invariably returning to those rhythms and themes. Its flurry of freedom, like that of the adolescent, is played out under the eye of the parent. This is the "regressive" aspect of modern music for Adorno.[5] Similarly in the montage sequence we find the appropriation of the graphic wizardry of Vorkapich by the ever present father, Capra, as though Capra had been holding in reserve a certain quantity of libidinal energy, not his own but borrowed, which he released at just the appropriate narrational moment. The sequence may strike us as free, but it points in only one direction. It leads us to the powerful gaze of the fascist D. B. Norton. Norton, who has been directing the action from behind the scenes all along and who now commands his motorcycle troops before dictating, with a more subtle rhetoric, the actions of Barbara Stanwyck and, hence, Cooper himself, is the story's counterpart to the storyteller Capra, whose presence we feel behind every gesture and every change of shot.

4. Slavko Vorkapich was revered and feared in Hollywood. An East European refugee, he had been associated with experimental projects in the twenties, most memorably in *The Life and Death of a Hollywood Extra* (1928). During the era of the classic Hollywood film he was responsible for numerous montage sequences and was regarded as a master when it came to montage. For an overview of his life and work see Vlada Petric, "The Vorkapich Effect," *American Film*, no. 3 (March 1978).

5. Theodor Adorno, "On the Fetish Character in Music and the Regression of Listening," in *The Essential Frankfurt School Reader*, ed. Andrew Arato and Eike Gebhardt (New York: Urizon, 1978), pp. 270–299.

Capra is not a great director of actors, but he is peerless in his use of stars. The difference is instructive, and it is clearly visible in the performance of the secondary players in the film. Aside from Stanwyck, Cooper, and Brennan, the other actors are fully utilitarian. Capra chooses them for their physiognomy, leaves them on screen long enough to deliver the proper speech and gesture, then opposes this to the next functional gesture of the next mechanical character. The relative success of this method must be credited to the casting department which he dominated. More than most of his thirties triumphs, *Meet John Doe* treats its actors as cogs in a machine, cutting to them for quick reaction shots, getting their speeches across, and getting them off screen. This is so apparent because Cooper, Stanwyck, and Brennan offer a different approach, one that we are tempted to say comes from them and is opposed to Capra.

Cooper, especially, struggles to be free within his role and within the strict limits of the camera's frame and the story's time. He is boxed in for the most part, but certain relaxed moments find him leading the film, deflecting our interest from the intrigue, as when he mugs for Stanwyck and her photographers or recounts his lengthy and all-too-telling dream. Here Capra has given to Cooper the same sort of leash he gave Harry Langdon in the twenties, a leash jerked back when necessary. After all, Cooper's character is written as quirky, spontaneous, with an instinct for truth and for the moment. This is what makes him so attractive to Barbara Stanwyck who shares all these qualities with the addition of ambition. Stanwyck brings to her character also a quantum of authenticity which takes her nearly beyond her role. She responds to certain situations hysterically while everyone else functions smoothly even in defeat. This is evident when she throws her shoe through Connell's window in the first sequence. While she generally knows how to control this energy, indeed knows how to use it to make others pay attention, it is with a certain ultimate hysteria that she cries to Cooper in the film's last scene, fainting in his arms when her voice can say no more. Capra doubtless saw himself in her, talented and powerful, within limits, authentic beyond her talent, persuading by the power of authenticity. More than Cooper, Barbara Stanwyck, especially in this role, is an emblem of the American personality, for her resourcefulness is checked by a basic sense of values which she is certain will win out in the end and which she feels, unreflectively, that she is pushing forward. Capra permits Stanwyck her hysteria because, like Vorkapich's quasi-anarchic montage sequences, he can lock this "other" discursive register into place, can cite it, we might say, as a reference to authenticity.

Walter Brennan represents the most recalcitrant case both as character and actor. A performer of great distinction, Brennan is nonetheless in the same paradigm with Sterling Holloway and other recognizable faces/voices which the film employs conventionally. But Brennan's style is so distinct, his position in the industry so unquestioned, that he challenges every film that tries to place him securely in its narrative. No doubt this stems from the uncouth directness he exudes, whether as poor sidekick as in this and so many other films, or as deranged but honest Judge Roy Bean, for instance, a year later in William Wyler's *The Westerner.* Unlike Cooper and Stanwyck, in other words, Walter Brennan's individual power comes from the type he has always played, as though he embodies that type. Cooper and Stanwyck exist beyond their characters and are available to a limited plurality of roles, all commenting on one another.

In *Meet John Doe* the Walter Brennan type gets its fullest play. For despite his sidekick standing, Brennan actually figures the most extreme pole of the possibilities offered by the film. He is the fully unsocialized human. His response to corruption and pettiness is a return to nature, Thoreau-like in its rugged individualism, yet without thought of social benefit nor even of the values of philosophical reflection. He is treated as the natural man, peripheral to society, yet central to any consideration of what society might be.

In this sense we must finally find in Walter Brennan the aptest figure for Vorkapich's discourse of montage. Both are spontaneous and playful, both are peripheral to the dominant system they nevertheless trouble and interrupt. Both operate according to some preposterous logic, with a libidinal energy threatening to the established order yet somehow necessary for that order to bring up and deal with. And just as Vorkapich returned his gift of freedom freely to Capra, actually promoting the narration of the film, so Walter Brennan makes a gift of his own freedom in the film's conclusion, a gift to the Christ child on Christmas Eve, as he stands (still on the periphery) beside the John Doe members, cheering John on, ushering in a new holistic image of society. He too has been integrated.

It is Walter Brennan, far more than Gary Cooper, whom the film has difficulty in socializing; the fact that Brennan's socialization arrives in the last moment, unexplained, barely noticed, and certainly not explicitly proclaimed, suggests that the film would prefer to think of him as a sidekick, going along with Gary Cooper as the Fool goes with Lear. But like Shakespeare's fools, Brennan really does refuse to be smoothed over. He is absurd in the dramatic equation, unbalanced by any ordinary scheme of character relations. An initial list of the opposing sides of characters in descending order of their commitment to the side would be:

Power and Technology	*Personal Values*
(*Politics*)	(*Intimacy*)
Hitler (implied)	Christ (implied)
D. B. Norton	Stanwyck's father
The Politicians	Stanwyck's family
Newspaper technocrats	citizens (club members)
Stanwyck	Cooper

Walter Brennan

The plot of course turns on the incongruity of Stanwyck's belonging to the world of personal values, via her father and family. By trying to appropriate Cooper at the film's outset, she hops to put her technology at the service of intimate, nonpolitical communication. At the end, of course, it is she who must beg to be taken, as once she took; it is technology that has failed and personal communication (an embrace, a body about to hurl itself to death) that brings her forever into the arms of Cooper. But by this time, of course, Cooper has indeed become her father, as once she wanted him to be, so that in his arms she is both taken by a lover and protected by a father.

All of this makes eminent Hollywood sense, and it successfully places every character function in the film, except Walter Brennan. No one woos the "Colonel," tempting him into the social order. He exists at the end, as he did at the outset, a permanent possibility to disorder, to ultimate liberty, a possibility of the imaginary. This is graphically apparent in several of Gary Cooper's moments of decision. As the beleaguered ego, literally on stage, Cooper looks to the Colonel who stands at the exit holding $5,000 with a mischievous gleam in his eye. In front of Cooper, though, is the word of the father, which he finally pronounces in a most dutiful way.

The temptation offered by Walter Brennan places him in inverse rapport with the film's most calculating figure, the villain D. B. Norton. Both men have disdain for citizenry, a fact underlined by a dissolve from Brennan screaming to John Doe members, "Out of my way, you helots" to Norton instructing his men how to do the "cleanup operations" on the John Doe clubs. Bot men act sheerly for themselves, exercising their own wills as they please. Both live in fully male societies, standing to the side and observing the everyday life they each in their own way despise. Both are, though in opposite manners, romantic figures, acting out of their own morality, or, better, their own amorality. The danger that each represents to the culture is the danger of the not-normal. It is the danger homosexuality poses to the heterosexual world, a danger seen on the one hand as attraction toward violence and fascism and on the other toward unproductive hedonism. In Capra's vocabulary Norton poses the threat from the right in strong-armed order, while the Colonel, slighter but more engaging, stands to the far left of democracy, almost to the point of anarchy.

Capra had hoped to preach a middle path, to speak with the voice of an ordinary citizen. Cooper was chosen as that citizen, placed in a battle for authority with D. B. Norton. There in the ballpark the logic of Capra's own plot and Norton's political machine reduce Cooper to a sniveling child with one snip of the wire-cutters. Cooper, castrated, returns to the Eden of hobo life, presexual and prepolitical.

Capra's dream that personal values might be packaged inside a Hollywood film, like John Doe's belief for a national reawakening outside of politics, is here cut short by its own logic. Those who live by amplification and organization must die by it, particularly if they are naive enough to use it for a "good cause." This is what we learned in a strictly filmic way when the free flow of images was seen as disciplined by Vorkapich's montage logic.

On the other side is Walter Brennan and the temptation, occasionally accepted by the major actors, to exist outside narrative desire altogether. No shot in the film has more poetic resonance than the narratively gratuitous silhouette of Cooper and Brennan playing their "doohickeys" and dancing on a freight car. This is the end of logic, the train leading to a campfire under the bridge, the smoking of a pipe, and other useless pleasures. Cooper's acting is a type of useless pleasure that Capra never fully drafted for his purposes.

It was precisely at this point (the castration of Cooper, the return to infantile life with Walter Brennan) that Capra despaired. His hundreds of pieces did indeed form that jigsaw puzzle no final scene could complete. But Capra's forthrightness here should not disarm us. A puzzle with a missing piece is not a masterpiece *manqué;* it is an incoherent work. Walter Brennan is the token of that incoherence and his gentle hold on Gary Cooper must mock every plot solution conceivable to the Hollywood mind.

It is here that the film shifts registers, leaving its public narrative tone at the ballpark and letting speak an intimate voice of conscience and a religious voice of renunciation. Vorkapich once again is called upon but now to remake the film in sixty seconds from the point of view of Gary Cooper. Whereas Norton ruled the first montage of Cooper's rise to fame and explicitly engineered the second montage chronicling the spread of the John Doe movement across the country, this final montage neither rises nor spreads in public strength but delves, swirls like water down a sewer into the troubled psyche of Long John Willoughby as he lies catatonic beside the Colonel's campfire.

This montage is composed primarily of shots we have already seen, but reorganized troublesomely as a threat and accusation, nightmarish, until it has an effect no logic could have on Cooper. The drama turns here not on external cause-effect but on a rhythmic accumulation of evidence and longing. Without pause, Vorkapich dissolves from Cooper retreating down a dark alleyway to a mystical view of city hall on a snowy Christmas eve.

The montage voice of Vorkapich has here shifted functions, from the public and political to the intimate and even psychoanalytic. This prepares the way for the final shift of registers into the hieratic. Atop city hall, Christmas bells in the air, Norton stands disarmed. When Stanwyck faints into Cooper's arms, her hysteria spent, the strains of Beethoven's "Ode to Joy" fall like snow from the sky. Gary Cooper is transformed into John Doe, into Stanwyck's father, and into Jesus himself.

Banking on the aphorism "Render unto Caesar, the things that are Caesar's, and unto God the things that are God's," Capra has tried to solve the conflict of personal purity and political effectiveness both in his plot and in his situation in Hollywood as he felt Christ solved it. Or rather, he hides behind Christ when neither of them are able to solve it. The hieratic register itself is meant to hush all doubts.

Meet John Doe is one of many Hollywood films that changes its tone, its narrational strategies, and even the rules of its genre to come to an acceptable conclusion. Far from vilifying this film or its type, we should see it as exposing a tension, present in every classic Hollywood film, between an authoritative voice of traditional logic and the more spontaneous tones of actors and visible technique. Too much of our analytical energy has gone into uncovering the source of narrative logic. From my point of view, Hollywood had always recognized the bankruptcy of the so-called classic approach, and challenged it in every film. If the spontaneous, the playful, the authentic subvoices in these films are put in choruses to support the same old song and singer, we ought to at least examine the productive tension between the two.

In *Meet John Doe* this tension is palpable when the chorus (Vorkapich and the principal actors) is forced to finish the song which Capra and his narrative logic have failed to end. Stepping back from a microphone that can only whistle in feedback, Capra lets us attend to acting as acting, technique as technique, if only to be able to close a film he had opened.

In the classic era Hollywood always stayed on top, even in such maverick independent productions as *Meet John Doe*. But the adjustments that it was forced to make to drown out or harmonize other voices, like Capra's adjustments in *Meet John Doe*, are ingenious and fertile. Hollywood is most interesting when its authoritative voice is in question. It is in question, I believe, a good part of the time. For spectators and analysts alike, the complications this struggle for unification produces ought to be of far more interest than the sameness of the system we have so prematurely labeled "classic."

System of Production/ System of Representation: Industry Context and Ideological Form in Capra's *Meet John Doe*

Nick Browne

With Edison's 1909 attempt to implement vertical integration of the American motion picture industry, the fundamental paradigm of a national system of film distribution and exhibition was set. The early industry structure was intended to bring together the fragmentary and dispersed mode of distribution, and to create and address a *national* audience. Though, in fact, this process of integration and consolidation of exhibition was not concluded until the mid-twenties, this national market structure constituted both the terms for assimilation, if not unification, of various diverse audiences and the conditions of film's reach of that audience. It is in this context—that of the transformation of the film industry—that I want to look at an aspect of one of the best known filmmakers of the classical period, Frank Capra, with a view toward an analysis of the discursive and cinematographic form implied in his work considered in its social relations.

The main body of Capra's work in the sound film is informed by what might be called an evolving "humanist" presentation of the inequalities of American society, inequalities figured conceptually and cinematographically as a conflict among Economy, Government, and the Media. These terms—presented more concretely as money, (political) representation, and speech—compose the coordinates of a certain version of an American Dream. They articulate an American mythos of an ascending, descending, and sometimes oppositional position for the central figure in which the chief signifier in the symbolic register is in one way or

An earlier version of this essay was published in Italian as "Sistem di produzione/sistema di rappresentazione: *Meet John Doe*," in *Hollywood in Progress: Itinerari cinema televisione,* ed. Vito Zagarrio (Venice: Marsilio Editori, 1984), pp. 53–72. It has been revised for this volume by the author.

another, money. Indeed the Bank is central to Capra's vision from *American Madness* to *It's a Wonderful Life,* from 1932 to 1946, insofar as it provides fundamental symbolic means for integrating, comparing, and dramatizing diverse ethnic and social interests. That *money* is central to Capra's work is obvious enough. What is perhaps not so apparent—curiously, it is never mentioned *as such* in Capra's writings, or in the writing on him—is the problem of American *speech.*

What I want to present, then, is a framework for analyzing the form of Capra's cinematic discourse in a paradigmatically central film of its period (*Meet John Doe,* released in 1941) with a view to characterizing its relation to the audience that Capra sought and to determining the institutional and historical circumstances within which this relation to the audience was constituted. As such, I need to reexamine the problem of modeling the relations between film form and the social intertext. This treatment is in two parts—one on context, and one on form.

Part I. The Problem and Interpretation of "Context"

Traditional thought about the relation of American film to American society has only in singular instances achieved theoretical or systematic rigor. The traditional film histories document style and technology, and rarely consider film as a social institution. The cultural histories, of course, do organize and present certain patterns of the cinema regarded as a social fact. These diverse assemblages, however, have rarely advanced a fully cogent paradigm of the film/society relation, or been informed by an explicit or distinct conception of the place of mass media in American society in ways that would allow film form itself to take on cultural significance. Yet a meaningful reconstruction of these specific historical and cultural materials, in view of a theory of the social formation, is a condition of interpreting changes in the evolution and function of film forms and for figuring in more rigorous ways the relation of texts to their social context. Arguably, the reinterpretation of the patterns of film history within the framework of institutional and social history constitutes the framework for understanding the function of film genres and modes of cinematic representation and, more particularly, of establishing the relation of groups of films, or the single film, to its historical and social subtexts.

The relationship of film and society, it seems evident, is not fully reducible to the traditional terms of the social history of film. Jowett's *Film: The Democratic Art* treats the social history of film through a study of the interaction of film as an institution (that includes both an organized system of production and a movie-going audience) with other institutions—the school, church, and State. As part of a general social change of industrialization, film introduces a disturbance in the established order, engendering "influences" and "effects" in the existing social system. On this account, the social history of film is tantamount to the changing response to it—its rise and fall—and above all, to its regulation. Robert Sklar's cultural history of the movies, *Movie-Made America,* is predicated on a fundamentally similar outlook. "The form that movie culture assumed grew out of interrelations with other social and economic institutions and with the State." [1] For Sklar, the cultural history of American film—the transformation and regulation of cultural power as information—is told according to three inter-related registers: social control, business arrangements, and forms/and languages. Sklar's narrative relates the challenge, transformation, and reassertion of middle-class cultural powers. The terms of the interpretation are provided by class and ethnicity. Specifically, the conflict over the social control of movies was a class struggle. [2] The form of movies, or more exactly, the work of "authors"— Griffith, de Mille, Capra, and Disney—are related temporally—either anticipating or following—general cultural change. "The pictures changed because audience taste changed, because American society changed." [3] Sklar is like Jowett in writing chiefly an analysis of the change of film's institutional relations.

A second type of social study of film foregrounds the narrative form of film (typically a "genre") in relation either to society in general or to the film industry. In the tradition of film criticism that begins with the problem of genre, the relation of films to the social ground has typically been figured as one of "reflection," or "correspondence." [4] Will Wright, for example, in *Six Guns and Society,* argues that changes in the narrative form of the Western correspond, temporally, with the (ideological) value requirements accompanying the transformation of the structure of the economy. That is, the mythic pattern of the narrative structure of the Western serves as a model of social action. As such it links and adapts the audience to general changes in socio-economic organization. The

1. Robert Sklar, *Movie-Made America* (New York: Vintage Books, 1975), p. 161.
2. Ibid., p. 213. "The struggle over movies, in short, was an aspect of the struggle between classes."
3. Ibid., p. 189.
4. See Michael Selig, "The Mirror Metaphor: Reflections on the History of Hollywood Film Genres," *Film Reader,* no. 6 (1985): 133–143.

audience/film/society relation undergoes an historical transformation led by the values and roles required by the economy. The concept of "popularity" of genre ties form and economy. In this way, the place of the studio and the production process are rendered transparent. Wright's logic of historical explanation in other words links "determination" with homological or chronological correspondence. Thomas Schatz's *Hollywood Genres* also treats film genres, but as the medium of exchange between audience expectations and the routines of industry production. Like Wright, genre is a specific form of a narrative of cultural conflict that "re-negotiates and reinforces American ideology." For Schatz, however, the audience constitutes the social context (and not the social institutions of the first tradition nor of the economy in general, as in Wright). The working procedures of the "studio system" are distinct from the force of the general economy as a major determinant of film form. Strictly speaking, of course, neither Wright's nor Schatz's books, based as they are on "genre," are traditional cultural histories in the sense of specifying evolving relations to other social institutions. Schatz's premise addresses Hollywood as mythmaking—via the studio—from an explicitly synchronic standpoint. Wright, on the other hand, presenting a strongly diachronic sequence, ignores the role of the studio and argues a single important correlation between film form and general economy.

A third approach undertakes to identify the social and historical context pertinent to understanding the form and significance of individual films. Often, this type of critical analysis takes place within an Althusserian frame, as with the *Cahiers du Cinéma* article on *Young Mr. Lincoln,* or the analyses in Robert Ray's *A Certain Tendency of the Hollywood Cinema, 1930–1980.* Both approaches interrogate and reject the premise of a simple reflection between film and society by underlining the ways the film—as ideology—excludes or distorts as much as it discloses. Though *Cahiers* treats in some detail the situation of the studio system (or more exactly, the personnel at Twentieth Century–Fox), the particularities of the production situation are finally and fully subordinated to the central thesis that Hollywood is "the main instrument of the ideological superstructure." In the *Cahiers* essay, the major determinations of the form of the film are ideological—artistic, philosophical and political—and not industrial.[5] The studio system is treated as an uncomplicated, transparent medium for the conduction

5. For a detailed analysis of *Cahiers'* critical method, see my "*Cahiers du Cinéma's* Re-Reading of Hollywood Cinema: An Analysis of Method," *Quarterly Review of Film Studies* 3 (Summer 1978): 405–416.

and representation of general financial interests. The *Cahiers* account is, moreover, restricted to determinations on the side of production. Similarly, for Robert Ray, the studio system is not a consideration as such, but only insofar as it is the vehicle that creates (ideological) "correlates" for common "wishes and fears." As with Wright, popularity is explained through the model of myth. In neither account is "the audience" or "the studio" an important theoretical category of film/society relations.

What seems clear from a critical reading of the social histories of film in contrast to the studies and analyses of genre is that the film industry in its operations and effects is nonaligned with, indeed often disjunct from, other major American social and economic institutions, and indeed has, historically, been at odds with them. It is this conclusion that must inform our idea of "context." The supposition of the existence of a discrete sphere of studio operations and interests is then the first premise of a cultural analysis proper, of cinematic discourse produced by the studio system. The second premise is to regard the studio system as extending beyond production—as it did in fact—through practices of distribution and exhibition to the *point of audience reception*. The "studio" system should be understood, in other words, to include the integration of production with distribution and exhibition. Finally, for a social reading, the cinematic "institution" in its entirety—both its industrial structures and its forms and meanings—must be taken up within a "context" and treated as part of the larger culture, the social intertext. The third premise, in other words, is to treat the dynamic of the "film institution" as part of the larger culture that frames it. Specifically, we might represent significant structural change in relation to the film industry in two ways—in the reorganization of the internal relations among its constituent parts, and in the shifting relation of the industry as a whole to other social/economic institutions. Both kinds of transformation compose the framework of mediations that must be invoked to (re-)construct the historical dimension of Capra's work in the late thirties. That is, a mode of reading responsive to context must both locate the film within the network of mediations specific to the operations and modes of representation of the institution through which it is produced and consumed, and remain committed to the analysis of the conditions of general social significance—the discourses of the other neighboring institutions—which the text adopts and addresses. Such a mode of interpretation must assign the text a place within these networks in such a way as to demonstrate the premises of the audience's place in its reading.

Chiefly, such a social mode of critical reading must conceptualize the text's relation to a determinant "situation" and figure that situation as a socio-historical subtext. Following Jameson, one can say this "situation" constitutes a framework for the social dimension of the text's intelligibility.[6] Specifically, the text can be reviewed as a dialogue—a restructuration and rewriting of the problem posed by the social ground. In this sense the text is in the Burkean sense "symbolic action," the result of a discursive rhetoric, at a distance from purely instrumental action, that both answers to that situation and defines and projects it. With respect to the text, the symbolic subtext—the relations that comprise the social ground and is different from the "empirical real" by narrativization—is both inscribed within and projected by the text. Narrative structure—*both narrative and narration*—negotiates these relations between text and context. The conditions of intelligibility and of audience position are inscribed conceptually and formally within the framework of this dialogue of questions and answers. The mode of address, the text's rhetoric, is itself a form of the social.

The relevant subtext then is necessarily a reconstructon of social ground implied by the symbolic act of the text; it is constructed as a kind of referent by a textual process that links it with the historical record. Establishing the domain of historical relevance and delimiting its scope—that is, establishing the criteria as well as the specifics for the construction of the relevant subtext—is the task of an historiographic imagination. In situating the text in history, Jameson's *The Political Unconscious*[7] affirms the relevance of three principal semantic horizons in respect to the form of textuality, which give point and direction to the contemporary project of cultural readings:

1) The political order, in which the work as a symbolic act is regarded as an imaginary formal resolution of real contradictions

2) The class order, in which the text is regarded as a statement in an ideological confrontation between classes

3) The historical order, in which the form of the text as a diverse assemblage of signs is viewed as the consequence of a complex, determined mode of sign production

In accord with our social perspective, we might say that the film institution ("studio system"), whatever other determinations operate, comprises the initial,

6. Fredric Jameson, "The Symbolic Inference; or, Kenneth Burke and Ideological Analysis," *Critical Inquiry* 4 (Spring 1978): 507–523.
7. Fredric Jameson, *The Political Unconscious: Narrative as A Socially Symbolic Act* (Ithaca: Cornell University Press, 1981), pp. 75–76.

central, but by no means comprehensive mediation of the relation between text and history, and text and society. Jameson's three semantic themes noted above provide the terms for specifying the relation of the system to the text.

Analysis of Capra's *Meet John Doe,* an independent production done at Warner Brothers in 1941, provides a concrete way of examining the situation of the studio system at that time, and of modeling, theoretically, the relations among the system of production, the historical context, and the textual order of an individual film. Doing so necessitates an analysis of the problem of Hollywood's audience.

The social-industrial context relevant to situating the "symbolic action" of *Meet John Doe* is broader and more longstanding than that of the years 1940–1941, and consists in fact of the two major continuing social and economic themes of American film's social history: the attempt to fashion film as an explicit moral form of public entertainment, an instrument of social/libidinal regulation; and the effort to institute, and to maintain against the wishes of the so-called "independents," an integrated economic system that dominates and controls the market for films.

These two general forces—social and economic—coincided with and were formative of the institution of American cinema in the 1909–1913 period, and in various changing relations significantly shaped the relations between film and society up to and through the 1940 period.

In the early period, the film institution became indissolubly linked socially and thematically to the family and school—which, following Donzelot and Foucault, we might call the "tutelary complex." [8] Film in the early period, we might say, was in the process of displacing and redefining, structurally, the processes and sites of socialization. Broadly speaking, that part of the traditional pedagogical function having to do with regulating manners and morals—previously vested in the family, church, and school—was taken up and reformulated within the cinema-institution. The historical coincidence and convergence of Griffith's moralistic cinematic form with the positive reception, and revision, of psychoanalysis in America were articulated around a set of common popular themes in the social subtext—the troubled situation of the family, the redefinition of familial positions, and the refiguration of domestic authority in an emerging industrial order. Cinema both continued and intensified these early twentieth-century

8. Jacques Donzelot, *The Policing of Families* (New York: Pantheon Books, 1979).

themes of popular culture, refiguring its dynamic tensions in a mode of increasing subjectivity. In this way cinema was constituted as a popular narrative institution and charged, we might say, with negotiating relations between morality (law) and romance (sexuality) in a new, emerging cultural order. The movies provided a design for living, a regulation of images, a language for imaginative conduct on the terrain of the social.

The reach and public effect of the cinema was linked to and ultimately assured by the early imperatives of its economic organization. Indeed, the elaboration of cinematic subject matter, narrative form, and pictorial style took place in a specific economic framework, namely the attempt by the Motion Picture Patents Company to establish a monopoly of the movie market.[9] The independent producers' opposition to various marketing practices of the Company, and the government antitrust suit in 1913 alleging illegal restraint of trade,[10] set a pattern of conflict and controversy that was to persist in the film industry in various forms for the next thirty-five years, until the resolution of the Paramount case.

By the late thirties, an industry composed of vertically integrated production and distribution parts, tied together by the traditional practices of block booking and a system of contracted stars, had long been linked structurally and financially to ownership of theaters. The ownership and control of first-run theaters had proved to be the linch pin in organizing and controlling the film markets. Nearly 90 percent of the assets of the industry were in theaters. The major studios not only produced 85 percent of the feature films, but also owned or controlled nearly 80 percent of the first-run theaters in the twenty-five largest markets. Access to screens controlled by majors and submajors was available almost exclusively (at the rate of 95 percent) to those eight producing companies.[11]

In fact, the circumstances leading to filing of the Paramount case in July 1938 constitute a significant part of the relevant context for placing *Meet John Doe* and its figuration of the role of the media. The Government's complaint defined the

9. See Ralph Cassady, Jr., "Monopoly in Motion Picture Production and Distribution 1908–1915," in Gorham Kindem, ed., *The American Movie Industry* (Carbondale: Southern Illinois University Press, 1982), pp. 25–68.

10. Jeanne Allen, "The Decay of the Motion Picture Patents Company," in Tino Balio, ed., *The American Film Industry* (Madison: University of Wisconsin Press, 1976), pp. 119–134.

11. Detailed descriptions and analyses of this monopolistic structure contemporaneous with the Paramount suit can be found in: Temporary National Economic Committee, *Investigation of Concentration of Economic Power: The Motion Picture Industry—A Pattern of Control,* Monograph No. 34 (Washington, D.C.: United States Government Printing Office, 1941); and Mae D. Huettig, *Economic Control of the Motion Picture Industry: A Study in Industrial Organization* (Philadelphia, University of Pennsylvania Press, 1944).

operation of the studio system through enumerating seven "competitive conditions," six of which had to do with control of marketing.[12] The government alleged a "monopoly of exhibition in first-run metropolitan theaters," a "nationwide monopoly of exhibition by producer-exhibitor dependents," the imposition of unfair trade practices upon unaffiliated exhibitors, as well as a "monopoly of production" by placing under exclusive contract stars, featured players, directors, technicians. In sum, the complaint alleged that the majors systematically dominated exhibition and production in a way that effectually excluded both independent exhibitors and producers from the market. The Government brief asserted that "free competition can exist . . . only when all producers and exhibitors, large as well as small, are assured of a fair opportunity to sell their respective motion pictures on their merits in a free, open and untrammeled market" and argued that under the existing circumstances such competitive conditions could be restored only with the "complete permanent, and effectual separation of the production and exhibition branches of the industry." In November 1940, a consent decree was entered that proscribed, in degree, the onerous practices of blind selling, block booking, and unreasonable clearances while leaving the system of ownership intact. The economic logic of the industry, and the framing of the Government complaint, converged on a central point: that the articulation of power in the industry consisted of control and access to screens.[13]

From the perspective of the social history of film, the interpretation of the Paramount case seems to require terms that go beyond the legal framework, strictly speaking, as well as a business framework, to terms that raise larger cultural questions about the media's relation to society.[14] The striking fact about

12. *Petition,* "United States of America vs. Paramount Pictures, Inc. et al." District Court of the United States for the Southern District of New York, 20 July 1938. See especially pp. 69–78, "Competitive Conditions in the Industry" and pp. 83–111, "Part IV, Offenses Charged," especially "A. Monopoly of exhibition in first-run metropolitan theaters" and "B. Nationwide monopoly of exhibition by producer-exhibition defendants." This document underlines the major importance the government gave to the *monopoly in exhibition* at the time of the filing of the case.

13. The U.S. Supreme Court did not challenge the District Court's finding that the government had not proven a monopoly in production. The main issue, at the final stage, according to the Court was "monopoly of exhibition, restraints on exhibition, and the like," and in particular, the monopoly of the first-run metropolitan theaters. "United States vs. Paramount Pictures, Inc. et al." 334 U.S. 131, 1948, p. 166.

14. The social histories of film generally treat the Paramount case exclusively as an industry issue, and do not pose in any significant detail the question in terms of the general transformation of the media. Jowett in *Film: The Democratic Art* does indicate in an important paragraph the "symbiotic" relation film established with radio ([Boston: Little, Brown, 1976], p. 280). Though the Paramount case is almost always raised with the matters of television, television is treated exclusively as a factor

the Paramount case, in a broader cultural context, is that the state, in the name of the "independents" and under the principle of "open" competition, moved to dismantle the cinema-institution at the height of its ideological hegemony. Confronted by this crucial historical moment—the filing and prosecution of the Paramount case—the basic models of film and society, *reflection, correspondence,* and (simple) *determination* (as in *Cahiers'* unmediated link of state, capital, and ideology), become graphically problematic.

Though the precise historical logic of the changing relation of the state and the economy to the studio system is far from clear, this process of deconstruction of the cinema institution coincided historically, over a considerable period from the mid-thirties to the mid-fifties, with the preparation, development, and introduction of network television. In 1940, film had reached an accommodation with radio, though more generally the relation between newspapers, radio, television, and film was complex, changing, and heterogeneous.[15] It is evident that the conjuncture of the final divestiture of film production from exhibition in 1948, with the advent of network television, radically altered and realigned the structure, definition, and powers of the American mass media. The 1940 period, however, represents a specific moment in the development and articulation of film to the other mass media. The studio system was in the process of being challenged from within the system by the state in the name of independent producers and exhibitors, and forced to acknowledge the disturbing potential of broadcasting and the imminence of television from without.

It is in this general media context that Capra made *Meet John Doe* for Warner

---

that contributed to the decline of the size of the film audience. Jowett: ". . . the fact remained that movie audiences were declining long before television became a major competitor on the American entertainment scene" (p. 344). Sklar in *Movie-Made America* also treats the Paramount case primarily as a business matter though he opens a curious new perspective: "With the advent of television, the history of motion-picture production and exhibition appeared in an entirely new light, not so much a fulfillment of the nation's entertainment needs as a diversion, an accidental detour caused by a temporary technological inadequacy" (p. 276). In these instances the social dimension so prominent in other sections of these books is eclipsed and the larger cultural significance of the case left unexplored.

15. It seems increasingly evident that the social history of film cannot consist only of the large and traditional themes of regulation and control, but must with the Paramount case also consider the broader cultural intertext composed of the other news and entertainment media—most importantly, radio, television and today, popular music. In particular the rise of advertiser-driven broadcasting, considered in relation to film, signals a significant reconfiguration of the domain of consumption, and hence of ideology, a transformation which is largely outside of the meaning given to economic and business categories that inform the traditional social histories.

Brothers. Since this relation between Capra and Warners has structural implications and provides a further specification of context for placement of the symbolic action of the film, let us review its genesis and structure.

In February 1940, when Frank Capra Productions, Inc., and Warner Brothers signed an agreement to produce *The Life and Death of John Doe* at Warner Brothers Studios and to distribute it through Warners' production arm, Vitagraph, Warner Brothers was in every structural aspect a major studio. "Capra" was also an institution. In 1938 he had been elected president of the Directors Guild and charged with seeking recognition from the Producers Association as the bargaining agent for directors and assistants. By 1939, the directors were for first time accorded a general legal role with respect to conditions and wages of work—thus institutionalizing a particular power position of the director within the studio system. Capra, besides being a notably successful director of hit movies, thus occupied a significant structural position within the system of Hollywood at this moment.

The Warner Brothers records show that the production deal, apart from talent, was structured through four separate but interlocked contracts, encompassing both production and exhibition, all signed 21 February 1940.[16] These records indicate the structure of a relation between the independent and the studio at this time and is considerably more intricate than Capra remembers in his autobiography. Capra made contracts with the bank, Warners, and Vitagraph; and the bank made a contract with Warners.

The production side first: The Bank of America was to advance Frank Capra Productions, Incorporated, $750,000 for the production of *The Life and Death of John Doe,* secured by a pledge of the negative and an assignment of returns from distribution. Warner Brothers agreed to furnish Capra with $500,000 to complete the film after the expenditure of the bank loan ($1,250,000 was the budgeted ceiling), agreed to make available such contracted talent as reasonably was required (at cost), and to furnish studio facilities on a rental/lease basis not to include overhead or carrying charges that included sets, electrical equipment, cameras, and the necessary technicians. Warner Brothers, under Harry Warner's signature, further agreed to complete the film if Capra didn't, and to subordinate its rights to payment until after recoupment by the bank. The legal title was vested in the Producer (Capra), as was the physical control of the negative,

16. Warner Brothers Archive of Historical Papers, Volume 1138, Doheny Library, University of Southern California. "Production Agreement," "Warner Bros. Agreement," "Mortgage, Pledge and Assignment," and "*Meet John Doe* Distribution Agreement."

subject only to the bank lien. The production of the photoplay, it was explicitly stated, was under Capra's exclusive control. Capra's agreement with the bank provided $100,000 for the writers, $150,000 for Cooper, and Capra received $250,000 for direction. The producer, Capra, would go into profit after full payment to the bank, and of production and distribution monies advanced by Warners.

Distribution was structured through an agreement between Frank Capra Productions and Warners' distribution arm in New York, Vitagraph, Incorporated. It provided five years' exclusive domestic and international rights. In return, Capra pledged 80 percent of gross receipts to the studio (20 percent went to Vitagraph), against which there were full charges for an initial 236 prints, the cost of the trailer, any censorship fees or expenses, and 80 percent of the costs of general advertising.[17] In addition to the strictly financial arrangement, Capra contracted for certain other significant conditions of distribution. The billing: "The photoplay shall not be designated as a Warner picture, but as a picture produced by Frank Capra." All titles, including the main credit title, would be prepared by the producer, and the distributor could make no change. The producer agreed to give distribution credit on the main title sequence.

There were in addition three specific stipulations in the Capra-Vitagraph contracts that addressed current, structural industry conditions, and provide a further immediate sense of the transitional character of the industry. Capra required distribution to agree "to procure the highest prices and rentals *in a free and open market* [my emphasis]."[18] Capra further stipulated ". . . that [the] contracts from the photoplay in any and all territories throughout the world shall be made

17. Capra's contract with Vitagraph provided for Capra's extensive control over advertising of the film and is very detailed in formulating an approach to the various different segments of the market. In the address to the broad public through general newspapers and magazines, Capra stipulated that "the nature of the campaign and the final control thereof . . . shall rest with the producer." Eighty percent of these expenses were to be paid by Capra, twenty percent by Vitagraph. In the address to the specialized audience—the fan magazines and the trade press—the advertising campaign was "subject to [Capra's] approval" and Vitagraph agreed to carry 100 percent of the cost. See "*Meet John Doe* Distribution Agreement," provision IX, pp. 11–14.

18. On this point, the language of Capra's contract incorporates that of the Government's initial *Petition* in the Paramount case: "Free competition means a *free and open market* among both buyers and sellers . . . ," *Petition. United States of America vs. Paramount Pictures, Inc., et al.*, section 217, p. 111; "free competition can exist . . . only when all producers and exhibitors, large as well as small, are assured of a fair opportunity to sell their respective motion pictures on their merits *in a free, open, and untrammeled market* . . ." *Petition*, section 226, p. 114.

separately and individually and apart from exhibition contracts of any other photoplays distributed by the Distributor." [19] Finally, and more generally, Capra stipulated that "distributor shall make distribution as complete and efficient as
practicable so that the gross receipts thereof shall be as large as possible, and in
this connection, if it becomes the commercial practice to employ *television in the
distribution or exhibition of photoplays* [my emphasis], the Distributor shall tele-
vise, or arrange for the television of, said photoplay."

It is in this historical media context that "Capra" as independent producer and
as a signifying practice is inscribed.

Part II. Text/Narrative/Studio-System

Meet John Doe exemplifies the contradictions of independent production and of
audience position within the studio system at a significant moment in its history—at precisely that point when the issue of that relationship is being explicitly thematized by the judiciary of the state. Moreover, the film's determined
efforts at contemporaneousness, established at the beginning of the film by continuing reference to domestic unemployment, and the decay of the world social
order ("the state of civilization"), indicates an ambition to engage, comment on,
and take action within the contemporary historical situation. More specifically,
the film pictures an historical scene at a moment of conflict between the powers
of state and of economy, as considered by the press.

The discursive form of the film, considered from a social-historical perspective, results from the integration of two narrative levels: that of the story proper
(that of the character and events), and that of rhetoric (the filmmaker's mode of
address to an implied audience). Narratively, the film is cast, like *Mr. Deeds
Goes to Town* and *Mr. Smith Goes to Washington,* within the genre of comedy—
the mode of social reintegration—and, like the previous films, adopts the world
of the newspaper as a medium for its treatment of the world of romance, and
ultimately of national politics. Schematically, the narrative form of the film

19. Capra is here refusing "block booking." The practice was defined by the Government as ". . .
the simultaneous licensing of a number of pictures to exhibitors for exhibition, the pictures being
offered together and the aggregate price for all the pictures being dependent upon the quantity taken
by the exhibitor, and requiring the exhibitor to contract for all of the pictures offered in order to get
any of them." *Petition,* section 87, p. 51. The Government characterzed it as "harsh, onerous, and
unfair trade practice which tends to restrain . . . interstate commerce" *Petition,* section 214, p. 101.

consists of the production, discovery, deconstruction, and resurrection of a "character" and the assertion of his value through a conflict between two different representations of social order—the civic and the religious. The civil order itself consists of a conflict between the economic interests of oilman D. B. Norton, who is seeking a constituency, and the representatives of the existing political establishment—both the mayor and the governor whose constituencies seem the well-to-do. Each faction has control of or has an association with a newspaper, either the *Bulletin* or the *Chronicle,* and each has access to a radio network. The two sides joust over the meaning of the John Doe figure and his protest against the "slimy politics" that cause unemployment, and attempt either to utilize, or defeat, his specifically political connotations. The media—the press and radio— are the vehicles for the presentation of these views to the general public. That is, the news media serve a mediating function between the political programs of its owners/sponsors and the terms of public belief.

This political conflict for state power between the two opposed forces is structured and focused in the text through two interconnected registers of signs: the order of the personal and subjective, a language of family genealogy and position including the domain of the unconscious, the dream; and the order of the public language of national iconography—baseball, the Constitution, Abraham Lincoln.

The explicit context for scripting the production of the central figure of the film, the anonymous everyman John Doe, is the family: the diaries of Ann's dead father and his persona of benevolent simplicity as a doctor serve as material for the radio speeches that Long John Willoughby performs and comes to inhabit. Ann scripts a radio persona—"John Doe"—based on the image of the healing powers of a dead father of the nuclear family. The romantic substance of the film comes to be articulated quite literally through the fictionalization of the daughter-father relationship. Ann declares that she has fallen in love with the figure she created in the radio speech, that is, the image of the father. Doe indeed assumes the position of the father. The multiplication and incongruity of fictional personalities—as Long John Willoughby, as John Doe, as father, and as justice of the peace—emerges most clearly in the moment of deepest subjectivity of the John Doe figure, in his report of his dream, which symbolizes both desire for and irresolution about marriage. The scene of the dream's narration is important in the process of the film's production of "character" in that it shows that private person who projects "John Doe" in his speeches. Through his dream of the woman and of his assumption of responsibilty for her, John comes to refigure himself, in accord with the requirements of the public script, in a way that condenses and unifies the public and private roles in an "authentic" cinematic figure—the star, Gary Cooper. Two forces—both of which are opposed to the lure of social irresponsibility embodied in the Walter Brennan figure—bind John Doe, as it were, libidinally, to his social mission: the "contract" with the woman, and the "contract" with the public. Through this condensation, John Doe becomes an image for the public. The religious discourse of the film, the ensemble of preachments and social practices delivered by this public image, John Doe, in his mode of American public speech, emerges from and is anchored in Willoughby's binding libidinal, and finally symbolic, inscription into a surrogate familial position—Ann's family—as a repetition and duplication of the ideal paternal authority.

The second large "mythos" that, like the language of the familial structure, serves to form and articulate the image of Doe's mission and its social significance, is the mythos of America, more particularly of American constitutional freedoms figured, as in baseball, as the rules of "fair play." Chiefly and centrally, the abstract constitutional guarantee of "freedom" is presented as the ultimate social and moral reference. The concept of fair play of business and of sport is embedded in a view of democracy as the working of small groups, like the neighborly, nonpolitical John Doe clubs, and is presented as necessarily antithetical to the authoritarian, fascist design on the body politic of the kind represented by D. B. Norton. Through the grand metaphor of baseball ("What," someone exclaims, "could be more American!"), a certain kind of American community is celebrated.

The film's narrative of a conflict between politics and religion comes by extended analogy, to constitute a parable or sermon on the increasingly evident master plot—the analogy between John Doe and the life of Christ. As such, the film projects and undertakes to validate a civil religion based on a Christian community. This analogy, culminating in the identification of John Doe with the second Christ through a symbolic resurrection, results at the end of the film, in a stark and unreconciled opposition between the interests of the economic machine (and its strategies of social domination and control) and the freedom of the "people." The media, it is clear, remains on the side of "the system."

The form of address of the film—its presentation of the story and its manner of conceptualizing and establishing relations with its hoped for audience, the rhetoric of its narrative point of view—is itself an historical/social form indicative of the situation of the studio system in 1940. The major features of the rhetorical organization indicate an unexpected form of reflexivity by which the film as a medium of communication, as a form of public speech, situates itself, ambiguously to be sure, within the relations of production and within a social context. The very story the film tells—the development of a fictional figure, John Doe, contracted in service to business enterprise (that is, newspapers) because of his special, believable American look, a figure played by just such a figure, Gary Cooper—establishes the terms of a basic structural analogy between the events of the film and the film itself as an event in its context. We can read an explicit dramatization of directorial activity in those scenes where Cooper actually meets the media. Stanwyck writes his scripts, produces his performance, and in her public relations capacity determines the situations in which he will be interviewed and photographed. She puts him in a hotel, combs his hair, supplies a motivation (from baseball) and elicits a performance which she causes to be photographed and reported in word and image in the press.

Though there had been many films of newspaper life and of lives of performers in the thirties, including Capra's own, it is arguable that *Meet John Doe* analyzes as explicitly and comprehensively as any of these performing and directional functions as integral parts of the economic and power relations by which the media conducts its relations with the public. The film presents, through its extended treatment and citation of "the press" and "radio," an exhaustive analogue to the situation of studio filmmaking that aspired to contemporary relevance in 1940. It figures not only the situation of the media but the problem of fascism abroad and at home, and each in relation to each other.

This general reflexive structure forcefully extends to the conceptualization of the film's intended audience as well. It is clear that Capra addresses his audience as "America" (by which he means middle-class adults who care about citizenship, that is to say, the electorate). This audience is depicted in its social diversity under the titles, and in the systematically deployed reverse shots of John Doe's speeches in parks and auditoria. The most elaborate, formal definition of the audience is provided at the occasion of John Doe's first radio address—first, by the invocation "the people" and the recitation of their history in the speech itself, and second, by visual representation of the distinctive, but anonymous persons in the auditorium, who, it seems clear, are stand-ins for the listening public, and like the audience of the film, are off-screen.

The strategy of the film's characterization of the audience alternates between nearly faceless anonymity and typification. Long John Willoughby, identified as a recognizable type of American hero, is fictionally rendered in a specifically American formula of nomination, "John Doe," in order to indicate his everyman character. The persons he encounters represent a number of distinctively American types. The audience as such, however, is figured as a mass. Given the size of American democracy, everyman is invisible or inaudible. Thus the mode of address to his audience that John Doe adopts depends upon an amplification of his voice, in the sense provided by a radio network.

The film's title (changed from *The Life and Death of John Doe* to *Meet* [my emphasis] *John Doe*) indicates not just the story of everyman as an American but a very special mode of address to the audience, almost tantamount to a physical gesture of introduction. That is, title is a performative in a social situation—a greeting—"Meet." The design of the film enacts this relation. In the scene, for example, of Doe's first radio performance, the film both in its visual composition and actual miking of sound presents and features Willoughby's face and voice. The systematic frontality of the visual design of those scenes in which Doe speaks puts us as movie viewers in almost the very same "place" as the depicted audience. In the reverse shot, we see the sign "Meet John Doe." We are asked in this mirroring, reflexive way to recognize a well-known celebrated figure as our fictional delegate, as everyman, as ourselves projected. It is in this sense that the Doe figure is a medium for the formation and conduct of audience interests and identifications. In this sense, we are asked as members of the audience, in accord with Capra's populist project of filmmaking, to recognize ourselves and each other as a congregation having an unknown and unrecognized virtue of the kind that John Doe dramatizes at the conclusion of the film. The audience addressed by Capra is the mass of Americans unknown to each other.

The ideological mode of reading—of seeing text and the historical intertext together—situates the specifics of the text within the mediations of production and certain networks of signification and social power. The history of the American media, of which the studio system is an important part, constitutes in turn an important part of the intertext of the film. The film's mode of address, its rhetoric, is an index of its symbolic project, the relation it seeks to the social.

Within its industrial and its social/historical framework, *Meet John Doe* constitutes a singularly explicit and contradictory intervention. While located fully within the American studio system, existing within its technical and financial resources, as an "independent production" it at the same time both adopts and contests the business principles through which the cinema historically assumed its institutional form.

The "deal" assigns the first position to the Bank of America (making its agreement the first condition of the possibility of the film) and makes the production component of the Warners studio a rental house and the bank's guarantor. Power, in the sense of institutional arrangements, consists of a network that depends on Vitagraph's capacity to engage significant theatrical bookings through the existing system of distribution. Though the director "owns" the film, exhibition remains the final condition of success and of profit. The inducement for the studio, reflected in the billing, the name above the title, is the profit and prestige to be derived from director as star.

The film appears at a moment in the history of the industry when the vertically integrated system fully controlled and dominated its markets. Though the labor problem, as illustrated by the formation at this time of the Directors Guild under Capra's direction, seems to constitute a point of disorder, it can also be regarded as putting into place a system of negotiation that was part of the internal process of studio rationalization and consolidation. If in 1940 the system in relation to its own parts was more or less resolved and ordered, the resumption of longstanding antitrust action, accompanied by the appearance of potentially competing media (with an alternate system of distribution, and a uniquely private place of consumption—the home), signalled an alteration and redefinition of the terms on which cinema existed in relation to other media institutions and to society at large. The social ground was itself, in ways we have indicated, in transformation. The shift seemed to be from a Depression America to a wartime America. Yet beneath that change was the ongoing transformation of the basic market system in the direction of a consumer economy. Radio and television, insofar as they realized an efficient mode of advertising of the American way to the nation, through its networks served as the agents and media of this larger social transformation. Radio and television promised a significant realignment of the public and private spheres, putting the home and the family in a new relation to "the social." In this sense the transformation of "the social" took place both on and within the "tutelary complex," a further social displacement of the one inaugurated by film and dramatized by the social response to it.

Regarded then as a statement within a certain historical mode of sign production (the Hollywood studio system including the star system, the banks, procedures of distribution, etc.), the film's mode of self-reflection corresponds to a certain kind of understanding of the place of the industry within the social formation, and of the position of the independent producer in relation to that system. Indeed, we have argued, the form of the film is an analogue of contradictions operating within the studio system itself. Yet these contradictions are multiple and mobile ones. This form of narrative reflexivity does not nor can it resolve its central problematic—its real relation to the real power of distribution/exhibition system. The film's system of address to the audience is founded on a similar contradiction. The film aims—at every level, from narrative to star—at the mass audience, as a congregation of virtuous neighbors, in opposition to monopoly. Yet the mode of addressing this audience is through film's specific institutional mode of amplification, that is, the comprehensive distribution provided by monopoly organization. For Capra, there is no national audience and no possibility of achieving his project of national self-renewal except through a national distribution system. Reaching these people in large numbers, as his Warners contract shows, is the very possibility of "Capra," if not as director, then certainly as an independent producer. Capra's wish in *Meet John Doe* to provide a voice for this mass, and to offer it a look at itself, presumes the stability, continuity, and reach of the studio system.

Yet there are other general conditions of significance which compose yet another subtext for *Meet John Doe,* one that is explicitly political. The film is an effort in a symbolic register to effect a reordering of American social relations, by replacing or substituting an ideal, religiously grounded social order for the existing and fully established economic one. The narrative, by opposing the individual hero to the power of the system (as it were, the image to the apparatus), models the social relations that compose the historical mise-en-scène of the film itself and evaluates it in accord with a moralist perspective offered by the promise of Christian communalism. The cluster of narrative contradictions evident through the film condense around the efforts to resolve and end this antagonism.

As in other American films, the opposition between self/system is finally "resolved" not on the economic/political terms in which the conflict was initially conceived and inscribed, but, in the film's chief textual displacement, by the substitution of one conflict (political-political) by another (political-theological). The chief ideological strategy is the substitution of a moralist discourse (the battle between a good and a bad father, Christ and anti-Christ) for both a political struggle (between two parties) and an economic struggle (between two classes, summarized ambiguously in the discussions of unemployment and philanthropy). The initial version of the film released projected a different ending by underlining the violence of the conflict. Doe shouted to the men at Norton's dinner party: "I'm beginning to understand why decent people have had to take up guns and give their lives to protect themselves from vultures like you," and a final unseen chorus sang of brothers "marching side by side." [20] The film's actualized "resolution," such as it is, is the result of John Doe's sacrifice and ritual renewal via public reawakening, a resurrection. At the end, the utopian or populist call for civil transfiguration of the body politic, to be marshalled against the forces of intrenched economic opposition, can be answered in Capra's filmic order literally and only by a miracle.

Capra's film, regarded as a symbolic act, is an intervention within the American social order of the early 1940s. It acts both within and on the sphere of the media, and by extension on the wider political life of the nation. It compares and evaluates two models of community, and urges, on behalf of its audience, a restructuring of the social ground (the nation) along the lines of American and Christian populism. In this it confronts monopoly and fascism. This intervention, however, can only resolve the conflicts it dramatizes through a rhetoric of individualism, one that depends on the studio system for an audience. The conflict within the social ground—in the various relations between the individual, the studio system, the state, and the audience—is taken up by the film in a complex and contradictory mode of ideological address. The form seeks to merge the narrative languages of family, nation, politics, and religion. Yet a comparison between the project of the film and the real reveals a conclusion governed by Christian ritual. The film's narrative instrumentality in relation to the social inter-text remains opposed to domestic fascism and yet contained by the terms of ritual form.

20. Warner Brothers Archive of Historical Papers, Capra Script File, Doheny Library, University of Southern California.

Filmography and Bibliography

Capra Filmography, 1922–1961

The list that follows includes the release date, title, screenwriter, and script source for all fiction films directed by Frank Capra. Not included here is information concerning the documentaries Capra supervised or directed for the U.S. Army during World War II and his series of science documentaries sponsored by Bell Telephone in the 1950s. For a comprehensive filmography of work by Capra, with full credits for all films directed by him, see Charles Wolfe, *Frank Capra: A Guide to References and Resources* (Boston: G. K. Hall, 1987).

1922 *Fultah Fisher's Boarding House*
Screenplay by Walter Montague, from the poem "The Ballad of Fisher's Boarding House" by Rudyard Kipling.

1926 *The Strong Man*
Screenplay by Arthur Ripley, Hal Conklin, Robert Eddy.

1927 *Long Pants*
Screenplay adapted by Robert Eddy from a story by Arthur Ripley; comedy construction by Clarence Hennecke.

1928 *For the Love of Mike*
Screenplay by J. Clarkson Miller, from the story "Hell's Kitchen" by John Moroso.

1928 *That Certain Thing*
Screenplay by Elmer Harris.

1928 *So This Is Love*
Screenplay adapted by Elmer Harris from a story by Norman Springer; continuity by Rex Taylor.

1928　*The Matinee Idol*
Screenplay adapted by Elmer Harris
from the story "Come Back to Aaron"
by Robert Lord and Ernest S. Pagano;
continuity by Peter Milne.

1928　*The Way of the Strong*
Screenplay by William Counselman;
continuity by Peter Milne.

1928　*Say It with Sables*
Screenplay story by Capra and Peter
Milne; continuity by Dorothy Howell.

1928　*Submarine*
Screenplay adapted by Winifred Dunn
from a story by Norman Springer;
continuity by Dorothy Howell.

1928　*The Power of the Press*
Screenplay adaptation and continuity
by Frederick A. Thompson and Sonya
Levien, from a story by Frederick A.
Thompson.

1929　*The Younger Generation*
Screenplay by Sonya Levien, dialogue
by Howard J. Green, from the play *It
Is to Laugh* by Fannie Hurst.

1929　*The Donovan Affair*
Screenplay continuity by Dorothy
Howell, dialogue and titles by
Howard J. Green, from the play of
the same title by Owen Davis.

1929　*Flight*
Screenplay scenario by Howard J.
Green, dialogue by Capra, from a
story by Ralph Graves.

1930　*Ladies of Leisure*
Screenplay adaptation and dialogue
by Jo Swerling, titles by Dudley
Early, from the play *Ladies of the
Evening* by Milton Herbert Gropper.

1930　*Rain or Shine*
Screenplay dialogue and continuity
by Jo Swerling and Dorothy Howell,
from the play of the same title by
James Gleason and Maurice Marks.

1931　*Dirigible*
Screenplay adaptation and dialogue
by Jo Swerling, continuity by Dorothy
Howell, from a story by Cmdr. Frank
Wilber Wead, U.S.N.

1931　*The Miracle Woman*
Screenplay by Jo Swerling, continuity
by Dorothy Howell, from the play
Bless You, Sister by John Meehan and
Robert Riskin.

1931　*Platinum Blonde*
Screenplay adaptation by Jo Swerling,
continuity by Dorothy Howell,
dialogue by Robert Riskin, from a
story by Harry E. Chandler and
Douglas W. Churchill.

1932　*Forbidden*
Screenplay adaptation and dialogue by
Jo Swerling, from a story by Capra.

1932　*American Madness*
Screenplay by Robert Riskin.

1933　*The Bitter Tea of General Yen*
Screenplay by Edward Paramore,

from the novel of the same title by Grace Zaring Stone (Indianapolis: Bobbs-Merill Co., 1930).

1933   *Lady for a Day*
Screenplay by Robert Riskin, from the story "Madame La Gimp" by Damon Runyon (*Cosmopolitan,* October 1929).

1934   *It Happened One Night*
Screenplay by Robert Riskin, from the story "Night Bus" by Samuel Hopkins Adams (*Cosmopolitan,* August 1933; reprinted in *Stories into Film,* edited by William Kittredge and Steven M. Krauzer [New York: Harper & Row, 1979]).

1934   *Broadway Bill*
Screenplay by Robert Riskin, from a story by Mark Hellinger.

1936   *Mr. Deeds Goes to Town*
Screenplay by Robert Riskin, from the story "Opera Hat" by Clarence Buddington Kelland (serialized in *American Magazine,* April-June 1935 and July-September 1935).

1937   *Lost Horizon*
Screenplay by Robert Riskin, from the novel of the same title by James Hilton (New York: William Morrow & Co., 1933, and frequently reprinted).

1938   *You Can't Take It with You*
Screenplay by Robert Riskin, from the play of the same title by George S. Kaufman and Moss Hart (published in

The Pulitzer Prize Plays, edited by Kathryn Cordell and William Howard Cordell [New York: Random House, 1938]; *Twenty Best Plays of the Modern American Theatre,* edited by John Gassner [New York: Crown, 1939]; *Six Plays* by George S. Kaufman [New York: Random House, 1958]; *Three Comedies of American Family Life,* edited by John Mersand [New York: Pocket Books, 1961]).

1939   *Mr. Smith Goes to Washington*
Screenplay by Sidney Buchman, from the story "A Gentleman from Montana" by Lewis R. Foster.

1941   *Meet John Doe*

Screenplay by Robert Riskin, from the treatment "The Life and Death of John Doe" by Richard Connell and Robert Presnell, based on Connell's story, "A Reputation" (*Century Magazine,* August 1922; reprinted in Connell's *Apes and Angels* [New York: Minton, Blach & Co., 1924]).

1944   *Arsenic and Old Lace* (made in 1941)
Screenplay by Jules J. Epstein and Philip G. Epstein, from the play of the same title by Joseph Kesselring (published in *S.R.O.: The Most Successful Plays in the History of the American Stage,* edited by Bennett Alfred Cerf and Van H. Cartmell [Garden City, N.Y.: Doubleday, Doran & Chapman, 1944] and *Best*

Plays of the American Theatre, edited by John Gladhorn [New York: Crown, 1947]).

1946 *It's a Wonderful Life*
Screenplay by Frances Goodrich, Albert Hackett, and Capra, with additional scenes by Jo Swerling, from the story "The Greatest Gift" by Philip Van Doren Stern (collected in Stern's *The Other Side of the Clock* [New York: Van Nostrand Reinhold, 1969]).

1948 *State of the Union*
Screenplay by Anthony Veiller and Myles Connolly, from the play of the same title by Howard Lindsay and Russel Crouse (New York: Random House, 1946).

1950 *Riding High*
Screenplay by Robert Riskin, from a story by Mark Hellinger, first filmed by Capra as *Broadway Bill* in 1934 (see above); additional dialogue by Melville Shavelson and Jack Rose.

1951 *Here Comes the Groom*
Screenplay by Virginia Van Upp, Liam O'Brien, and Myles Connolly, from a story by Liam O'Brien and Robert Riskin.

1959 *A Hole in the Head*
Screenplay by Arnold Schulman, from his play of the same title.

1961 *Pocketful of Miracles*
Screenplay by Hal Kanter and Harry Tugend, from Robert Riskin's 1933 screenplay for *Lady for a Day* (see above).

Selected Bibliography

Andrew, Dudley. "*Meet John Doe.*" *Enclitic,* nos. 10–11 (Fall 1981–Spring 1982): 111–119. Revised and reprinted as "Productive Discord in the System: Hollywood *Meets John Doe,*" in *Film in the Aura of Art.* Princeton: Princeton University Press, 1984.

Bergman, Andrew. "Frank Capra and Screwball Comedy, 1931–1941." In *We're in the Money: Depression America and Its Films.* New York: New York University Press, 1971. Reprinted in: *Frank Capra: The Man and His Films,* edited by Richard Glatzer and John Raeburn. Ann Arbor: University of Michigan Press, 1975. *Film Theory and Criticism,* edited by Gerald Mast and Marshall Cohen. 2nd ed. New York and Oxford: Oxford University Press.

Black, Louis. "*Meet John Doe.*" *CinemaTexas Program Notes* 13, no. 2 (24 October 1977): 71–78.

Browne, Nick. "Sistem di produzione/sistema di rappresentazione: *Meet John Doe.*" In *Hollywood in Progress: Itinerari cinema televisione,* edited by Vito Zagarrio. Venice: Marsilio Editori, 1984.

Capra, Frank. *The Name Above the Title.* New York: Macmillan, 1971.

Carney, Raymond. *American Vision: The Films of Frank Capra.* Cambridge: Cambridge University Press, 1986.

Clune, Henry A. *Monkey on a Stick.* New York: William Morrow and Co., 1940.

Codelli, Lorenzo. "Liberty Films Inc." Translated into French by Paul-Louis Thirard. *Positif,* no. 133 (December 1971): 68–75.

Connell, Richard. "A Reputation." In *Apes and Angels.* New York: Minton, Blach, & Co., 1924.

Corliss, Richard. "Capra and Riskin." *Film Comment* 8, no. 4 (November–December 1972): 18–21. Reprinted as "Robert Riskin," in *Talking Pictures.* Woodstock, N.Y.: Overlook Press, 1974.

Coursodon, Jean-Pierre. "Frank Capra." In *American Film Directors, Vol. I.* New York: McGraw-Hill, 1983.

Dickstein, Morris. "It's a Wonderful Life, But . . ." *American Film* 5, no. 7 (May 1980): 42–47. Revised and reprinted as "Frank Capra: Politics and Film," in *The Artist and Political Vision,* edited by Benjamin R. Barber and Michael J. Gargas McGrath. New Brunswick and London: Transaction Books, 1982.

Edgerton, Gary. "Capra and Altman: Mythmaker and Mythologist." *Literature/Film Quarterly* 11, no. 1 (Spring 1983): 28–35.

El Guedj, Frederic. "*L'Homme de la rue:* Frank Capra. *Cinématographe,* no. 97 (Spring 1984): 61–62.

Flaherty, Joe. "Jimmy Carter: John Doe Born Again." *Soho Weekly News* (3 February 1977): 8–9.

Glatzer, Richard. "*Meet John Doe:* An End to Social Mythmaking." In *Frank Capra: The Man and His Films,* edited by Richard Glatzer and John Raeburn. Ann Arbor: University of Michigan Press, 1975.

Glatzer, Richard and John Raeburn, eds. *Frank Capra: The Man and His Films.* Ann Arbor: University of Michigan Press, 1975.

Griffith, Richard. *Frank Capra.* New Index Series No. 3. London: British Film Institute, 1950.

Handzo, Stephen. "Under Capracorn: A Decade of Good Deeds and Wonderful Lives." *Film Comment* 8, no. 4 (November–December 1972): 8–14.

Maland, Charles J. *American Visions: The Films of Chaplin, Ford, Capra, and Welles, 1936–1941.* New York: Arno Press, 1977.

———. *Frank Capra.* Boston: Twayne Publishers, 1980.

Masson, Alain. "Une demonstration et une critique: sur *La Vie est belle* et *L'Homme de la rue.*" *Positif,* nos. 317–318 (July–August 1987): 13–16.

Pechter, William S. "American Madness." *Kulchur* 3, no. 12 (Winter 1962): 64–77. Reprinted in: *Twenty-four Times a Second: Films and Film-makers.* New York, Evanston, and London: Harper & Row, 1971. *Frank Capra: The Man and His Films,* edited by Richard Glatzer and John Raeburn. Ann Arbor: University of Michigan Press, 1975. *Movie Comedy,* edited by

Stuart Byron and Elisabeth Weis. New York: Grossman Publishers, 1977. *Great Film Directors: A Critical Anthology,* edited by Leo Braudy and Morris Dickstein. New York: Oxford University Press: 1978.

Pells, Richard. *Radical Visions and American Dreams.* New York: Harper & Row, 1973.

Phelps, Glenn Alan. "Frank Capra and the Political Hero: A New Reading of *Meet John Doe.*" *Film Criticism* 5, no. 2 (Winter 1981): 49–57.

————. "The 'Populist' Films of Frank Capra." *Journal of American Studies* 13, no. 3 (December 1980): 377–392.

Poague, Leland. *The Cinema of Frank Capra.* Cranbury, N.J.: A. S. Barnes and Co.; London: Tantivity Press, 1975.

Richards, Jeffrey. "Frank Capra and the Cinema of Populism." *Cinema* (London) 5 (February 1970): 22–28. Reprinted in: *Visions of Yesterday.* London: Routledge & Kegan Paul, 1973. *Movies and Methods,* edited by Bill Nichols. Berkeley: University of California Press, 1976.

Roffman, Peter, and Jim Purdy. *The Hollywood Social Problem Film.* Bloomington: Indiana University Press, 1981.

Rose, Brian Geoffrey. *An Examination of Narrative Structure in Four Films of Frank Capra.* New York: Arno Press, 1980.

Schatz, Thomas. "The Screwball Comedy." In *Hollywood Genres: Formulas, Filmmaking and the Studio System.* New York: Random House, 1981.

Scherle, Victor, and William Turner Levy. *The Films of Frank Capra.* Secaucus, N.J.: The Citadel Press, 1977.

Sklar, Robert. "The Imagination of Stability: The Depression Films of Frank Capra." In *Frank Capra: The Man and His Films,* edited by Richard Glatzer and John Raeburn. Ann Arbor: University of Michigan Press, 1975.

Tyler, Parker. "John Doe; or, the False Ending." In *The Hollywood Hallucination.* New York: Creative Age Press, 1944. Reprinted, New York: Simon and Schuster, 1970.

Willis, Donald C. *The Films of Frank Capra.* Metuchen, N.J.: Scarecrow Press, 1974.

Willson, Robert. "Capra's Comic Sense." In *Frank Capra: The Man and His Films,* edited by Richard Glatzer and John Raeburn. Ann Arbor: University of Michigan Press, 1975.